Intention in Talmudic Law

The Brill Reference Library of Judaism

Editors

Alan J. Avery-Peck (*College of the Holy Cross*)
William Scott Green (*University of Miami*)

Editorial Board

Herbert Basser (*Queen's University*)
Bruce D. Chilton (*Bard College*)
José Faur Z"l (*Netanya College*)
Mayer I. Gruber (*Ben-Gurion University of the Negev*)
Ithamar Gruenwald (*Tel Aviv University*)
Arkady Kovelman (*Moscow State University*)
Baruch A. Levine (*New York University*)
Allan Nadler (*Drew University*)
Jacob Neusner Z"l (*Bard College*)
Maren Niehoff (*Hebrew University of Jerusalem*)
Gary G. Porton (*University of Illinois*)
Aviezer Ravitzky (*Hebrew University of Jerusalem*)
Dov Schwartz (*Bar Ilan University*)
Güenter Stemberger (*University of Vienna*)
Michael E. Stone (*Hebrew University of Jerusalem*)
Elliot R. Wolfson (*University of California, Santa Barbara*)

VOLUME 65

The titles published in this series are listed at *brill.com/brlj*

Intention in Talmudic Law

Between Thought and Deed

By

Shana Strauch Schick

BRILL

LEIDEN | BOSTON

Cover Illustration: Detail from Sarcophagus with a Greek Physician, made in Ostia, Rome, in the early 300s. Metropolitan Museum of Art. CC0 1.0 Universal (CC0 1.0) Public Domain Dedication.

Library of Congress Cataloging-in-Publication Data

Names: Strauch Schick, Shana, author.
Title: Intention in Talmudic law : between thought and deed / by Shana Strauch Schick.
Description: Boston ; Leiden : Brill, 2021. | Series: The Brill Reference Library to Judaism, 1571-5000 ; vol. 65 | Includes bibliographical references and index. | Summary: "In Intention in Talmudic Law: Between Thought and Deed, Shana Strauch Schick offers the first comprehensive history of intention in classical Jewish law (1st-6th centuries CE). Through close readings of rabbinic texts and explorations of contemporaneous legal-religious traditions, Strauch Schick constructs an intellectual history that reveals remarkable consistency within the rulings of particular sages, locales, and schools of thought. The book carefully traces developments across generations and among groups of rabbis, uncovering competing lineages of evolving legal and religious thought, and demonstrating how intention gradually became a nuanced, differentially applied concept across a wide array of legal realms"– Provided by publisher.
Identifiers: LCCN 2021001078 (print) | LCCN 2021001079 (ebook) | ISBN 9789004433038 (hardback) | ISBN 9789004433045 (ebook)
Subjects: LCSH: Talmud–Criticism, interpretation, etc. | Intention in rabbinical literature. | Intention–Religious aspects–Judaism.
Classification: LCC BM509.I54 S77 2021 (print) | LCC BM509.I54 (ebook) | DDC 296.1/2–dc23
LC record available at https://lccn.loc.gov/2021001078
LC ebook record available at https://lccn.loc.gov/2021001079

Typeface for the Latin, Greek, and Cyrillic scripts: "Brill". See and download: brill.com/brill-typeface.

ISSN 1571-5000
ISBN 978-90-04-43303-8 (hardback)
ISBN 978-90-04-43304-5 (e-book)

Copyright 2021 by Koninklijke Brill NV, Leiden, The Netherlands.
Koninklijke Brill NV incorporates the imprints Brill, Brill Hes & De Graaf, Brill Nijhoff, Brill Rodopi, Hotei Publishing, mentis Verlag, Verlag Ferdinand Schöningh and Wilhelm Fink Verlag.
All rights reserved. No part of this publication may be reproduced, translated, stored in a retrieval system, or transmitted in any form or by any means, electronic, mechanical, photocopying, recording or otherwise, without prior written permission from the publisher. Requests for re-use and/or translations must be addressed to Koninklijke Brill NV via brill.com or copyright.com.

This book is printed on acid-free paper and produced in a sustainable manner.

Printed by Printforce, the Netherlands

Dedicated to the memory of Professor Yaakov Elman z"l.

∴

Contents

Preface XI

Introduction 1
1. Summary of Findings 2
2. Previous Scholarship and Methodology 4
3. Methodological Concerns 7
4. Historical Context of the Bavli: Hellenistic, Christian, Zoroastrian 11
5. Outline of Chapters 15
6. A Note on Gender Pronouns 17

1 From Tannaitic to Early Amoraic Law: Contrasting Systems of Tort Law in the Yerushalmi and Bavli 18
1. Overview of Tort Law in Tannaitic Sources 18
2. M. Bava Qama 2:6: "A Person Is Always Forewarned" 21
   2.1 *Yerushalmi: R. Isaac on the Necessity of Fault* 22
   2.2 *Bavli: Strict Liability* 24
3. M. Bava Qama. 3:1: Exemption for Accidental Damages 27
   3.1 *Yerushalmi: Rav, Samuel and R. El'azar: Liability Determined by Fault* 27
   3.2 *Bavli: Rav, Samuel and R. Yohanan: Strict Liability* 31
   3.3 *Bavli and Yerushalmi: Identical Traditions, Divergent Rulings* 37
4. Contextualizing Tort Liability in the Yerushalmi 41
5. Contextualizing Tort Liability in the Bavli 43

2 The Third Generation of Babylonian Amoraim: A Period of Transition 48
1. Overview: The Emergence of Competing Schools of Thought in Pumbedita and Mahoza 48
2. Pumbedita: Negligence and Deliberate Action in the Rulings of Rabbah 49
   2.1 *B. Bava Qama 26b-27a: Strict Liability and Negligence* 50
   2.2 *B. Bava Qama 56a: Liability for Negligence* 57
   2.3 *B. Bava Qama 28b-29b: Intent to Act* 59
3. Mahoza: Negligence and Purposeful Action 62
   3.1 *R. Nahman: Purpose Defines the Prohibition* 63

		3.2	*Mitasseq and Melakhah She-eina Tzerikha Le-gufa*: Exemptions in the Laws of the Sabbath 64
		3.3	*R. Hisda: Intention in the Fulfillment of Religious Precepts* 67
	4	Summary 70	

3 **The Fourth Generation of Babylonian Amoraim: A Period of Innovation** 72
   1. Overview 72
   2. Pumbedita: Abaye 73
      - 2.1 *Challenge to Rabbah's Strict Liability* 73
      - 2.2 *Challenges Regarding the Laws of the Sabbath* 77
   3. Mahoza: Rava 81
      - 3.1 *Tort Law* 81
         - 3.1.1 B. Bava Qama 27b: Rights of Pedestrians 82
         - 3.1.2 B. Bava Metzia 96b: Borrower's Rights 82
         - 3.1.3 B. Bava Metzia 83a: Borrower's Oath 84
         - 3.1.4 B. Bava Qama 62a: Guarding a Golden Dinar 85
      - 3.2 *Religious Law: Intention in the Laws of the Sabbath* 86
   4. Rava in Contrast to Abaye in Religious Law 89
      - 4.1 *B. Sanhedrin 61b: Idol Worship out of Love and Fear* 89
      - 4.2 *B. Sanhedrin 74a-b: Martyrdom* 90
      - 4.3 *B. Shabbat 72b-73a: Davar She-ein Mitkavvein* 92
      - 4.4 *B. Menahot 64a: Action versus Intention* 94
   5. Rava's Emphasis on Intention: Precedents and Parallels 97
      - 5.1 *Land of Israel Precedents* 98
      - 5.2 *Parallels in Zoroastrian Literature* 99
   6. Rava's Jurisprudence and Aristotelian Corrective Justice 100
      - 6.1 *Aristotle on Corrective Justice* 100
      - 6.2 *Parallels with Rava* 103
      - 6.3 *Reading Aristotle in Mahoza?* 108

4 ***Mitzvot Ein Tzerikhot Kavvanah*: Divorcing Ritual Performance from Intention** 110
   1. Overview: A Radical Change in Ritual Law 110
   2. The Development of *Mitzvot Ein Tzerikhot Kavvanah* 111
      - 2.1 *The Mishnaic View: Shema, Shofar, Megillah* 111
      - 2.2 *Early Amoraic Views: Accidental Immersion* 113
      - 2.3 *Rava's View* 118

CONTENTS

- 3 Rava's Ruling in Context 131
  - 3.1 *The Bavli Context: Intent in Tort Law and Religious Violations* 131
  - 3.2 *Cultural Context: Zoroastrian and Monastic Texts* 133
- 4 Summary 136

5 Views in the Bavli after Rava 137
1. Overview: The Late Amoraim and the Bavli's Redactors 137
2. Rava's Students 137
   - 2.1 *Continuity* 137
   - 2.2 *Innovation: Manslaughter* 138
3. The Redactors 142
   - 3.1 *Intent to Derive Benefit/Pleasure:* Davar She-ein Mitkavvein *and* Hana'at Atzmo 143
4. Summary 150

Conclusion: Intentionality in Rabbinic Law in Historical and Cultural Perspective 151
1. Transitions from Subjective to Objective Standards in Legal Thought 151
2. The "Evolution" of Legal Systems 153
3. Intention and the Self 154
4. Intention, Argumentation, and Conceptualization 155

Bibliography 157
General Index 173
Source Index 174

Preface

I am honored to be able to thank all those who have helped me, and without whom this book could not have been written. First and foremost, my teacher and advisor Yaakov Elman *z"l*, whose recent passing has left a terrible void. His scholarship and methodology are manifest on practically every page of this book: Not only did he teach me how to read Talmudic passages in a critical way, but he has done far more than could ever be expected of an academic mentor, such that I do not think I can fully do justice to the gratitude I owe to him. His unflagging guidance and encouragement did not waver over the course of years and miles. Throughout what I now know were his final months, he was reading and commenting on my work, writing letters on my behalf, and rallying others to support me. What I will always be most grateful for is the belief that he had in me, which continues to inspire me to today.

I would also like to express my gratitude to David Brodsky, Jeffrey Rubenstein, and Shai Secunda who read earlier versions of this book as part of my doctoral dissertation, and whose feedback and critiques greatly helped my dissertation and the revisions I have subsequently made. I am grateful to Oktar Skjærvø for hosting me as his student at Harvard University and for teaching me Middle Persian. It was well worth my weekly roundtrip from Detroit to Boston for the opportunity to learn under such a dedicated scholar and lucid teacher. The late Zvi Arie Steinfeld *z"l*, who served as an early member of my committee, was essential in teaching me the critical methodology of reading Talmudic *sugyot*, for which I will always be grateful. I am also honored to thank David Weiss Halivni for discussing several of the *sugyot* in this study with me.

Suzanne Last Stone guided me in exploring legal theory, both one-on-one and along with Aryeh Edrei, at their research seminar at the Van Leer Institute in Jerusalem. I am grateful for her guidance, support, and friendship. Steven Friedell kindly read several passages, offered his insights, and explained to me the nuances of negligence law.

I am grateful to Ishai Rosen Zvi who shared his unpublished works with me and discussed some of the issues of intentionality, and Moshe Halbertal for discussing with me his work on intention in Talmudic law. Leib Moscovitz introduced me to the work of David Daube and has frequently offered his guidance and advice.

A special debt of gratitude is owed to Steven Fine for helping me in the final processes of writing this book. I thank him for his mentorship and along with his wife Leah, for their close friendship, for which I feel to be mostly on the receiving end. Barak Cohen likewise offered indispensable support and advice in the final stages, for which I am grateful. The editors at Brill, Alan Avery-Peck, Katie Chin and especially Erika Mandarino have been supportive, attentive, and exceedingly thoughtful throughout the entire process.

I would like to thank several friends and colleagues who read parts of this study in earlier versions including Yonatan Feintuch, Rebecca Feldman, Rachel Furst, Ayelet Hoffman Libson, Sara Labaton, Pinchas Roth, and Moshe Shoshan. I thank the editors of *Dinei Israel*, *JLAS*, and *JSQ* for allowing me to make use of material published previously for Chapters One, Three, and Four.

My students, both in the US and Israel, helped me to sharpen many points and offered new perspectives that I would have otherwise overlooked. This study has been improved by their insight and enthusiasm. In particular, I wish to thank Yona Berzon, Eliana Hirsch, Ruchama Katz, and Tehilla Katz as well as Arielle Listokin Achdut, for proofreading.

I am indebted to Rabbi Moshe Kahn, my *rebbi* in Stern College and in the Graduate Program in Advanced Talmudic Studies, who taught me how to learn *gemara* with a careful eye. My research draws from the skills I have learned from him and the faith and high expectations he has in all his students to acquire high proficiency in learning *gemara*.

Finally, I must give thanks to my family. My incredibly loving parents, Joseph and Cheryl Strauch, who provided me with every opportunity I could ever need and particularly my mother, who has always encouraged me to pursue my dreams. My in-laws, Allen and Miriam Schick, have constantly been supportive and never ceased to express their great pride. My sweet and adorable children, Saadyah, Noa, Aviyah, and Avraham Chananel are the most wonderful blessings in my life and through their excitement, curiosity, and love enhance my life in every way. *Aharon Aharon haviv:* my husband, Ari, introduced me to the field of academic Talmud and to Dr. Elman, and took time from his own research to painstakingly edit large swaths of this study, offering astute observations and critiques. I cannot adequately express the love and support he gives me and how grateful I am to have him as my partner in life.

Introduction

Every legal system has its particular standards for establishing guilt and obtaining fair compensation for the wrongfully harmed. Ideally, such standards will account for the needs of injured parties without placing an undue burden on the flow of daily activities that allow a society to function. Jurists must therefore determine whether the bare fact of having inflicted harm is sufficient for assigning culpability, or whether damages must be caused intentionally. They must also decide whether the character or motivations of the accused ought to be weighed as criteria for judging their conduct. Systems of religious law have the additional task of deciding how such criteria factor into the fulfillment and violation of religious precepts.

The Babylonian Talmud (Bavli), the most voluminous and influential text of rabbinic Judaism, dedicates considerable attention to these issues and to the role of intention in discussions concerning cases of (what in modern terms we would classify as) religious, criminal, and civil law.[1] Although the Bavli is arranged topically and thematically based on the Mishnah, a concise and carefully edited collection from rabbis who lived in the Land of Israel during the first through third centuries, the oral composition of the Bavli over several centuries, combined with the active hand of the anonymous redactors, result in a recombination of material, often without regard to chronology or history. Moreover, topics that may be closely related can be scattered throughout the Talmudic corpus. The resulting amalgam of conflicting rulings on the assessment of guilt and the relevance of intention and negligence in judgment has posed a challenge to readers of the Bavli for more than a millennium. Where some passages impose liability for all damages, even in the absence of evidence that the one who caused the damage (the tortfeasor) was at fault, others propose exemptions from responsibility in such instances.[2]

This book seeks to disentangle the many voices preserved in the Bavli, demonstrating that the conflicting rulings follow discrete chronological and

---

[1] By religious law, I refer to areas that involve rituals and religious institutions such as the Sabbath, holidays, and the ban against idolatry. Civil law pertains to social and economic matters between people such as cases of property and personal damages, custodianship, and contracting marriage. I offer these classifications for the sake of clarity, though it is not clear that the rabbis would make such distinctions, as all of Talmudic law is seen as having a divine source. See Hayes, *What's Divine about Divine Law?*, 170 in particular.

[2] See differing opinions expressed by the medieval Talmudic commentators e.g. Tosafot B. Bava Qama 27a, s.v. *U'Shmuel* and *Hiddushei Ha-Ramban* B. Bava Metzia 82b.

geographical axes. By tracing the development of the role of intention in various aspects of Talmudic law,[3] from the Amoraic era (220-circa 500 CE) through the generations of the anonymous redactors who further develop and systematize the Bavli's discursive units (*sugyot*),[4] this study constructs a legal-intellectual history that highlights the distinct positions of the Amoraim expressed in their statements and rulings (identifying each according to generation, cultural environment, and school of thought) as well as the approaches favored by the redactors. This careful process of reconstruction reveals a decided shift in rabbinic thinking that ramifies across many aspects of Talmudic law.

1 Summary of Findings

Throughout the Mishnah, for the majority of tannaitic sages associated with the House of Hillel, intention plays a crucial role in determining the status of an action in diverse areas ranging from sacrifices and ritual impurity, to the Sabbath and daily prayer, to manslaughter.[5] Most rulings regarding tort law

---

3   The philosophical aspect of intention is beyond the scope of this study. For a discussion of the distinctions and commonalities between legal and philosophical notions of intention, see Naffine, Owens, and Williams, *Intention in Law and Philosophy*.

4   There are a range of opinions as to the dating of the Bavli's redaction. David Weiss Halivni, who maintains that the redactors postdate the amoraic period, has offered several chronologies throughout the years: initially positing a stammaitic period that spanned the years 427 to 501/520, followed by the period of the Saboraim (Halivni, *Meqorot U-Mesorot: Yoma to Hagigah*, 7–10; Halivni, *Midrash, Mishnah, and Gemara*, 83–84.) He later proposed that the stammaitic period began roughly in 550 and ended in the mid-eighth century, which includes the Saboraim (Halivni, *Meqorot U-Mesorot: Bava Metsia*; Halivni, *Formation*, 26; and see Rubenstein, "Introduction," xxix who presents a table outlining Halivni's views of the different stages of the stammaitic period.)

   Martin Jaffee and Charlotte Fonrobert date the final redaction to 620, while Yaakov Elman argued for an earlier final date, no later than 542, the outbreak of the Justinian Black Plague, which devastated the Byzantine and Sasanian Empires, and whose recurrences continued to ravage the region for another two centuries. Elman, "The Babylonian Talmud in Its Historical Context," 19; Jaffee and Fonrobert, *The Cambridge Companion to the Talmud and Rabbinic Literature*, xvi.

   Robert Brody has recently challenged Halivni's late dating of the redactors, arguing for a *Stam Qadum*, which was active already during the amoraic period (Brody, "The Anonymous Talmud and the Words of the Amoraim.") For a summary of the scholarly views regarding the dating of the anonymous strata, see Vidas, *Tradition and the Formation of the Talmud*, 45–51.

5   The importance of intention is not unanimous among the Tannaim. According to Itzhak Galit, the House of Shammai assessed events based on action, while the majority of tannaitic sages embraced the view of the House of Hillel which emphasized intention. Gilat, "Intent and Act in Tannaitic Teaching."

(with, as we shall see, one crucial exception) similarly seem to limit liability to instances of awareness and negligence (behavior that fails to mitigate foreseeable risks).[6] Evidence from the Palestinian Talmud suggests that this dominant tendency continues in the Land of Israel during the early centuries of the Common Era. By contrast, the early generations of Babylonian Amoraim, who lived during the third century, apply a system of strict liability in civil cases, assigning liability even without evidence of negligent behavior or intent to inflict harm.[7] By the early fourth century, although some rulings of third-generation Babylonian sages continue to evince a standard of strict liability, statements attributed to Rabbah, R. Nahman b. Jacob, and R. Sheshet, among others, begin to gradually introduce subjective factors such as intention and negligence. In fact, a number of principles relating to the intentions and foresight of an agent as well as the foreseeability of harm first appear in statements attributed to this period. In a related manner, R. Hisda makes intention a key factor in the performance of various ritual obligations. During the third generation, we also begin to see the emergence of two distinct Babylonian schools, each with its own approach to intentionality. Sages from the city of Pumbedita tend to focus on action and intentional behavior, whereas those from Mahoza stress motive and purpose.[8]

A turning point occurs during the fourth generation of Amoraim (early to mid-fourth century), in rulings attributed to two prominent sages: Rava (of Mahoza) and Abaye (of Pumbedita). In their rulings intention becomes a decisive factor for determining culpability in both civil and ritual law, and the divisions between the two schools come into sharp focus. Rava in particular ushers in a new legal

---

[6] More specifically, negligence refers to carelessness and the failure to exercise the standard of care expected of a reasonable person in a particular society, thereby creating foreseeable risks of unreasonable injury to the person or property of others, even when done unintentionally or through indirect contact. Wright, "The Standard of Care in Negligence Law," 249; Kelley, "Restating Duty," 1061; Garner, *Black's Law Dictionary*, 846 s.v. Negligence.

[7] Strict liability is defined as the requirement to compensate another for damages even when the loss is not intentionally or negligently inflicted, and there is no fault on the part of the defendant. Garner, *Black's Law Dictionary*, 741 s.v. Strict Liability.

The parameters dividing negligence from strict liability are not always apparent since both consider the unintended consequences of a person's actions. If defined broadly and at a high level of abstraction, almost any harm can be deemed foreseeable and as resulting from negligence, since all actions have a potential for causing harm. Negligence could therefore look like a ruling which reflects strict liability. Conversely, if the focus is on the particular facts of a case, a more limited judgment of negligence will emerge with far less risks being deemed foreseeable. Friedell, "Nobody's Perfect."

[8] A distinction similar to that found between the rulings of the Houses of Shammai and Hillel in the Mishnah. See n. 5.

paradigm by determining the disposition of cases in a broad range of areas of civil, criminal, and religious law in accordance with the specific intention of an agent. He imposes full liability only when one purposely harms another's property, whereas one who acts negligently, or without full knowledge of the implications of his actions, faces diminished penalties. In religious violations as well, Rava only deems one who purposely and knowingly violates a prohibition to be guilty, be it transgressing the Sabbath, worshipping idolatry, or engaging in illicit sexual relations. Curiously, however, regarding the performance of ritual obligations (*mitzvot*), Rava systematically discounts the necessity of intention, which not only conflicts with his own rulings in all other areas of law, but contradicts explicit tannaitic law which unambiguously requires intention when performing specific rituals. The later Amoraim of the mid-fourth and early fifth centuries who represent the students of Rava, espouse his positions regarding intention in these various arenas. Similarly, the anonymous material belonging to the redactional strata—including the interpretation of amoraic statements as well as the organization of rulings into the *sugyot* we now have—effectively codify the views articulated by Rava. The redactors apply existing principles to new cases, formulate explicit principles that were perhaps inherent in amoraic dicta, and use them to explain debates among earlier sages.[9]

2 Previous Scholarship and Methodology

Throughout this book I draw on work that has contributed to our understanding of intention in rabbinic thought. Several previous studies have explored intention as a factor in rabbinic law—albeit more narrowly focused on discrete topics and themes in the two Talmuds—including those by Shaul Kalcheim, David Brodsky, Yaacov Habba, Irwin Haut, Jacob Bazak, Avraham Goldenberg, and Shalom Albeck, which I refer to throughout this study.[10] As well, a

---

9 This conforms to Leib Moscovitz's description of redactorial activity as "the explicit formulation of complex, abstract concepts and legal principles." Moscovitz, *Talmudic Reasoning*, 350.
10 Kalcheim, "Davar Sh'ain Mitkaven"; Brodsky, "Thought is Akin to Action"; Habba, "Intention as Part of the Actus Reus in Jewish Law and Israeli Law"; Haut, "Some Aspects"; Bazak, "The Element of Intention in the Performance of Mitsvot Compared to the Element of Intention in Current Criminal Law"; Goldenberg, "Commandment and Consciousness in Talmudic Thought."

A more general study of intention throughout Talmudic law was conducted in a 1927 doctoral dissertation, Higger, "Intention in Talmudic Law." However, a more current study is in order which considers the different generations, locations, and schools of the rabbis.

number of works have analyzed how intention factors into rulings found in the Mishnah, Tosefta, and tannaitic law more generally, or in midrashic texts.[11] The present study offers the first comprehensive picture of intention as a major factor in Talmudic jurisprudence. As Ephraim Urbach and Leib Moscovitz have noted, only in amoraic sources does intention become a fundamental concept—both underlying the rationale for amoraic rulings themselves and being invoked in explanations of tannaitic debates.[12] This study is particularly notable in describing a distinct process of development in legal thinking and the emergence of conflicting approaches that came into sharp relief as intention became more central to amoraic jurisprudence, including the rise of different schools of thought under the influence of particular sages. By showing consistencies across different realms of civil and religious law, it becomes evident that the intention of an agent is precisely what is at stake in many aspects of amoraic jurisprudence. Through this analysis, the legal discourses

---

Shalom Albeck examines the role of intention in the Bavli in a variety of contexts. Albeck, "Is there a Category of Intention in Talmudic Criminal Law?" Because he defines *kavvanah* as the willingness and desire to do an act for the purpose of doing what is required/prohibited, he excludes statements which discuss awareness. As such he asserts that the Bavli only discusses the notion of *kavvanah* in regard to the performance of positive commandments and the violation of the Sabbath, but not in regard to civil and criminal law. In a number of both mishnaic and Talmudic sources the position that emerges is that one's awareness that an action is prohibited is sufficient in order to be held liable. Albeck concludes that in the Bavli, one need only be aware but not intend to commit a wrong in order to be held liable in the areas of civil and criminal law and religious violations. While Albeck's conclusions are true in some rulings, as I will show, they do not consistently follow through for all of the decisions or all of the Amoraim recorded in the Bavli. Moreover, intention often can refer to both willingness and awareness, and in legal thought the two are generally linked. See Finnis, "Intention in Tort Law."

[11] Jackson, "Liability for Mere Intention in Early Jewish Law" which discusses whether or not early Jewish law considered intention alone grounds for liability; Zeitlin, "Studies in Tannaitic Jurisprudence: Intention as a Legal Principle"; Montefiore and Loewe, *A Rabbinic Anthology*, 272–94 in the section entitled "The Importance of Motive or Intention. Kawwanah, and Lishmah. The Love, the Fear, and the Praise of God"; Gilat, "Intent and Act in Tannaitic Teaching." Howard Eilberg-Schwartz discusses the role of intention in a number of contexts in Eilberg-Schwartz, *The Human Will in Judaism*. See Bernard Jackson's review in Jackson, "Eilberg-Schwartz's 'The Human Will in Judaism.'"

More recent works include Boyarin, *Socrates and the Fat Rabbis*, and Stein, *Textual Mirrors* who examine how the very genre/structure of rabbinic midrash and discourse implies its self-reflexivity. The prominence of intention in tannaitic law and aggadic texts has been discussed recently by Balberg, "Recomposed Corporealities"; Balberg, *Purity, Body, and Self in Early Rabbinic Literature*; Levinson, "From Narrative Practice to Cultural Poetics"; Rosen-Zvi, *Demonic Desires*; Rosen-Zvi, "The Mishnaic Mental Revolution"; Hoffman Libson, *Law and Self-Knowledge*. I will discuss these studies in the final chapter.

[12] Urbach, *The Halakhah*, 179; Moscovitz, *Talmudic Reasoning*, 353.

of the Bavli (constituting the bulk of Talmudic literature) become a conduit of rabbinic thinking more generally,[13] and reveal the significant changes that can occur over the course of only a few generations.

The core thesis of this book is therefore necessarily grounded in systematic analyses of Talmudic texts. I apply a source critical approach in an effort to identify the original meaning of statements attributed to particular sages, independent of the glosses and interpretations of the redactors. The most influential accounts of this methodology in American scholarship have been advanced by David Weiss Halivni and Shamma Friedman, who each emphasize the role of the later redactors in shaping the Bavli into its present form. Halivni describes the "forced explanations" of the Bavli's redactors, termed the "Stammaim," who lived at a later time than the Amoraim, and often misinterpreted their sources.[14] He contends that amoraic statements were disseminated as isolated rulings devoid of explanations, and their original contexts were often forgotten or amended due to the process of oral transmission. In later elaborations of his theory, Halivni describes the Stammaim's main program as a process of reconstructing the forgotten dialectical argumentations behind brief amoraic statements.[15] Friedman similarly stresses the role of the redactors in forming complex *sugyot*,[16] but understands their activity as the result of literary creativity (found in all the strata of the Bavli), as opposed to misunderstanding.[17] He also places greater emphasis on identifying original amoraic statements, and to that end provides a number of criteria for distinguishing between them and redactional elaborations. This, he explains, allows for grouping the former together and arriving at a clearer understanding of "Talmudic law, Jewish history, the language of the rabbis, (and) a true corpus of traditions."[18] I incline toward Friedman's approach in identifying and analyzing amoraic strata, and follow his view that redactional comments, even when

---

13 On the use of Talmudic legal texts as a source of rabbinic thought see Urbach, *The Sages: Their Concepts and Beliefs*, 17; Neusner, *Theology of the Oral Torah*; Cohen, *From the Maccabees to the Mishnah*, 34–35.

14 See his introductions to Halivni, *Meqorot U-Mesorot: Seder Nashim*; Halivni, *Meqorot U-Mesorot: Yoma to Hagigah*.

15 See his introductions in Halivni, *Meqorot U-Mesorot: Erubin and Pesahim*; Halivni, *Mekorot U-Mesorot: Baba Kama*; Halivni, *Meqorot U-Mesorot: Baba Metsia*; Halivni, *Meqorot U-Mesorot: Baba Batra*; as well as Halivni, *Midrash, Mishnah, and Gemara*; Halivni, "Sefeqei de-Gavrei," 67–93; and Halivni, "Iyunim beHitavut Hatalmud."

16 Friedman, "A Critical Study," 283–321; Friedman, *Talmud Arukh*, 11:7–23.

17 Friedman, "A Critical Study," 313; Friedman, "A Good Story Deserves Retelling," 57.

18 Friedman, "A Critical Study," 301–8.

INTRODUCTION 7

diverging from the likely meaning of amoraic statements, do not necessarily result from misinterpretation.

Friedman further diverges from Halivni in attributing some compositional and organizational activity to earlier periods, but both agree that the redactors who shaped the *sugyot* into their current form postdate the amoraic period;[19] a view that is generally accepted among American scholars. Robert Brody has recently challenged this, arguing that cases where Amoraim appear to respond to anonymous questions are evidence for an early Stam.[20] Whether the redactors began operating soon after the fourth generation of named sages, as Brody maintains, or significantly later, there is general agreement regarding the core view that drives my reconstruction: that the redactors came after the generation of Rava and Abaye.

3 Methodological Concerns

This study is predicated on the reliability of attributions in both Talmuds as accurate reports of the sages being cited or, at minimum, their respective generations and/or locales. Such a methodological premise should not be mistaken for an assurance that the Bavli is free from attributed statements that were composed or inserted from external sources at a later stage, inaccuracies that may have arisen during the process of oral transmission, and the redactors' reworking of amoraic material into *sugyot*.[21]

Jacob Neusner first questioned the reliability of attributed statements in the Talmud, deeming it naïve to take them at face value, and arguing that it is more worthwhile to focus on the larger editorial framework of each work as a single coherent text.[22] Several studies have responded to Neusner's skepticism including those by David Brodsky, Barak Cohen, Yaakov Elman, David Kraemer, and Richard Kalmin,[23] demonstrating that the picture presented by the Bavli

---

19 Friedman, "Al Titma," 58; Friedman, "Wonder Not at a Gloss," 115–19; Halivni, *Midrash, Mishnah, and Gemara*, 76–92.
20 Robert Brody, "The Anonymous Talmud and the Words of the Amoraim"; Brody, "The Contribution of the Yerushalmi to the Dating of the Anonymous Material in the Bavli." See discussion in n. 4.
21 Brodsky, Bride Without a Blessing, 386–88, 415.
22 Neusner, *Talmudic Biography*; Neusner, *Reading and Believing*, 21; Neusner, "Talmudic History: Retrospect and Prospect," xxviii–xxxv; Green, "What's in a Name? The Problematic of Rabbinic 'Biography'" also espouses Neusner's skeptical position.
23 Brodsky, *Bride Without a Blessing*, 386–88, 415. Cohen, *For Out of Babylonia Shall Come Torah*, 24–26. Elman, "Babylonian Heresy." Also see Kraemer, *The Mind of the Talmud*, 20–25; Kraemer, "On the Reliability of Attributions in the Babylonian Talmud," 175–90;

is complex and layered, making it problematic to claim that it was the product of one author or a small circle of redactors. For instance, it contains contradictions and patterns that preserve the voices of different generations, such as cross-generational praise, but criticism of contemporaries.[24] Kalmin traces consistencies among the statements of specific Amoraim as well as differences in "literature, personalities, and institutions," which all affirm the distinction between Amoraim of different generations.[25] As these studies have shown, there may be a certain degree of fallibility with regard to attributions due to the limitations of oral transmission,[26] such that we cannot be certain of them or their history, nevertheless, contra Neusner, they were not late fabrications but well-meaning attempts to accurately report them.

A number of studies have proposed methodological tools that contribute to the authentication of attributed statements in the Bavli,[27] including verification by external witnesses such as datable archeological evidence or non-Jewish sources,[28] along with rabbinic text witnesses, particularly manuscripts and incunabula. The Yerushalmi, whose process of redaction is generally thought to have been concluded in the second half of the fourth century,[29] is often viewed as having preserved materials in a less altered form than the

---

Kalmin, *Sages, Stories*, 21–23. Though Kraemer later espoused the more skeptical approach in Kraemer, *Responses to Suffering in Classical Rabbinic Literature*, 11.

David Brodsky suggests that errors in attributions often result from oral transmission, which does not correspond to generation, as Kraemer and Kalmin maintain.

24 Kalmin, *Sages, Stories*, 21–23, n. 1; Kalmin, "Formation"; Kalmin, "Rabbinic Literature of Late Antiquity as a Source for Historical Study"; Kraemer, *The Mind of the Talmud*, 20–25; Kraemer, "On the Reliability of Attributions in the Babylonian Talmud."

25 Kalmin, "Formation," 840–76; Kalmin, "Rabbinic Literature of Late Antiquity as a Source for Historical Study."

26 On orality theory see Lord, *The Singer of Tales*. However, the theories of Lord and Perry have since been modified. Regarding orality and rabbinic literature, see Jaffee, "How Much 'Orality' in Oral Torah? New Perspective on the Composition and Transmission of Early Rabbinic Tradition"; Jaffee, "The Oral-Cultural Context of the Talmud Yerushalmi"; Jaffee, "Oral Tradition in the Writings of Rabbinic Oral Torah: On Theorizing Rabbinic Orality"; Jaffee, *Torah in the Mouth*; Jaffee, "Writing and Rabbinic Oral Tradition: On Mishnaic Narrative, Lists and Mnemonics"; Shanks Alexander, *Transmitting Mishnah*; Shanks Alexander, "The Orality of Rabbinic Writing."

27 For a discussion of the various methodological approaches, see Chernick, *A Great Voice*, 14–20.

28 See Levine, *The Rabbinic Class of Roman Palestine in Late Antiquity*, 17–19.

29 There are several opinions as to when the Yerushalmi reached its final form, with the earliest dates ranging from: 360 (Sussman, "Ve-shuv Li-yerushalmi Neziqin," 132.) 380 (Moscovitz, "The Formation and Character of the Palestinian Talmud," 663–77; Brody, "The Contribution of the Yerushalmi to the Dating of the Anonymous Material in the Bavli," 29.) Others propose a later date in the early fifth century, including 410–20 (Epstein,

Bavli, since it was subject to a lower degree of redactional activity. As such, the amoraic statements cited in the Yerushalmi are often considered to reflect a higher level of accuracy, if not the sages' precise wording.[30] Tractate Bava Qama in the Yerushalmi (part of the single tractate Neziqin together with Bava Metzia and Bava Batra, as it originally appeared in the Mishnah)[31] is particularly important on account of its terse discussions and simple presentations of both amoraic statements and *baraitot*, which suggest transmission in forms that preceded their incorporation into larger *sugyot* by the Bavli's redactors.[32] However, the Yerushalmi also contains numerous instances of textual corruption due to typical scribal errors, its unique penchant for duplicating parallel *sugyot* (often not copied fully or correctly),[33] as well as the dominance of the Bavli which both influenced the text of Yerushalmi manuscripts and led to its neglect.[34] These factors can make its meaning and the originality of its language difficult to ascertain.

Attributions may also be deemed accurate when they corroborate with other statements from the generation or school of the rabbi being cited elsewhere in the Talmud and in other independent rabbinic sources.[35] The attributed statements examined in this study demonstrate consistencies with material from their respective generations and, in another indicator of authenticity, are often

---

Introduction to Amoraitic Literature: Babylonian Talmud and Jerusalem Talmud, 274.), or 429, linking the redaction with the end of the patriarchate (Ginzberg, "Mabo," 83.).

[30] Moscovitz, "The Formation and Character of the Jerusalem Talmud," 672. This may be seen from the state of the text of Yerushalmi Sanhedrin published by Moshe Assis (Assis, "A Fragment.")

[31] Kraemer, "The Mishnah," 301; Balberg, *Gateway to Rabbinic literature*, 54–56.

[32] See Sussman, "Ve-shuv Li-yerushalmi Neziqin," 104–13. Many scholars have tried to account for the brevity of Y. Neziqin. Saul Lieberman suggested that it is the oldest Palestinian tractate in the Talmud, having been edited prior to the composition of amoraic explanations and the formation of *sugyot* (Lieberman, *Greek and Hellenism*, 7.) Sussman and Yaakov Epstein challenge this position, citing the absence of definitive proof for Lieberman's early dating. Furthermore, many late Amoraim are cited in Y. Neziqin. (Sussman, "Ve-shuv Li-yerushalmi Neziqin," 72–73.) Lieberman attributed the differences between Y. Neziqin and all other Yerushalmi tractates as resulting from the school that allegedly produced Y. Neziqin. Moreover, Y. Neziqin is the sole Yerushalmi tractate by a distinct coterie of rabbis in Caesarea. Although Epstein counters this hypothesis, many others, including Sussman, concur with Lieberman on this last point. Saul Lieberman, *Talmuda Shel Kesarin*; Lieberman, *Sifrei Zuta B: Talmuda Shel Kesarin*, 125–36; Epstein, *Introduction to Amoraitic Literature: Babylonian Talmud and Jerusalem Talmud*, 282ff.

[33] Lieberman, *On the Yerushalmi*, 7–21; Assis, "The Jerusalem Talmud," 244.

[34] Strack and Stemberger, *Introduction to the Talmud and Midrash*, 181.

[35] Kraemer, "On the Reliability of Attributions in the Babylonian Talmud," 182–86; Kalmin, *Sages, Stories*, chap. Two, Three and Seven; Goodblatt, "Towards the Rehabilitation of Talmudic History," 37–38.

commented upon by later Amoraim. I have applied current methods to affirm the reliability of these attributions, while also acknowledging that certain concepts and themes coalesced during the later processes of redaction. Ultimately, demonstrating that theories of liability appear to have developed along different trajectories according to specific generations and locales provides further support for the reliability of attributed statements. As to the specific problem raised by Shamma Friedman of correctly identifying the rulings of the fourth-century sages Rabbah (R. Abba b. Nahmani) and Rava (R. Abba b. R. Joseph b. Hama),[36] I assess the evidence on a case-by-case basis using appropriate methodologies and consider the arguments that have been made in previous studies, in order to make a determination. These considerations can be found in the notes for each relevant case where these names appear. Moreover, as this study points to the fact that the rulings of Rava and Rabbah diverge from each other in a consistent manner, we now have additional criteria by which to make a determination.

The selections from the Bavli presented result from my examination of the relevant manuscripts and textual witnesses in an effort to determine the correct or, in some cases, most easily readable text. Of particular importance for this study are: MS Hamburg 165 (Gerona, 1184) for the three Babot, which is considered the most reliable extant manuscript for these tractates, as attested by its equivalence to certain Genizah fragments,[37] and is the source used when citing from these tractates; MS Oxford 2673, 8, which contains texts from half of B. Keritut, and is the earliest firmly dated Talmudic manuscript; and, MS Munich 95, the only complete[38] manuscript of the Bavli.[39]

---

[36] Shamma Friedman has pointed out that the orthographic distinction between the names "Rabbah" and "Rava" was a later development in order to differentiate between the two rabbis, for both were originally referred to as "Rava." It is therefore common to find differences among the text witnesses when their names appear, making it difficult to determine the correct attribution. Friedman, "Writing of the Names." See also Weissberg, "Ketiv Ha-Sheimot Rabbah ve-Rava: Shitat Rav Hai Ga'on ve-Shitot Holkot."

[37] Friedman, "Geniza Fragments and Fragmentary Talmud MSS of Bava Metzia – A Linguistic and Bibliographic Study."

[38] The fact that there is only one complete extant manuscript of the Bavli is typically understood to reflect the fact that not only was copying an arduous and costly endeavor, but not all tractates were regularly studied. (See R. Menahem ha-Meiri's commentary, *Beit ha-Behira al Masekhet Berakhot*, p. 32; Kanarfogel, "Study of the Order of Qodashim," 68–69; Krupp, "Manuscripts of the Babylonian Talmud," 347.) The numerous episodes when Hebrew texts were burnt by order of the Church (as in Paris, 1242) contributed to a lack of manuscripts more generally. Furthermore, Saul Lieberman has observed that many Jews repurposed the parchment of their manuscripts as printing became established (oral communication from Yaakov Elman).

[39] For a comprehensive list of extant manuscripts of the Bavli, see Krupp, "Manuscripts of the Babylonian Talmud," 351–61.

The citations from the Yerushalmi in this volume are from the Rosenthal edition, based on MS Escorial, whose high level of accuracy is demonstrated by its consistency with Genizah fragments, affirming its reliability over MS Leiden, on which the printed edition is based.[40] All other Yerushalmi passages are cited from the transcribed text of MS *Leiden, Scaliger* 3 provided by the Academy of Hebrew Language in Jerusalem. While MS *Leiden* is not the most reliable MS due to its many omissions—including whole sentences[41]—as well as the changes made based on the Bavli, it served as the basis for all of the printed editions of the Yerushalmi. Citations from the Mishnah are reproduced from MS Kaufmann A 50, a complete, and the earliest, manuscript of the Mishnah.[42]

4 Historical Context of the Bavli: Hellenistic, Christian, Zoroastrian

My focus is the development of rabbinic legal thought, largely as reflected in the self-contained discourses of Bavli *sugyot*. Yet the Jewish communities of the Talmudic period were far from self-contained. Several of the most influential sages of the Bavli display knowledge of Persian legal, social, and religious norms.[43] By examining relevant texts that were written (or in circulation) roughly during this period, we can better understand how surrounding groups and cultural communities factored intention into aspects of civic and religious life. Significant parallels or divergences between rabbinic texts and works of Zoroastrianism, Greek philosophy, Roman law, and early Christian monasticism can therefore shed light on some of the underlying ideas and processes that may have also shaped rabbinic legal thinking.

---

40 Rosenthal and Lieberman, *Yerushalmi Neziqin*. See the Introduction, where Rosenthal also describes the merits of MS Escorial for its preservation of Galilean Aramaic dialect and Greek loan words, as opposed to MS Leiden, which shows influence from the Bavli.

41 Evidenced by comparisons with citations of the Yerushalmi in medieval rabbinic texts, Genizah fragments, as well as in the Vatican MSS of *Zera'im* and *Sotah*.

42 This manuscript, dating from the tenth to eleventh centuries, probably from the Land of Israel, reflects spoken Hebrew of second-century Palestine. Krupp, "Manuscripts of the Mishnah," 253.

43 As Yaakov Elman has highlighted, this was especially true of those rabbis who lived in the city of Mahoza, including R. Nahman and his student Rava. Mahoza was part of the most important metropolis of the Empire, situated across the river from the Sasanian winter capital of Ctesiphon, and was a meeting ground for peoples of different ethnic and religious affiliations. Elman, "Middle Persian"; Elman, "Acculturation to Elite Persian Norms in the Babylonian Jewish Community of Late Antiquity," 33.

Throughout this book I discuss relevant passages from Zoroastrian sources. As the dominant and official religion of Sasanian Persia, these texts offer a significant point of reference for understanding the wider culture in which the sages of the Bavli lived. Since the late nineteenth century, comparative studies have explored Iranian parallels to Bavli texts, beginning with Alexander Kohut and Jacob Levy, and continuing in the late twentieth century with Moshe Beer, Isaiah Gafni, Moshe David Herr, and Jacob Neusner.[44] Irano-Talmudic studies has greatly benefited from Shaul Shaked's work on Middle Persian texts,[45] and over the past two decades it was advanced considerably by Yaakov Elman, whose research program revealed a wide range of parallels between the Bavli and Middle Persian literature, as well as marks of a shared Persian culture. Continuing in this vein are studies by Geoffrey Herman, Yishai Kiel, Reuven Kiperwasser, Jason Mokhtarian, Sara Ronis, Shai Secunda, and myself.[46] To be sure, comparing Bavli and Zoroastrian works presents certain obstacles,[47] particularly because many such texts, including *Dēnkard* and *Bundahišn* (discussed in several chapters) were written after the Bavli's

---

44 Levy, *Wörterbuch Über Die Talmudim Und Midraschim*; Beer, *Amora'ei Bavel: Peraqim Be-Hayei Kalkalah*, 64; Gafni, *Jews of Babylonia*. See in particular Gafni's appendix on "Iranian and Roman Influence on Family Life: The Attitude towards Marriage among Babylonian Jews," pp. 266–73. Neusner, *Judaism and Zoroastrianism*. Though Neusner acknowledges that he used only those Middle Persian texts that had been properly translated into Westerns languages (pp. 9–11).

45 For a sampling of his many studies devoted to both Iranica and Irano-Judaica, see Shaked, *The Wisdom of the Sasanian Sages: Dēnkard VI*; Shaked, "Iranian Influence"; Shaked, "First Man, First King"; Shaked, "Religious Actions"; Shaked, *Dualism in Transformation. Varieties of Religion in Sasanian Iran (The Jordan Lectures in Comparative Religion)*; Shaked, "Some Notes on Ahreman, the Evil Spirit, and His Creation"; Shaked, "Esoteric Trends in Zoroastrianism"; Shaked, "Judaeo-Persian Notes"; Shaked, "Ambiguous Words in Pahlavi"; Shaked, "Zoroastrian Polemics Against Jews in the Sasanian and Early Islamic Period"; Naveh and Shaked, *Amulets and Magic Bowls. Aramaic Incantations of Late Antiquity*.

46 Herman, *A Prince without a Kingdom: The Exilarch in the Sasanian Era*; Herman, "Table Etiquette and Persian Culture in the Babylonian Talmud"; Herman, "Ahasuerus, the Former Stable -Master of Belshazzar and the Wicked Alexander of Macedon: Two Parallels between the Babylonian Talmud and Persian Sources"; Kiel, "Cognizance of Sin and Penalty in the Babylonian Talmud and Pahlavi Literature: A Comparative Analysis"; Kiel, "Reimagining Enoch"; Kiel, "Creation"; Kiperwasser, "Three Partners in a Person"; Kiperwasser and Shapira, "Irano-Talmudica I"; Mokhtarian, *Rabbis, Sorcerers, Kings, and Priests*; Ronis, "A Seven-Headed Demon in the House of Study"; Strauch Schick, "From Dungeon to Haven: Competing Theories of Gestation in Leviticus Rabbah and the Bavli"; Strauch Schick, "Beruriah." For a thorough introduction to the field of Talmudo-Iranica, see Secunda, *The Iranian Talmud: Reading the Bavli in Its Sasanian Context*.

47 For a critique of the relevance of Zoroastrian texts for the study of the Bavli, see Brody, "Irano-Talmudica: The New Parallelomania?"

INTRODUCTION   13

redaction.⁴⁸ Critical methods that identify older oral traditions preserved in these later writings open the possibility of establishing how Zoroastrian Persians during the Sasanian period addressed related sets of issues in their own religious-legal thought.

The Greco-Roman context of rabbinic texts from the Land of Israel (Mishnah, Talmud Yerushalmi, and various midrashic works) has long been viewed as a vital consideration in modern Talmud scholarship.⁴⁹ Yet, the idea that Hellenistic thought and culture had a significant influence on the Babylonian rabbis has been less well established.⁵⁰ In recent years, however, scholars such as Daniel Boyarin, Shaye Cohen, Charlotte Fonrobert, and Richard Kalmin,⁵¹ have demonstrated that rabbis living in the Persian Empire had some degree of engagement with Greek thought. This is relevant to my discussion of the notable parallels between Rava's body of rulings and Aristotelian corrective justice (Chapter 3).

Aside from the evidence from rabbinic texts, the broader question of how and when Hellenic knowledge spread through Sasanian Persia is also relevant. Although a major dissemination occurred under king Xūsro (sixth century),⁵²

---

48 *Dēnkard* is dated to the ninth century, but is based on earlier versions and includes ancient traditions. See Rezania, "The Dēnkard Against Its Islamic Discourse," 343–49; Shaked, *The Wisdom of the Sasanian Sages: Dēnkard VI*, 225. The tenth-century *Bundahišn* similarly contains older Iranian traditions, including Old Avestan as well as Sasanian material. Henning, "An Astronomical Chapter of the Bundahishn," 229. In general, Avestan traditions were transmitted orally for centuries and were written only once Zoroastrian priests created an alphabet in the mid-sixth century. H. Bailey postulates that this was the result of Manichaean influence. H. W. Bailey, *Zoroastrian Problems in the Ninth-Century Books*, 159–76; Yaakov Elman, "Middle Persian Culture and Babylonian Sages: Accommodation and Resistance in the Shaping of Rabbinic Legal Tradition," 167.

49 Many studies have been devoted to this topic. For a recent bibliography see Hidary, *Rabbis and Classical Rhetoric*, 9, n. 38.

50 For example, Catherine Hezser considers the "extent of their (Babylonian Amoraim's) knowledge of and ways of adapting Greco-Roman philosophy" and concludes that such knowledge belonged to the Palestinian rabbis alone. Hezser, "Interfaces between Rabbinic Literature and Graeco-Roman Philosophy," 186.

   Hellenism refers to Greek texts and ideas. See Becker, "Positing a 'Cultural Relationship' between Plato and the Babylonian Talmud," 258.

51 Boyarin, *Socrates and the Fat Rabbis*, 349; Boyarin, "Hellenism in Jewish Babylonia"; Cohen, "Patriarchs and Scholars"; Fonrobert, "Plato in Rabbi Shimon Bar Yohai's Cave"; Kalmin, *Jewish Babylonia*.

52 Walker, "The Limits of Late Antiquity: Philosophy between Rome and Iran," 55–56. Sasanian interest in Greek scientific and philosophical works reached its climax during

well after the time of the Amoraim, several factors indicate that by the third century denizens of Persian lands would have been exposed to Greek thought and learning. Persia had already been part of the Greek empire under Alexander the Great and then the Seleucids from the fourth century until 140 BCE when it was conquered by the Parthians. Both they and their Sasanian successors demonstrated an affinity with the Hellenic past of Iran.[53] Consistent with this picture, *Dēnkard* IV.19 depicts the second Sasanian king, Šābuhr I (third century),[54] engaging with Greek philosophical and scientific works, and issuing an edict to collect them in the royal treasury.[55] In spite of the continuous battling between Persia and Rome and fluctuations in the borders between the Tigris and the Euphrates during the reign of Šābuhr I, travel, trade, and marriage between members of the two empires continued.[56] The many wars with Rome resulted in an influx of non-Persians, with Šābuhr I resettling large numbers of inhabitants from the eastern provinces of the Roman Empire to Mesopotamia, eastern Syria, and western Persia.[57] These former residents of the Roman Empire contributed to the economic, cultural, and intellectual life of Sasanian Persia,[58] described by Eva Riad as a "milieu imbued with Hellenistic thought patterns."[59]

Beyond the wider trends in Persian culture, Syriac Christians, who held a presence in the city of *Weh-andīōg-šābuhr* (built during the reign of Šābuhr I), served as a conduit for Greek texts into regions of the Sasanian Empire, during the fourth and sixth centuries.[60] They were especially influential in their

---

the reign of Xūsro I Anūširwān who sponsored Pahlavi translations of Aristotelian works. Gutas, *Greek Thought, Arabic Culture*, 25–28.

53 Daryaee, *Sasanian Persia*, 2–6.
54 Šābuhr I became co-regent with his father Ardashir in 240 CE, and fought and defeated the Romans in 244.
55 Shaki, "The Dēnkard Account of the History of Zoroastrian Scriptures," 119. Although the *Dēnkard* was composed centuries after the time of Šābuhr, Kevin van Bladel has argued for the authenticity of this account. Bladel, *The Arabic Hermes*, 38–39.
56 Bladel, *The Arabic Hermes*, 45.
57 This is described in an inscription. Wiesehöfer, *Ancient Persia*, 155; Frye, *The History of Ancient Iran*, 296–303, 371–73; Kalmin, *Jewish Babylonia*, 7, notes 45–46. Kalmin gives a list of sources documenting Roman evidence of Šābuhr I's policy of relocating Roman inhabitants into Sasanian Iran in the third century. More recently, he argues for a strong connection between Jewish Babylonia and the eastern provinces of the Roman Empire due to several of such forced resettlements from the third to sixth centuries. Kalmin, *Migrating Tales*.
58 Daryaee, *Sasanian Persia*, 40, 53–55.
59 Riad, *Studies in the Syriac Preface*, 40.
60 Boyarin, "Hellenism in Jewish Babylonia," 350; Rubenstein, *The Culture of the Babylonian Talmud*, 35–38; Becker, *Fear of God and the Beginning of Wisdom*.

emphasis on Aristotelian logic, which was a central component of the curriculum at the academy of Nisibis.[61] Several studies have noted a common interest in Greek thought and rhetoric between late Babylonian sages and East Syrian Christian schools including those by Adam Becker, Daniel Boyarin, Isaiah Gafni, Richard Hidary, and Moulie Vidas.[62] Arguing for the wider relevance of Syriac Christian texts for the study of the Talmuds (beyond earlier studies focusing on religious polemics),[63] Michal Bar-Asher Siegal contends that the Bavli includes "analogies, literary borrowing, and parallel developments" with Syriac Christian writings.[64] Her discussion of the parallels between monastic and Palestinian rabbinic texts concerning prayer and their joint emphasis on proper intention is addressed in Chapter 4.[65]

5 Outline of Chapters

The first chapter discusses intention as a component of tannaitic law as approached by the first two generations of Amoraim in the Palestinian and Babylonian Talmuds. By examining two ostensibly conflicting positions in Mishnah Bava Qama (2:6 and 3:1) and their corresponding *sugyot* in the

---

For a critique, see Gutas, *Greek Thought, Arabic Culture*, 21. Becker also notes that it was not likely shared with their rabbinic contemporaries. Becker, *Fear of God and the Beginning of Wisdom*, 260.

61   Becker, *Fear of God and the Beginning of Wisdom*, 92; Brock, "From Antagonism to Assimilation: Syriac Attitudes to Greek Learning," 21–22; Gutas, *Greek Thought, Arabic Culture*, 21; Walker, *The Legend of Mar Qardagh*, 187.

62   Becker, "The Comparative Study of 'Scholasticism' in Late Antique Mesopotamia"; Boyarin, "Hellenism in Jewish Babylonia"; Gafni, "Nestorian Literature as a Source for the History of the Babylonian Yeshivot"; Hidary, *Rabbis and Classical Rhetoric*, 112–30; Vidas, "Greek Wisdom in Babylonian." Though others have countered that the Bavli refers to the study of the Greek language, as appears in the parallel Yerushalmi account, or grammar/rhetoric. See Rokeah, *Jews, Pagans and Christians in Conflict*, 204; Rappel, "Greek Wisdom-Rhetoric"; Visotzky, *Fathers of the World*, 3.

63   E.g. Naomi Koltun-Fromm, "A Jewish-Christian Conversation in Fourth-Century Persian Mesopotamia"; Adiel Schremer, "Stammaitic Historiography," 224; Schäfer, *Jesus in the Talmud*, 15–22; Schäfer, *The Jewish Jesus*; Boyarin, *Socrates and the Fat Rabbis*, 246–66; Holger Zelletin, "Margin of Error"; Rosenberg, "Sexual Serpents"; Rosenberg, "Penetrating Words."

64   Bar-Asher Siegal, *Early Christian Monastic Literature and the Babylonian Talmud*, 17. See also Yifat Monnickendam's recent study on the relation between matrimonial law in Syriac Christianity in Ephrem's legal traditions and Jewish law. Monnickendam, *Jewish Law and Early Christian Identity*.

65   Bar-Asher Siegal, "Prayer," 69–71.

Yerushalmi and Bavli, we will discern two competing approaches to liability that were promoted by the Palestinian and Babylonian Amoraim, respectively. The chapter then turns to examining the systems of fault and culpability evidenced in the Yerushalmi and Bavli in relation to Roman and Zoroastrian law and their differing cultural contexts.

The subsequent chapters focus on Babylonian Amoraim. Chapter 2 analyzes statements attributed to third-generation Amoraim, demonstrating that certain rulings adhere to the strict stance held by previous generations, whereas others begin to weigh the intention and fault of actors; in this context, the technical term for "negligence" (*peshi'ah*) is coined. These differing approaches suggest that the third generation may be regarded as a transition point between legal paradigms, when the system of strict liability remained in place while the inroads of an emergent system were taking root. We also begin to see the formation of two distinct schools, each with its own approach to intentionality: sages from Pumbedita tend to prioritize actions irrespective of motive, whilst their counterparts from Mahoza display a nascent interest in the intentions that underlie actions.

The third chapter documents a major shift during the fourth generation of Babylonian Amoraim. A survey of a substantial body of rulings attributed to Rava, arguably the most creative and influential Amora of the Bavli, indicates that he instituted that intention is a necessary condition for establishing guilt for civil and ritual transgressions. In some instances, his position is juxtaposed with a stance from Abaye, his senior contemporary, which highlights a rising interest in the role of intention among these fourth-generation sages. Their recurring disputes on this subject will be shown to reflect more fundamental differences between the schools of Mahoza and Pumbedita on the prioritization of action versus intention; a tension that was already evident in the rulings of their respective third-generation teachers. This discussion concludes with an examination of Rava's consistent emphasis on intentionality in jurisprudence in light of the Aristotelian theory of corrective justice in the *Nicomachean Ethics*.

An analysis of intention in cases that involve the performance of ritual acts and religious obligations is the focus of Chapter 4. It is striking that, unlike his positions regarding civil and ritual violations, in the realm of religious praxis Rava did not consider intention requisite to fulfill an obligation, even though this position conflicts with tannaitic precedents. This chapter explores Rava's departure from the Mishnah's unambiguous requirement of intentionality, with particular attention to how his position on the performance of *mitzvot* may be understood vis-à-vis his rulings concerning religious and tort violations analyzed in the previous chapter. Several possible explanations are offered, which are informed by current approaches to ritual theory and by comparative analyses with contemporaneous Zoroastrian and Christian monastic literature.

In Chapter 5 we examine rulings attributed to the final two generations of Amoraim as well as anonymous glosses by the Bavli's redactors. These later generations of Babylonian Amoraim reinforced and expanded the fourth generation's emphasis on intentionality and maintained many of Rava's positions and principles regarding intention. They further applied his standards to other aspects of law not discussed by Rava. The Bavli's redactors similarly continued to sustain the positions promulgated by Rava as they formulated distinct legal principles and applied them in a widening range of cases.

6   A Note on Gender Pronouns

This study employs gender pronouns consistent with those found in the source texts. Although a balanced use of gender pronouns is generally welcome in contemporary scholarship, it is important to stay true to the texts in question, as doing otherwise would misrepresent the nature of rabbinic discourse. Hence, in the vast majority of cases the pronouns are male, and in the rare cases where the subjects are female, these cases are appropriately conspicuous.

CHAPTER 1

From Tannaitic to Early Amoraic Law

Contrasting Systems of Tort Law in the Yerushalmi and Bavli

1   Overview of Tort Law in Tannaitic Sources[1]

The Mishnah demonstrates great concern for the presence or absence of intention in a number of areas,[2] including: manslaughter,[3] ritual impurity,[4] *eruv*,[5] sacrifices[6]—especially *piggul*,[7] *sha'atnez*,[8] and numerous areas of religious violations and appropriate ritual observance.[9] Yet, with respect to torts, it is unclear whether tannaitic law applies a standard of strict liability or one that considers fault.

Two seemingly conflicting positions are presented in Mishnah Bava Qama. On the one hand, M. Bava Qama 2:6 ostensibly presents a doctrine of strict liability, famously stating that a person is ever forewarned and that legal responsibility is categorically imposed, even for non-volitional acts that occurred

---

1   An earlier version of this chapter appeared in *Dinei Israel*, as Strauch Schick, "Negligence and Strict Liability in Babylonia and Palestine."
2   As Leib Moscovitz notes, the Mishnah does not present "intention" as a conceptual principle that undergirds various laws; rather, it arises in a casuistic style. Moscovitz, *Talmudic Reasoning*, chap. 1.
3   M. Sanhedrin 9:2; M. Bava Qama 4:6.
4   Biblical law stipulates that food must come into contact with water to become susceptible to impurity. Tannaitic law limits this to cases where the contact is brought about intentionally. See M. Makhshirim 1:6, 3:4–8, 4:1–7, 5:3–8, 6:1–8; T. Makhshirim 1:1–2. 2:15–16; T. Taharot 3:1. Noam, "Ritual Impurity in Tannaitic Literature." Tannaitic law also rules that having a plan for using an object renders it susceptible to impurity (M. Keilim 25:9). See Balberg, *Purity* for an extensive discussion on the role of will, intention, and thought in mishnaic laws of purity and impurity.
5   I.e. creating an enclosure that allows carrying on the Sabbath. M. Bava Metzia 4:12.
6   See Chapters One and Two in M. Zebahim.
7   *Piggul* is the prohibition against bringing a sacrifice with the intention of consuming it at an incorrect time; even though the sacrifice was offered under proper conditions, it is rendered invalid. See M. Zebahim 2:2–5 and chapter two of B. Zebahim.
8   I.e. the prohibition against wearing garments made of mixed fibers. M. Kilaim 9:5.
9   M. Peah 6:11; M. Erubin 4:4; M. Sheqalim 3:3; M. Yebamot 16:5; M. Bava Qama 3:1, 8:1; M. Negaim 7:5. For civil and criminal law, see M. Bava Metzia 4:12; M. Shabuot 4:10; M. Makhshirim 1:2, 5, 5:6; M. Sanhedrin 9:2. See Haut, "Some Aspects." As noted earlier, this represents the view of the majority of Tannaim who followed the House of Hillel; sages from the House of Shammai, by contrast, tend to focus on action. Gilat, "Intent and Act in Tannaitic Teaching."

during sleep.[10] This opinion is echoed in the *Mekhilta de-Rabbi Ishmael,* which suggests that intentional and accidental damage are treated equally:

כי תצא אש למה נאמר עד שלא יאמר יש לי בדין הואיל וחייב ע"י קנוי לו
לא יהא חייב על ידי עצמו אם זכיתי מן הדין למה נאמר כי תצא אש אלא בא
הכתוב לעשות את האונס כרצון ושאינו מתכוין כמתכוין ואת האשה כאיש לכל
הנזקין שבתורה

'If a fire breaks out ...' (Exodus 2:6).

Why is this said? Even if it had not been said, I could have reasoned: Since he is liable [for damage done] by what is owned by him, shall he not be liable [for damage done] himself? If, I succeeded [in proving it] through reasoning, why was it said, 'If a fire breaks out'? Rather, Scripture comes to establish that one acting under duress is [regarded] as one acting willfully, and one acting unintentionally is [regarded] as one acting intentionally, and a woman is like a man regarding all [liability for] damages in the Torah.[11]

Yet, the majority of mishnayot that address torts as well as Tosefta Bava Qama acknowledge varying levels of negligence,[12] presenting a framework that calibrates culpability according to the circumstances and the degree of fault in a given incident. Even in the opening mishnah of Bava Qama (1:1) fault and negligence appear as the basis of assigning liability for injuries caused by indirect actions and one's property.

ארבעה אבות נזיקים השור והבור והמבעה וההבער ... הצד השוה שבהן שדרכן
להזיק ושמירתן עליך וכשהזיק חב המזיק לשלם תשלומי נזק במיטב הארץ

There are four principal categories (*avot*) of damages [mentioned in Scripture]: the ox, the pit, the *mav'eh*,[13] and the fire ... common to all is

---

10   Haut, "Some Aspects," 8–11.
11   *Mekhilta de-Rabbi Ishmael* on tractate *Neziqin* 14. Jacob Lauterback, trans., *Mekhilta de-Rabbi Ishmael,* vol. 2 (1935; repr., Philadelphia: Jewish Publication Society, 2004), 432. The Yerushalmi references an analogous teaching attributed to Tanni R. Ishmael (discussed below). That this teaching of R. Ishmael conflicts with the majority of mishnayot (as we will shortly see) is not at all surprising, given that the Mishnah belongs to the opposing Aqivan School. See Kahana, "The Halakhic Midrashim," 28–35. The Tosefta too is largely based on sources from the school of R. Aqiva. Kahana, 57.
12   The dictum "a person is always forewarned" does not appear in T. Bava Qama.
13   The meaning of this term is unclear and subject to debate in the Talmud. The Bavli presents two interpretations of ox and *mav'eh*. Rav interprets 'ox' as a category that encompasses all damages caused by oxen (i.e. tooth, leg and horn) and other types of livestock,

that they are prone to damage, and they must be under your watch, and if damage is done, the damager must pay restitution from his best estates.

The four primary categories of damages listed here introduce a system that prioritizes negligence when evaluating torts by virtue of its assertion that all "are prone to damage, and they must be under your watch." Precisely because they are likely to cause damage, one is considered negligent should they not be supervised properly, and hence liable to pay restitution.

The third chapter of M. Bava Qama continues with a discussion of how to determine tort liability, with an implicit assumption that each actor's level of fault and negligence is a contributing factor. Namely, whether an owner adequately secured his potentially damaging property or followed expected norms when operating in the public domain, or whether the injured party engaged in an inherently dangerous activity. M. Bava Qama 3:1 rules that one who stumbles upon and breaks a jug left in a public thoroughfare is absolved from responsibility—presumably because he did not purposely act to harm another's property and is thus not at fault.

As with other apparent conflicts between mishnayot, the dissonance between M. Bava Qama 2:6 and the way in which torts are discussed elsewhere is met with attempts at harmonization in the two Talmuds. In particular, M. Bava Qama 2:6 and 3:1 are interpreted in relation to one another, but with contrasting goals in the Yerushalmi and Bavli. In the Yerushalmi, M. Bava Qama 2:6 is viewed through the prism of 3:1, where legal responsibility hinges on fault and negligence; whereas in the Bavli, M. Bava Qama 3:1 is understood based on an assumption of strict liability as the baseline, in accordance with 2:6.

The remainder of this chapter is dedicated to a detailed analysis of how each of the Talmuds treats M. Bava Qama 2:6 and 3:1, examining each mishnah and the amoraic attempts to reconcile them. Contrasting the development of the parallel *sugyot* on 3:1 provides us with a clear demonstration of how the early Amoraim from Babylonia and the Land of Israel took very different approaches to liability, and how later Babylonian Amoraim revised their understanding in a manner that was more consonant with the approach of the Yerushalmi. As we shall see in later chapters, the generations of Babylonian Amoraim who reject strictly liability in the context of M. Bava Qama 3:1 did so in a range of cases, and likewise introduced intention into other areas of law.

---

whereas he interprets *mav'eh* as human-caused harm. Samuel interprets ox and *mav'eh* as two categories of damage done by livestock: 'leg' (trampling) and 'tooth' (eating). See B. Bava Qama 3b.

2   M. Bava Qama 2:6: "A Person Is Always Forewarned"

אדם מועד לעולם בין שוגג בין מזיד בין ער בין ישן סימא את עין חברו ושבר את הכלים משלם נזק שלם

A person (*adam*) is always forewarned (*mu'ad*), whether [the injurious act was] inadvertent (*shogeg*) or malicious (*meizid*) whether awake or asleep. If he blinded his friend's eye or broke vessels, he pays full compensation for damages.[14]

On its surface, this mishnah expresses a doctrine of strict liability in its assertion that every person is considered forewarned at all times, even extending to non-volitional acts that occur during sleep.[15] Although, as noted above, such an understanding renders this mishnah at odds with the majority of tannaitic rulings regarding torts, the presence of internal contradictions and differing views within the Mishnah is not uncommon.[16] M. Bava Qama 2:6 may represent a dissenting view in line with that of R. Ishmael, as against the rest of the rulings in M. Bava Qama on this matter which, like the Mishnah overall, represent the Aqivan School.[17] Nevertheless, the fact that this mishnah mentions

---

14   The final clause demonstrates the scope of a person's liability; it refers to damages inflicted on both persons and objects. The example of blinding an eye is a reference to Exodus 21:24, which opens with: "an eye for an eye." Weiss, *Diyyunim u-Verurim*, 382.

15   Mira Balberg points out that in mishnaic literature, *adam*, a person, is used to denote either a legal subject or a human body that is the object to which things happen, in tandem with artifacts or animals "making the object-like nature of humans in the given context quite apparent." In this way, a person is distinguished either as a "willing, active, self-reflective entity" or an "object-like body." Balberg, *Purity, Body, and Self in Early Rabbinic Literature*, 50–51. The mishnah in question conforms to both, by delineating the compensation required when a person is the legal agent of the damage; he is culpable even where he does so unwillingly. The latter use of *adam* mirrors what Balberg describes as its primary use in mishnaic laws concerning impurity, where human bodies are juxtaposed with and described in identical manners to objects (Balberg, chaps. 1–2.) There indeed is a connection between the realms of ritual impurity and tort liability; just as a body becomes impure through unwilling and unknowing bodily emissions, contacts, etc., in the view of M. Bava Qama 2:6, one is liable for damages their body, even unwillingly and unknowingly, causes.

16   Hanoch Albeck and Yaakov Epstein maintained opposing views regarding Rabbi's editorial role when compiling the Mishnah. For Albeck, Rabbi rarely altered his sources even when they contradict, while Epstein argued for a heavy hand. The internal contradictions in the Mishnah are an important factor for Albeck's position. Albeck, *Introduction To The Mishna*, 99–115; Epstein, *Introduction to Tannaitic literature*, 212–25; Bokser, "Jacob N. Epstein's Introduction to the Text of the Mishnah" offers a summary of Epstein's view.

17   See Kahana, "The Halakhic Midrashim," 28–35. *Supra* n. 11.

inadvertent (*shogeg*) and malicious actions and leaves out the category of coercion (*ones*) may suggest some degree of fault on the part of the tortfeasor corresponding to the balance of mishnayot in M. Bava Qama.[18] *Ones* refers to an action that was coerced by a third party or by circumstances beyond the agent's control, whereas *shogeg* is understood as an action that was performed knowingly and intentionally by the agent, but under mistaken assumptions.[19]

Furthermore, the intent of the mishnah may not be to categorize a person as always liable, but to point out that once found liable, a tortfeasor always pays full compensation, in line with the rule for the owner of a *mu'ad* animal (an animal that has caused injury on three consecutive occasions).[20] Abraham Weiss understands the mishnah as intending to limit compensation for inadvertent injuries to damages alone. The four other compensatory payments (pain, medical expenses, loss of income, and humiliation) are required only when the injury was intentional, and not when the harm is caused by one's animal. This reading is suggested by the mishnah's use of the term *mu'ad*, typically applied only to animals, and by ruling that a person who blinds his friend's eye is liable for "full compensation for damages" (*nezeq shalem*), without mention of the four other compensations.

Quite apart from the original meaning of M. Bava Qama 2:6, the two Talmuds attest to two strikingly different interpretations by early Amoraim.

2.1   Yerushalmi: R. Isaac on the Necessity of Fault

As typifies Yerushalmi *Neziqin*,[21] a single statement comments on M. Bava Qama 2:6 (Y. Bava Qama 3a).

---

[18] Other versions of this mishnah contain the phrase: "whether willing or coerced." See B. Sanhedrin 72a, *Tosafot* B. Yebamot 53b, s.v. "*hakha*." Halivni, *Mekorot U-Mesorot: Baba Kama*, 98. However, Abraham Weiss shows this to be a later addition that was influenced by the statement of Hezeqiah (see below section 2.2). Weiss, *Diyyunim u-Verurim*, 382. Halivni traces this addition to M. Yebamot 6:1 and to the Tosefta writ large, where this is a common phrase.

[19] See M. Nedarim 3:2; B. Nedarim 25b, where the actor understands the law but makes a vow due to a misunderstanding. Also see B. Horiyot 6b; M. Shabbat 7:1; and, for a general overview, Chapter Two of Maimonides' *Mishneh Torah: Hilkhot Shegagot*.

[20] Weiss, *Diyyunim u-Verurim*, 382. Elsewhere in M. Bava Qama and throughout T. Bava Qama, the term *mu'ad* appears in regard to animals and the types of damage that they cause (M. Bava Qama 1:4, 2:4; in T. Bava Qama, *mu'ad* refers to either animals or inanimate objects.) The owner of a *mu'ad* animal is deemed forewarned and hence obligated to pay full compensation. By contrast, when an animal is *tam*, innocent (it has not previously caused injury three times), its owner pays for half the value of the damages to the claimant (M. Bava Qama 1:4).

[21] *Supra* Introduction, n. 32.

אמ' ר' יצחק מתנית' בשהיו שניהם ישינין אבל אם היה אחד מהן ישן ובא חבירו
לישן אצלו זה שבא לישן אצלו הוא המועד

R. Isaac said: Our mishnah [involves a case] in which two were asleep (having gone to sleep at the same time). But if one of them was sleeping and his fellow came and lay down next to him, this [person] who came and slept next to him is the forewarned.[22]

R. Isaac, a third-generation Amora from the Land of Israel (mid-late third century), understands this mishnah to impose liability for damages caused while sleeping only in the event that a person is aware of his fellow or a nearby object before he goes to sleep; in other words, in the presence of fault or negligence.[23] In this circumstance, one must be attentive to the potential that damages can result from natural movements during sleep and take precautions to avert such an outcome. However, if neither another person nor object were present when an actor went to sleep, that person is deemed to have taken adequate preventive measures and is absolved from damages that may occur. According to R. Isaac's understanding of this mishnah, a principle of negligence seems to be the source of liability. This stipulation is thus read into M. Bava Qama 2:6.

R. Isaac's dictum is followed by a passage attributed to *Tanni* R. Ishmael (lit. R. Ishmael taught, though this should not be confused with R. Ishmael himself),[24] which is analogous to the (anonymous) selection from *Mekhilta de-Rabbi*

---

22 Following MS Leiden, since this passage is incomplete in MS Escorial.

23 Weiss views R. Isaac's exemption in relation to the principle articulated in M. Bava Qama. 1:2: "... anything that I have an obligation in guarding, I caused its damages." That is to say, liability is applied to items that one has pledged to watch. In a case where items have been placed beside one who is sleeping, he is not obliged to safeguard that property since he was asleep at the time and, thereby, unable to commit himself; thus, he is exempt if those objects subsequently are damaged. Weiss rejects the notion that this exemption is due to his having acted under duress (Weiss, *Diyyunim u-Verurim*, 383–84.) Nahmanides argues that this Yerushalmi passage does not reject strict liability in principle but, rather, imposes this standard on the second person who lies down beside him and is cognizant of the presence of this property (*Hiddushei Ha-Ramban al Masekhet Bava Metzia* 82b s.v. "*u-matzati*").

24 Although Porton (a student of Neusner) casts doubt on traditions attributed to R. Ishmael and argues that later redactors reworked them in accordance with the dominant school of R. Aqiva, making it impossible to determine with any certainty what R. Ishmael said, Menahem Kahana demonstrates the authenticity of R. Ishmael traditions and that the divisions between the teachings of R. Ishmael versus those of R. Aqiva are apparent. Porton, *The Traditions of Rabbi Ishmael*, 4:218–25; Kahana, "The Halakhic Midrashim," 39, n. 161. Indeed in this case, although the attribution to R. Ishmael is uncertain, it may be deemed a tradition from his school due to its parallel in *Mekhilta de-Rabbi Ishmael.*

Ishmael quoted above. Unlike R. Isaac, *Tanni* Rabbi Ishmael endorses liability even without fault:

תני ר' ישמעאל ... והאש מלמדת על כולהן שהוא חייב על האונסין

> *Tanni* R. Ishmael ... [The category of] fire [mentioned in Scripture] teaches that, for all of them (i.e. all of the primary categories of damages), one is [even] liable for [damages that occur] under coercion.[25]

As in the passage from *Mekhilta de-Rabbi Ishmael*, this citation in the Yerushalmi deduces from the primary category of fire that one is liable for damages, even those that result from acts done under coercion. Although this teaching represents an exception to the Yerushalmi's overarching tendency to require fault as a condition for liability, it appears only in the anonymous stratum as a possible rationale for why Scripture lists the primary categories of damages. Moreover, as it is clearly a teaching of the R. Ishmael School, it is not at all surprising that it conflicts with the dominant approach of the Mishnah which is attributed to the school of R. Aqiva.[26] Indeed, the Yerushalmi offers no indication that this stance was espoused by Amoraim from the Land of Israel; rather, the dominant position presented in the Yerushalmi bases liability on the presence of fault.

2.2   *Bavli: Strict Liability*

The parallel passage in the Bavli does not include the teaching by R. Isaac. Instead, B. Bava Qama 26b opens with the view of Hezeqiah,[27] a first-generation Babylonian Amora. Hezeqiah and his school are cited as bringing biblical support for the dictum of M. Bava Qama 2:6, "a person is always forewarned" (*adam muʿad le-olam*):

אמר חזקיה וכן תני דבי חזקיה אמר קרא פצע תחת פצע לחייבו על השוגג
כמזיד ועל האונס כרצון

> Hezeqiah said, and the school of Hezeqiah[28] likewise taught: Scripture states 'a wound for a wound' (Exodus 21:25) in order to make one liable for inadvertent [harm] as malicious [harm] and coerced as willing [acts].

---

25 Y. Bava Qama 2b (MS Leiden).
26 Kahana, "The Halakhic Midrashim," 28–40, 56–57. *Supra* n. 11.
27 Hezeqiah was born in Babylonia and immigrated to the Land of Israel with his father Hiyya. See Strack and Stemberger, *Introduction to the Talmud and Midrash*, 83.
28 Absent from MSS Munich 95 and Florence II I 7–9. In three other instances Hezeqiah and his school are credited with deducing legal rulings from biblical verses, all in the Bavli: B. Shabbat 24b; B. Sanhedrin 15b; and B. Temurah 4b.

In this teaching, which appears nowhere else in extant rabbinic literature,[29] Hezeqiah interprets the Torah's injunction that one is liable "a wound for a wound" to impose liability under any circumstance in which one causes injury, even in the absence of fault. Hezeqiah thus reads the mishnah as espousing absolute responsibility and furnishes it with a biblical proof text; foreclosing any reading of the mishnah that might imply otherwise. This position is underscored by his inclusion of the phrase "coerced as willing [acts]." Weiss notes that in contrast with the mishnah, Hezeqiah equates coerced, inadvertent, and intentional damage in every respect, thereby obligating one to pay for damages along with the four other compensations in cases of personal injury.[30]

Following a discussion of the validity of Hezeqiah's scriptural derivation, the Bavli presents several rulings in the name of Rabbah, a third-generation Babylonian Amora, that concur with Hezeqiah's reading of M. Bava Qama 2:6 by imposing liability for damages, even when harm was unintended. Although we will analyze this group of cases in Chapter 2, the first case merits attention here, due to its intrinsic association with the explanation ascribed to Hezeqiah:

אמ' רבה היתה אבן מונחת לו בחיקו ולא הכיר בה מעולם ועמד ונפלה לענין נזקין חייב לענין ארבעה דברים פטור...

Rabbah[31] said: If one had a stone resting on his lap, and he had never been aware of it,[32] and he rose and [the stone] fell; with regard

---

29 Both Talmuds record a related teaching in the name of Hezeqiah and his school (albeit with several differences), which states that one who kills another's animal, whether inadvertently or maliciously, is obligated to compensate that loss, whereas if the victim is a person, he is exempt from monetary compensation. This may not reflect Hezeqiah's stance on torts since it only applies to the laws of murder. See B. Bava Qama 35a and Y. Ketubot 27c. *Infra* Chapter 5 where I discuss manslaughter.

30 Weiss, *Diyyunim u-Verurim*, 383–84. See *Mekhilta de-Rabbi Shimon b. Yohai*, Exodus 21:22, which states that one who injures another person is liable for all five compensations, whether or not there was intent to cause harm.

31 Rava, according to MSS Munich 95, Vatican 116, Florence II 1 7–9. As noted in the introduction (*supra* n. 36 there), Shamma Friedman has pointed out that the orthographic distinction between the names 'Rava' and 'Rabbah' was a later development in order to differentiate between the two rabbis. Friedman, "Writing of the Names." Friedman maintains that Rabbah is the correct attribution in this case. Friedman, 154.

32 In such a case, one would have placed an object on a sleeping person's lap. Upon waking, he stands and the stone falls and causes damage. (*Shita Mequbetzet*, s.v. *ve-lo*.) Alternatively, Rabbah might have been describing a scenario where the actor was sifting or winnowing grain, and a stone landed on his lap without his awareness (M. Beitzah 1:8, B. Beitzah 13b B. Sotah 14b, B. Bava Batra 93b–94a). This latter possibility includes a certain degree of risk; thus, the actor should have taken precautions prior to standing, despite the minimal likelihood of danger. I am grateful to Steven Friedell for sharing this interpretation with me.

to damages, he is liable; with regard to the [other] four things (i.e. the four forms of compensation), he is exempt ... [33]

Despite being unaware of the stone resting on their lap, Rabbah deems the one who set it in motion liable.[34] Rabbah's ruling conforms to a framework of strict liability without regard for negligence. In a system of negligence, steps need not be taken to avoid far-fetched risks or unforeseeable consequences of a given action. Rather, a determination of liability depends on distinguishing "the potential for harm in the defendant's act from the background harms that are part and parcel of all action."[35] Although Rabbah's ruling conforms to strict liability by penalizing the "unintended consequences of intentional acts,"[36] it is not clear that he would go so far as Hezeqiah's statement in equating coercion with willful actions, since in this case the act itself (standing) was intentional. Still, the placement of Rabbah's ruling immediately following Hezeqiah's dictum (notwithstanding an intervening section questioning Hezeqiah's derivation), indicates that the redactors identified a similarity between their stances consistent with a reading of M. Bava Qama 2:6 that espouses strict liability. The teaching of Hezeqiah equating coercion with willful acts has no parallel in extant rabbinic literature, making its authenticity suspect;[37] nevertheless, it is congruent with other early amoraic rulings quoted in the Bavli and seems to represent the stance taken within early Babylonian jurisprudence. This characterization will be further supported in our discussion of Mishnah Bava Qama 3:1 below.

In sum, M. Bava Qama 2:6 is understood differently in the two Talmuds. The Bavli cites Hezeqiah's teaching which reads this mishnah as straightforwardly applying a standard of strict liability and extends it even to acts committed under coercion. Rabbah's strict ruling is next cited, which correlates with this view. In contrast, the Yerushalmi offers a ruling by R. Isaac, which restricts the apparent strict ruling of M. Bava Qama 2:6 regarding one who is asleep

---

33   B. Bava Qama 26b. The remainder of this statement discusses the ramifications of this case with regard to the laws of the Sabbath, slave manumission, and manslaughter, which I discuss in the next chapter.
34   However, unlike Hezeqiah, Rabbah does not extend liability to the other four compensations, echoing the Mishnah's position. See the discussion above.
35   Weinrib, *Private Law*, 167.
36   Haut, "Some Aspects," 39. This is not to say that Rabbah considered intent, for here the tortfeasor lacks the intent to inflict harm or even awareness of a potential risk.
37   Moreover, another teaching cited in the name of the house of Hezeqiah, which appears several times in the Bavli, makes no mention of *ones* (coercion) but imposes liability only when one damages another's animal in cases of *shogeg* and *meizid*. See Katz and Stern, "Hithayvut Muhletet: Toldot Adam Ha'mazik".

FROM TANNAITIC TO EARLY AMORAIC LAW

to instances where the responsible party demonstrates a degree of fault. The rulings ascribed to Hezeqiah and Rabbah are absent.[38]

3 M. Bava Qama 3:1: Exemption for Accidental Damages

In contrast with M. Bava Qama 2:6, M. Bava Qama 3:1 appears to make liability contingent on fault.

המניח את הכד ברשות הרבים ובא אחר ונתקל בה ושיברה פטור ואם הוזק בה
בעל החבית חייב בניזקו...

> One who leaves a jug in the public domain, and another comes, stumbles upon it and breaks it, he (the one who breaks it) is absolved [from paying for the broken jug]. If he is injured by it, the owner of the jug is liable to pay for his injury.

Unlike M. Bava Qama 2:6, the first case of this mishnah does not impose liability on a pedestrian who accidentally breaks a jug that was left out in the public domain, even though he caused direct damage to property.[39] Rather, it absolves him from legal responsibility, whereas the owner of the jug is held liable for injuries caused by this accident. As this analysis will show, like in the previous case, the discussions of this mishnah in the Talmuds reach divergent conclusions. Remarkably, these different approaches are reached with reference to near verbatim citations of the same amoraic statements.

3.1 *Yerushalmi: Rav, Samuel and R. El'azar: Liability Determined by Fault*
The Yerushalmi comments on this mishnah as follows:[40]

(a) ואין דרכו של אדם להיות מבחין[41] ברשות הרבים

---

38 In general, Rabbah is not mentioned in Y. Neziqin. Sussman, "Ve-shuv Li-yerushalmi Neziqin," 131, n. 179.
39 We will discuss the latter clause of this mishnah in Chapter 2.
40 Following the text of the Rosenthal edition, based on MS Escorial. Rosenthal and Lieberman, *Yerushalmi Neziqin*, 3.
41 MS Leiden presents an alternate formulation of the anonymous opening question: "Is it not customary for people to leave [belongings] out in the public domain?" Here the introductory query focuses on property owners' obligations rather than the expectations placed on pedestrians in such circumstances; by extension, this *sugya* reaches a contrasting conclusion from that found in the Rosenthal edition. This discussion emphasizes the responsibility of the owner who left his possessions in public, thereby making them

vulnerable to the resulting damage, and asks whether one has a right to place belongings out in this way and then seek redress if they are harmed. In MS Leiden, as in the Bavli, the anonymous voice inquires why a pedestrian would be exempt if property owners have the right to place their belongings in the public domain. In both versions, Rav's statement, "Where it fills the whole public domain" immediately follows. According to MS Leiden, Rav implies that one may leave belongings out and receive compensation for damages only where the public domain is filled with personal property. Otherwise, owners may neither leave their possessions in public nor collect compensation in case of damage. An opinion by Samuel then provides another instance when an owner may leave his property unattended in public: if he places them on a corner. R. El'azar's ruling follows:

(a) ואפי׳ אינה ממלא כל רשות הרבים
(b) אם יטלינה מיכאן ויתנינה כאן הרי זה בור
(c) ואפי׳ אינה נתונה על קרן זוית אין דרך אדם להיות מניחן ברשות הרבים.
(d) היתה ממלא כל רשות הרבים אם יטלינה מיכן ויתנינה כאן נעשה בור...

(a) And even if it does not fill the whole public domain,
(b) if one takes it from here and places it here; this is a pit [that is made] (*harei zeh bor*).
(c) And even if it is not placed on a corner, it is not customary for a person to leave [their belongings] in the public domain.
(d) Where it fills the whole public domain, if one takes it from here and places it here, a pit is made (*na'aseh bor*) ...

It is unclear how the final clause of R. El'azar's statement (d) relates to the preceding traditions, which address an owner's right to leave his belongings in public, since this closing comment seems to address a pedestrian's ability to navigate a public area that is overtaken by privately owned objects. The condition in (d), "if one takes it from here and places it here, a pit is made..." also appears in (b), as following the opening clause (a). Passages (a) and (b) form a highly problematic sentence since the first line seemingly refers to the pedestrian whereas the second explicitly addresses the property owner. This second line (b) may have been mistakenly copied from (d), where this conditional statement also follows the phrase "fills the whole public domain;" meaning that (a) and (c) originally appeared as an uninterrupted clause, as in MS Escorial. (Alternatively, since R. El'azar opens by remarking that "even" where the whole domain is filled with property, owners may not leave out their belongings, as in MS Escorial, an echo of Rav's ruling, it is conceivable that (b) was intentionally copied from (d) and inserted between (a) and (c) to separate these lines and distinguish this teaching from Rav's opinion.)

Although MS Leiden, which focuses on the owner of the property, differs from the Bavli's discussion, which is centered on the pedestrian, this manuscript variant may represent an attempt to reconcile this Yerushalmi *sugya* with the corresponding Bavli one (B. Bava Qama 27b). The Bavli and the Rosenthal edition of the Yerushalmi cite identical rulings by Rav and Samuel but they reach opposing conclusions on pedestrians' responsibilities. In the Rosenthal edition, Rav and Samuel cite exceptional circumstances that require pedestrians to pay attention and thus take precautions whereas, in the Bavli, these opinions represent the normative situations in which pedestrians are exempt from such attentiveness for no dependable precaution is available. By modifying one term throughout this *sugya* (*mavhin* to *manihan*) ("be attentive" to "leave [belongings] out"), the scribe of MS Leiden aligned these statements of Rav and Samuel with their significance in the Bavli, effectively shifting responsibility back to the pedestrian and asserting that owners have the right to leave their property out and that, therefore, pedestrians are normally liable. However, as noted above, the resulting text does not read coherently. Furthermore, the Rosenthal edition is corroborated by the parallel *sugya* in the Bavli, where R. Abba

(b) רב אמ'. בממלא לכל רשות הרבים אבל אם אינה ממלא את כל רשות הרבים אין דרכו של אדם להיות מבחין[42] ברשות הרבים

(c) שמואל אמ' בממלא את כל רשות הרבים או עד שתהא נתונה בקרן זוית

(d) אמ' ר' אלעז' ואפי' [אינה ממל]א[43] את כל רשות הרבים[44] ואפי' אינה נתונה בקרן זוית אין דרכו של אדם להיות מבחין[45] ברשות הרבים

(e) היתה ממלא את כל רשות הרבים שאם יטלינה מכאן ויתנינה כן נעשה בור אלא יטול את המקל וישברנה או יעבור עליה אם נשברה נשברה

(a) Is it not customary for a person to be attentive in the public domain?
(b) Rav said: 'When it fills the whole public domain'. But if it does not fill the whole public domain, it is not customary for a person to be attentive in the public domain.
(c) Samuel said: When it fills the whole public domain or when it is placed on a corner.
(d) R. El'azar said: And even if it does not fill the whole public domain, and even if it is not placed on a corner, it[46] is not customary for a person to be attentive in the public domain.
(e) Where it fills the whole public domain, if one takes it from here and places it here, a 'pit' is made (it qualifies under the category of 'pit').[47] One should rather take his stick and break it or pass over it, and if it breaks, it breaks.[48]

This *sugya* opens with an anonymous question, which frames the context for the amoraic citations that follow: (a) why does the mishnah absolve the pedestrian who breaks the jug if everyone is expected to be attentive while walking in a

---

reports in the name of R. Ila'i: " 'In the West', they say, 'Because it is not customary for people to pay attention on the roads,'" which quotes this same Palestinian tradition. For these reasons, along with the scholarly consensus that MS Escorial, which serves as the principal basis for the Rosenthal edition, is generally superior to MS Leiden, it seems likely that this edition is closer to the original text of the Yerushalmi and the tradition that was prevalent in the Land of Israel. See Rosenthal, *Yerushalmi Neziqin*, Introduction.

42 להיות מניחם] MS Leiden. See previous note.
43 Following MS Leiden. It seems highly probable that this is the text missing from MS Escorial as well.
44 הרבים אם יטלינה מיכאן ויתנינה כאן הרי זה בור] MS Leiden. See above.
45 להיות מניחן] MS Leiden. See above.
46 It is unclear whether this is a redactional gloss similar to that added to Rav's statement, or it is part of R. El'azar's statement. See note 50 below.
47 The implication is that, by moving the jug to a new location, one creates the paradigm of a pit, namely an obstacle in the public domain for which that agent would be liable for anyone or anything that might be damaged by it.
48 Y. Bava Qama 3b.

public domain?[49] The centrality of this issue is emphasized by the apparently redactional comment that immediately follows the quotation from Rav: (b) "But if it does not fill the whole public domain, it is not customary ..."[50] This response rhetorically directs Rav's statement toward the introductory query. Comments ascribed to Rav and Samuel, both first-generation Babylonian Amoraim (late second to mid-third century), are presented as replies to the initial question by each supplying the rare situations when a pedestrian must exercise caution while walking in public (b, c) thereby affirming that such vigilance is not generally normative. R. El'azar, a second-generation Amora,[51] then explains that pedestrians are *never* expected to be on alert when traversing a public domain (d).

There are several inconsistencies in this passage from the Yerushalmi. The statement credited to R. El'azar appears to reiterate Rav and Samuel's respective interpretations (i.e. that attentiveness is only demanded under exceptional circumstances) though he is presented as responding to them and ostensibly disagreeing. It is also unclear whether section (e) is a continuation of R. El'azar's statement, or (more likely) it belongs to the anonymous stratum. Despite these uncertainties within R. El'azar's quotation, he undoubtedly releases the pedestrian who broke the vessel from liability under any condition and either he or the redactors applies this exemption to one who deliberately breaks a jug impeding his path. This action is justified as an expression of a pedestrian's inherent right to travel through a public area unhindered.[52]

However, this *sugya* poses a more fundamental difficulty: neither of the statements of Rav and Samuel (nor R. El'azar's, if it is a response to theirs) explicitly addresses this mishnah's release from liability. Rather, they mention extraordinary conditions when it is expected that people will pay attention when walking in a public thoroughfare, implying that in such cases a pedestrian would be held to an unusual standard of liability. Yet, without the anonymous question that introduces them (a), these statements by Rav and Samuel would be incoherent since, considered independently, they appear as qualifications of M. Bava Qama 3:1, specifying the very few conditions under which the mishnah releases the pedestrian. It is therefore likely that the redactional gloss attached to Rav's statement ("But if it does not fill the whole public domain, it is not customary for a

---

49 See the commentary by Lieberman in Rosenthal and Lieberman, *Yerushalmi Neziqin*, 114.
50 Applying Shamma Friedman's criteria for distinguishing between amoraic and redactional statements: It is easily detachable from the rest of Rav's statement, it alters the meaning of Rav's statement, and it is repeated throughout the passage, including in the opening question. The second part of Rav's statement is also lacking in the Bavli's parallel version. Friedman, "A Critical Study," 301–8.
51 Originally from Babylonia, where he studied under Samuel and Rav, R. El'azar later immigrated to the Land of Israel, where he became a student of R. Yohanan.
52 See Owen, "Philosophical Foundations of Fault in Tort Law," 220.

FROM TANNAITIC TO EARLY AMORAIC LAW 31

person to be attentive in the public domain") offers an inaccurate inference, and that Rav and Samuel's statements were in fact originally intended to qualify the mishnah: a pedestrian is only exempt when a public thoroughfare is filled with jugs or if the jug had been placed on a corner. R. El'azar's response would thus counter that the plain meaning of the mishnah stands: pedestrians are never expected to pay such close attention as they walk in the public domain and are always exempt from liability for accidental damages. Not only does this provide a more cogent reading, but, as we will see below, this understanding is congruent with the comments of Rav and Samuel in the parallel *sugya* in the Bavli, suggesting that the Bavli preserves the correct context for their statements.

Notwithstanding the questionable coherence of this *sugya*, it is broadly consistent with the Yerushalmi's comment on M. Bava Qama 2:6 for its rejection of strict liability. This *sugya*, much like M. Bava Qama 2:6, considers pedestrians blameless in cases of accidental damages (and, in certain instances, even intentional ones).

3.2   Bavli: Rav, Samuel and R. Yohanan: Strict Liability

The parallel *sugya* in the Bavli conveys the same rulings by Rav and Samuel, but as direct responses to the mishnah, in this case by restricting exemptions to instances when the pedestrian is deemed to lack the ability to avoid causing harm. This *sugya* is particularly noteworthy for, in its ultimate redactional form, it illustrates how subsequent generations of Babylonian Amoraim understood this mishnah, encapsulating the shift from prioritizing strict liability to considering negligence and fault when determining liability, the legal trajectory that I suggest in this study. It is also the single Talmudic passage concerning torts that incorporates statements from all of the generations together. I therefore present this *sugya* in its entirety, including opinions by later Amoraim (which are analyzed in detail in subsequent chapters), to provide an overview of the chronological progression of this unified composition:

(A)   אמאי פטור לימא ליה איבעי לך עיוני ומיזל

(B)   אמרי בי רב משמיה דרב בממלא רשות הרבים כולה חביות ושמואל אמ' באפלה שאנו ר' יוחנן אמ' בקרן זוית שנו

(C)   אמ' רב פפא לא דיקא מתני' אלא או כשמואל או כר' יוחנן דאי כרב מאי איריא נתקל אפלו שבר נמי

(D)   אמ' רב זביד משמיה דרבא הוא הדין דאפלו שבר נמי[53]והאי דקתני נתקל משום דקא בעי למתנא סופא אם הוזק בה בעל חבית חייב ודוקא נתקל אבל שבר הוא והוזק הוא לא מאי טע' הוא אזיק נפשיה (וק)תני רישא נתקל

---

53   The switch to Aramaic along with the extensiveness of this section likely indicate a redactional addition to R. Zebid's statement. See Friedman, "A Critical Study," 301–8.

('D) אמ' ליה ר' אבא לרב אשי אמרי במערבא משמיה דר' אלעאי לפי שאין דרכן של בני אדם להתבונן בדרכים

('C) הוה עובדא בנהרדעא וחייב שמואל בפומבדיתא וחייב רבה

('B) בשלמא שמואל כשמעתיה אלא רבה לימא כשמואל סבירא ליה

('A) אמ' רב פפא התם קרנא דעצרא הוה כיון דברשות קא עבדי איבעי ליה עיוני ומיזל

(A) Why is he (the pedestrian who stumbles in M. Bava Qama 3:1) exempt? Let us say to him: you should look and walk!

(B) The school of Rav said in the name of Rav: [This mishnah speaks of a case] where the whole public domain is filled with jugs.
Samuel said: They taught [that this ruling applies when the public domain is] in darkness.
R. Yohanan said: They taught [that this ruling applies when the jug was placed] on a corner.

(C) R. Papa said: Our mishnah is not precise unless [we interpret it] according to Samuel or R. Yohanan. For if [we explain it] like Rav, why [does the mishnah] specify 'stumble' - even if he broke it [intentionally he would] also [be exempt].

(D) R. Zebid said in the name of Rava: It is the same rule, that even if he [intentionally] broke [the jug], [he is] also [exempt]. And [the reason] that [the mishnah] teaches 'stumbles' is because it wanted to teach the latter clause [of the mishnah]: 'If he (the pedestrian) is injured by it, the owner of the jug is liable.' And [this applies] specifically if he stumbles; but not if he breaks it [intentionally] and is injured by it. What is the reason? He injured himself. [Thus] the first clause of the mishnah taught 'he stumbles'.

(D') R. Abba said to R. Ashi: They say in the West in the name of R. Ila'i:[54] Because it is not customary for people to pay attention on the roads.

(C') There was an incident (like the simple case from the mishnah) in Nehardea and Samuel held [that one] liable. In Pumbedita, and Rabbah[55] held [that one] liable.

(B') It is well [for] Samuel, [for he is following] his own teaching. But as for Rabbah, should we say that he reasons like Samuel?

---

54   ר' אילעא] MSS Escorial G-I-3, Munich 95, Florence II I 7–9; ר' עולא] ed. Vilna; ר' אליעזא] MS Vatican 116. Piskei Ha-Rosh and the Rif also contain the attribution of ר' אלעאי. *Hiddushei HaRa'avad* states ר' אלעא.

55   רבא] MSS Hamburg, Vatican 116, ed. Vilna רבה] MSS Escorial G-I-3, Munich 95, Florence II-I 7–9, ed. Soncino, RiF Sefer Ha-Halakhot. See Chapter 2 for an elaborated discussion

(A')   R. Papa said: There (in Pumbedita), it was on the corner of a press; since he (the owner of the jug) acted with permission; he (the pedestrian) should look and walk.[56]

This *sugya* captures the changing views among Babylonian Amoraim from strict liability to fault, which is underscored by its chiastic structure:[57] Both (A) and (A') state that a pedestrian "should look and walk;" (B, C) and (B', C') examine aspects of this early amoraic stance; (D) and (D') present later Babylonian amoraic as well as Land of Israel rulings that consider fault. It is possible that the placement of these late Babylonian and Land of Israel positions at the center of this series of comments as the focal point of the *sugya* highlight their importance for the Bavli's redactors. It is noteworthy that despite its linguistic parallel to the introductory comment (A), the final passage (A') operates on an opposing assumption.

Like the Yerushalmi, this *sugya* begins with an anonymous question on the mishnah. This opening (A) expresses surprise at the mishnah's ruling with the rhetorical query: isn't he required to look while he walks? In other words, don't pedestrians have an obligation to watch where they go and therefore be held liable for stumbling? This remark assumes that an unintended fall is insufficient to absolve a tortfeasor of responsibility for the damages caused. The *sugya* next cites rulings (B) from the first-generation Babylonian sages Rav and Samuel, then R. Yohanan, a second-generation Amora from the Land of Israel.[58] All three statements are presented as qualifications to the case in this mishnah, to eliminate any suggestion that the pedestrian could have prevented this incident. According to Rav, the public domain was full of jugs; Samuel situates the event in darkness; R. Yohanan maintains that the jug was left on a corner, where the pedestrian was unable to see it. Thus, in any other condition, the pedestrian would have been liable.

---

on attributions of 'Rava' and 'Rabbah.' The fact that the incident is reported as having occurred in Pumbedita strongly suggests that Rabbah is the correct attribution.

56   B. Bava Qama 27b.
57   Ancient and classical texts typically utilize chiastic structures to highlight key points. Similar use of this literary devise has been demonstrated in biblical and rabbinic texts. For examples in biblical texts, see Cassuto, *A Commentary on the Book of Genesis, Part II*; Milgrom, *JPS: Numbers*; Steinmetz, *From Father to Son*, 60–87.

   For rabbinic texts, see Norman Cohen, "Structural Analysis of a Talmudic Story"; Fraenkel, *Darchei Ha-Aggada Veha-Midrash*, 23–269, 307; Steinmetz, "Must the Patriarch Know 'Uqtzin?," 171.
58   In several instances, R. Yohanan b. Nappaha, a second-generation Amora in third-century Palestine, is mentioned with Rav and Samuel, indicating that, irrespective of whether he belonged to their generation, he was considered their intellectual peer.

Despite these qualifications, the plain sense of the mishnah indicates that one who stumbles upon a jug that has been left in the public domain is not held accountable for damaging it. Moreover, it is the owner of that jug who is at fault and liable for injury to the pedestrian. In contrast to the Yerushalmi, which construes the amoraic statements as interpreting the mishnah to be broadly applicable to normal circumstances, the Bavli cites three amoraic statements (B) that limit the mishnah. The Bavli's assumption is that a stumbling pedestrian would normally be liable but for the fact that no precaution on his part could have averted the accident (Samuel and R. Yohanan), while still preserving the public domain as a viable thoroughfare (Rav).

These three amoraic rulings initially appear to subscribe to a system of negligence, in that they expect a pedestrian to exercise extreme caution under normal circumstances; his failure to do so results in liability for stumbling. However, the qualifications posed by Rav and Samuel in particular imply that liability always remains, unless it was absolutely impossible for the pedestrian to avoid stumbling. If in their view it is only when no preventative measures are available to a pedestrian that he would be absolved, this suggests that in the opinions from Rav, Samuel and R. Yohanan fault is not actually factored into the determination of guilt, thus reflecting a position much closer to one of strict liability.

Moreover, despite the apparent negligence on the part of one who leaves his possessions in a public thoroughfare where it is likely to be harmed, these early amoraic rulings focus on the direct cause of damage, namely the pedestrian. When faced with a negligent act that precipitates an accident and its immediate cause, these early Amoraim place legal responsibility on the latter. This logic is in consonance with a doctrine of strict liability,[59] as is Rav, Samuel and R. Yohanan's view that in such cases where the owner of a jug creates a situation in which an accident is unavoidable, he is considered the sole actor and is responsible. This adherence to strict liability brought Rav, Samuel and R. Yohanan to develop an understanding of M. Bava Qama 3:1 that hardly accords with a straightforward reading, though it may very well be an attempt to reconcile it with M. Bava Qama 2:6, which states that "a person is always forewarned" and hence must always pay full restitution for damages.[60]

Indeed, the next passage of the *sugya* (C) states that later Amoraim override this interpretation. R. Papa (a fifth-generation Babylonian Amora of the

---

59   Epstein, "A Theory of Strict Liability," 177–79.
60   In *Piskei Ha-Rosh* B. Bava Qama 3:1, R. Asher b. Yekhiel (late thirteenth to early fourteenth century) makes this point.

fourth century and student of Rava) challenges the reading ascribed to Rav: he contends that, following Rav's construal of this case, the pedestrian should be exempt from liability even if he broke (*shavar*) the jug; the use of an active verb form in this context emphasizes intent, implying that he deliberately broke a jug to proceed on his way. R. Papa's statement could be explained as highlighting a gap in Rav's application of absolute liability. Legal scholars have observed that, according to systems of strict liability, whoever generates a hazard is responsible for subsequent damages, even if another agent directly causes that injury, whether through negligence or even willfully, because the harm was an outcome of the dangerous condition produced by the first party, rendering the subsequent actor legally inconsequential.[61] R. Papa thereby asserts that Rav's interpretation is not supported by the mishnah, which states that the pedestrian is only exempt if he damages the jug accidentally.

R. Zebid (another fifth-generation Babylonian Amora and student of Rava) responds to R. Papa's objection by reporting a tradition from Rava (D), which either affirms that Rav's teaching is compatible with the mishnah—i.e. intentional harm is justified in such an instance, because it seems unavoidable and allows the pedestrian to pass through a public area as he is entitled to do—or offers an alternate, autonomous interpretation of this mishnah. One indication of the independence of R. Zebid's citation of Rava is the appearance of this same teaching as a direct interpretation of this mishnah on B. Bava Qama 28a, without reference to R. Papa or his question. The central placement of (D) in this chiastically structured *sugya* may also signal its autonomy from the other statements therein. If so, this passage would indicate that Rava always exempts pedestrians for the damages that they cause, even if their way is not complicated by jugs, darkness, or other impediments; such a position would represent a marked departure from the early Babylonian posture, since the pedestrian is never held responsible. It also conforms to Rava's general stance, which is discussed in detail in Chapters Three and Four. Importantly, his reading is congruent with the final ruling in the Yerushalmi *sugya*, which correlates with the broader tendency, observed by Yaakov Elman, that statements attributed to Rava often articulate Palestinian interpretations of the Mishnah.[62]

A more blatant rejection of the earlier amoraic approach is evident toward the end of this passage, in R. Papa's interpretation of the third-generation Babylonian Amora, Rabbah's ruling, which imposes liability on a pedestrian in a case that is comparable to the situation presented in our mishnah (C').

---

61 Epstein, "A Theory of Strict Liability," 181.
62 Elman, "Rava Ve-Darkei Ha-Iyyun Ha-Eretz Yisraeliyyot Be-Midrash Ha-Halakhah"; see also Gray, *A Talmud in Exile*, chap. six.

This ruling is consistent with Rabbah's decisions that assign liability in the absence of fault (discussed above in regard to M. Bava Qama 2:6).[63] Nevertheless, R. Papa limits the application of Rabbah's judgment to the instance of a jug that is left on the corner of a press, which is clearly within the prerogative of its owner (A'). In this setting, pedestrians are expected to proceed with caution while, in all other instances, R. Papa understands Rabbah to view them as exempt. Although the same logic is applied (by R. Papa or more probably added by the redactors)[64] as that found in the anonymous question, its meaning is reversed in this conclusion: This *sugya* opens by reasoning that, despite the mishnaic teaching, pedestrians are normally responsible for accidental damages since they are expected to pay attention to their surroundings. R. Papa argues that Rabbah typically absolves pedestrians, though he holds them responsible only in the limited case where owners are permitted to leave their jugs in public by the press. Thus, the principle that restricts exemptions at the beginning of this *sugya* is used to limit culpability at its conclusion.

Let us now return to the midpoint of this *sugya*, where the statements by R. Zebid and R. Papa are followed by R. Abba's report to R. Ashi (all sixth-generation Babylonian Amoraim) of another interpretation of this mishnah, in the name of R. Ila'i "from the West" (a third-generation Amora from the Land of Israel and student of R. Yohanan), that operates from a similar principle (D').[65] R. Abba grants a release for damages that are inadvertently caused when passing through a public domain, since it is not normative for pedestrians to be alert in this setting. This decision presumably applies even if the harm incurred is preventable. This view represents a clear departure from earlier Babylonian interpretations of M. Bava Qama 3:1, since R. Abba neither obligates pedestrians to take precautions nor does he hold them responsible to remit compensation. Unlike his Babylonian predecessors, R. Abba's understanding of this mishnah maintains its plain meaning. Moreover, it is virtually

---

63 Haut, "Some Aspects," 28. In Chapter 2 I address Rabbah's approach in detail.
64 It is detachable from the beginning of R. Papa's statement and repeats the opening question. See Friedman, "A Critical Study," 301–8.
65 Several texts mention R. Abba reporting Palestinian teachings to R. Ashi. During the careers of fourth- and fifth-generation Babylonian Amoraim, numerous sages from the Land of Israel immigrated to Babylonia and brought traditions from their homeland with them. Sussman, "Ve-shuv Li-yerushalmi Neziqin," 113, n. 211. The Bavli also reports that a number of his decisions were dispatched to Babylonia (B. Erubin 96a; B. Bava Batra 144b). In the Yerushalmi, this statement is attributed to R. El'azar, whereas the Bavli contains several possible variants in manuscript and print editions. Richard Kalmin has also noted the "influx of Palestinian traditions" into Babylonia during the fourth century. Kalmin, *Jewish Babylonia*, chaps. 7 and 8.

identical to the opinion of R. El'azar (the teacher of R. Ila'i),[66] as presented in the Yerushalmi. Given many similarities between 'Ila'i' and 'El'azar'—their names, lifetimes, residences and their close association with R. Yohanan—and the general tendency for the Bavli and Yerushalmi to offer different attributions for the same statement, it is hardly surprising that the ascriptions to these Amoraim may have been reversed.[67] Moreover, the textual witnesses transmit various forms of the name 'Ila'i' for this particular attribution, with MS Vatican 116 referring to 'El'aza,' much like the Yerushalmi. However, it is also possible that R. Ila'i held this opinion, accepting the stance of his teacher R. El'azar. Regardless of whether 'Ila'i' is a corruption of 'El'azar' or a reliable attribution, the Palestinian tradition reported by R. Abba is both consistent with and corroborated by the Yerushalmi.

The ordering of this *sugya* presents a chronological progression of the Babylonian amoraic system of liability. The first three generations cited — Rav and Samuel, R. Yohanan, and Rabbah, respectively — each impose responsibility on the pedestrian despite the absence of fault. Rava, in the fourth generation, considers the pedestrian exempt, and his students reverse earlier amoraic decisions that ruled otherwise. The position from the Land of Israel referenced in this *sugya* similarly deems the pedestrian in the mishnah to be free from liability.

3.3   *Bavli and Yerushalmi: Identical Traditions, Divergent Rulings*

As this analysis has shown, the discussions of M. Bava Qama 3:1 in both Talmuds include near identical quotations, although they reach contrasting conclusions. This raises questions regarding the context and authenticity of these traditions, particularly the earlier teachings, which touch on broader issues with respect to the redactional history of the Talmuds. It is tempting, and in many ways compelling, to suggest that the Bavli presents the statements by Rav and Samuel with greater authenticity where their rulings directly address and offer qualifications of M. Bava Qama 3:1 (B). By contrast, the Yerushalmi situates these decisions as responses to an anonymous inquiry, which then offer exceptions to the mishnaic teaching (b, c); without such contextualization, these ascriptions to Rav and Samuel would be enigmatic at best. Moreover, R. El'azar's response (d) is readily comprehensible only if the comments by Rav and Samuel are read as they appear according to the Bavli. These factors would suggest a reframing by the redactors of the Yerushalmi to support the system of liability based on fault that was preferred in the Land of Israel, as

---

66   See Y. Terumah 2:1 (41b).
67   Frankel, *Mevo*, 41b.

evidenced by the *sugya* on M. Bava Qama 2:6, which cites R. Isaac limiting the strict connotation of *adam mu'ad le-olam*. Moreover, the version of Rav's statement that appears in the Bavli is affirmed by R. Papa's challenge of that earlier sage's severe interpretation (C), which indicates that this reading was not a product of later redactional filtering but a teaching that had already become established during the amoraic period. Samuel's reading is also confirmed, albeit anonymously, by a tradition in which he too issues a strict decision (C'). R. Papa's attempt to harmonize a similar ruling issued by Rabbah (A'), further verifies the fifth-generation understanding of this early amoraic position. Furthermore, the version of Samuel's statement that appears in the Yerushalmi reiterates the ruling ascribed to Rav as well as the teaching that is attributed to R. Yohanan in the Bavli (B), though the interpretation attributed to Samuel in the Bavli is absent from the Yerushalmi. Since material is more likely to be omitted than created afresh, this textual evidence might indicate that the Bavli transmits a more authentic quotation from Samuel. Given that Rav and Samuel both lived in Babylonia and presumably issued their dicta there, it is conceivable that their traditions would have been preserved more accurately in their original context, especially since the positions presented in the Bavli would surely correspond with other Babylonian traditions of that period.

The fact that R. Yohanan's ruling in the Bavli runs counter to the prevailing Land of Israel posture could suggest that either R. Yohanan expressed an opposing stance or this attribution in the Bavli is unreliable, whereas the Yerushalmi more accurately ascribes this teaching to Samuel. It is conceivable that the Bavli correctly credits these three comments to three different tradents but, in the course of transmission, the author of the final one was lost. Subsequently that view was attributed to R. Yohanan, whose rulings often are placed following those of Rav and Samuel,[68] whereas in the Yerushalmi, its content was combined with Samuel's statement (c).[69] The standpoint that the Bavli associates with R. Yohanan may therefore represent that of the early Babylonian Amoraim despite its (erroneous) Palestinian ascription.[70] Whether R. Papa was aware of this discrepancy or whether his query (C) was also shaped by the Bavli's redactors remains unclear. On the one hand, this counter that was allegedly posed by R. Papa may in fact be a redactional construct that was

---

68   E.g. B. Shabbat 37b, 145a, B. Hullin 95b.
69   David Brodsky identifies a number of variant attributions that he traces to the process of oral transmission. Brodsky, *Bride Without a Blessing*, 386–88, 415.
70   It is not uncommon for the Bavli to present and attribute a ruling to a Palestinian authority, which is not found in the Yerushalmi, and vice versa. See Frankel, *Mevo*, 41a.

designed to introduce R. Zebid's citation of the statement by Rava (D), thus creating literary balance for this chiastic structure. Since R. Papa is mentioned at the end of the *sugya* (A'), the redactors could have placed him at the beginning as well. Yet Zvi Dor has noted several passages in the Bavli where R. Papa reports teachings in the name of R. Yohanan that are either absent from the Yerushalmi or attributed to other Palestinian tradents in the Yerushalmi, and that R. Papa often demonstrates an awareness of early redactional treatment of Palestinian traditions.[71] Thus, such an attribution to R. Yohanan by R. Papa is not unprecedented.

If the Bavli in this instance does transmit these teachings closer to their original context, this might suggest that the redactors of the Yerushalmi had a heavier editorial hand than has previously been thought and that most scholars have reserved for the Bavli.[72] Scholars have typically assumed that this *sugya* from the Yerushalmi represents an earlier version that was subsequently restructured by the redactors of the Bavli, who incorporated later Babylonian amoraic comments. This latter claim is supported by the fact that all of the rulings in the Yerushalmi appear in the Bavli's parallel *sugya*. In addition to the statements by Rav and Samuel, which appear in both Talmuds (as mentioned above), the concluding tradition in the Yerushalmi (e) parallels Rava's statement reported by R. Zebid (D), and the teaching ascribed to R. El'azar (d) is cited by R. Abba in the name of R. Ila'i (D'). Moreover, as noted earlier, the Yerushalmi, especially tractate *Neziqin*, was subject to considerably less redactional activity than the Bavli and therefore generally presents more original versions of amoraic sources. However, the difficulties posed by the Yerushalmi's citations from Rav and Samuel, in addition to the Bavli's detailed chains of transmission when reporting traditions by Rava and R. Ila'i are all indicative of greater authenticity rather than an effort to create the appearance of reports from Babylonian tradents. Indeed, the anonymous ruling cited in the Yerushalmi may quote a teaching by Rava whose attribution has been omitted, rather than the inverse phenomenon.[73] However, given the competing evidence, any conclusion concerning which Talmud conserves a more authentic context necessarily remains tentative.

---

71   Dor, *The Teachings of Eretz Israel in Babylon*, 94–113. Dor also notes that R. Papa alone knew the tradition which attributes this ruling to R. Yohanan, whereas neither Rava nor the "Palestinian *Beit midrash*" did, as the Yerushalmi reports. Dor, 97–98.
72   See Friedman, "A Critical Study," 283–321; Halivni, "Sefeqei de-Gavrei," 67–93; Halivni, *Midrash, Mishnah, and Gemara*; Halivni, "Aspects of the Formation of the Talmud," 117–69. Also see Halivni's introductions in his various volumes of *Meqorot u-Mesorot*.
73   For examples of this phenomenon, see Frankel, *Mevo*, 41a.

What the textual evidence affirmatively demonstrates is the existence of two distinct traditions among early Amoraim in Babylonia and the Land of Israel that were known to fifth-generation Babylonian Amoraim and the redactors of the Bavli. These later Amoraim ultimately questioned their Babylonian predecessors and endeavored to synchronize those earlier stances with the plain sense of M. Bava Qama 3:1 and their own view toward determining liability on the basis of fault. Consistent with their rejection of the earlier Babylonian view, these later generations of Amoraim reported a Palestinian interpretation of the mishnah that is compatible with the corresponding *sugya* in the Yerushalmi.[74] While we cannot identify with complete confidence the original contexts of the rulings by Samuel and Rav from the versions of their statements that have been shaped by the redactors, we can confirm the pattern that emerges from the Talmuds of two different approaches to liability.

In sum, two distinct systems of liability undergird the Babylonian and Palestinian *sugyot* concerning torts. In the Bavli, early amoraic teachings consistently impose liability, even in the absence of fault. Hezeqiah strictly interprets M. Bava Qama 2:6; Rav, Samuel, and R. Yohanan limit the criteria for exemption in their readings of M. Bava Qama 3:1; Rabbah issues similarly strict decisions in several cases that address damages. In contrast, the Yerushalmi cites these same opinions of Rav and Samuel (and R. Yohanan in the name of Samuel), yet places them in another context and thereby yields strikingly different conclusions. In the Bavli, these rulings restrict the exemptions from liability granted to pedestrians in the case presented by M. Bava Qama 3:1 while, in the Yerushalmi, they limit exceptions to this same mishnah. Furthermore, in the Yerushalmi, R. Isaac confines M. Bava Qama 2:6 to instances of negligence. These Yerushalmi *sugyot* suggest the existence of a Palestinian attitude of imposing liability only when one acted with some degree of negligence. This picture is affirmed in the Bavli by R. Abba's report of a Palestinian teaching that "it is not customary for people to pay attention on the roads" (D'). In Babylonia, however, the early Amoraim uphold a standard of

---

Alternatively, Friedman observes that both Talmuds ascribe citations to named sages, although that same quote is presented as a redactorial explanation of an amoraic statement in the other Talmud; see Friedman, *Tosefta Atikta*, 434–35, n. 52; Friedman, "Al Titma," 128. Friedman explains this pattern in the Bavli as an effort to formulate statements in more lucid, rather than more authentic, language.

74 I have observed other instances where the Bavli similarly aggregates Palestinian traditions with its own divergent views and arranges them into a *sugya* that forms a chiastic structure. See Strauch Schick, "From Dungeon to Haven: Competing Theories of Gestation in Leviticus Rabbah and the Bavli."

absolute liability. It is only later generations of Babylonian Amoraim and the Bavli's redactors who ultimately reject this received tradition and interpret earlier statements accordingly.

4 Contextualizing Tort Liability in the Yerushalmi

The differences discussed above may stem from the inconsistencies within the mishnayot and the different approaches of the rabbis of the Land of Israel versus those of the Bavli to reconcile them. Nevertheless, an examination of their differing cultural contexts as well as contemporaneous legal systems may shed light on why they favored their respective interpretations which ultimately led to two very different systems of liability.[75]

There is some historical evidence as to the material conditions of public thoroughfares in Roman Palestine.[76] Daniel Sperber notes that it was customary for vendors to display wares outside their shops, which was done at their own risk. As a result, the narrow streets would become so crowded with merchandise that ease of passage was regularly impeded.[77] This situation is reflected in Y. Neziqin (BQ) 2:5, 3a, where a man brings his couch (קלטירה) to the forum and it is subsequently broken by a donkey. R. Isaac b. Tablai ruled: "He (the owner of the ass) does not owe you anything. Further, if he (the ass) had been injured, you would have been responsible for damages."[78] *Genesis Rabbah* 19.5 similarly records:

ותפקחנה עיני שניהם וכי סומין היו אתמהא ר' יודן בשם ר' יוחנן בן זכיי ר'
ברכייהו בשם ר' עקיבה לעירוני[79] שהיה עובר לפני חנות הזגג והיתה לפניו קופה
מליאה כוסות ודייטרוטין והפשיל במקלו ושברן עמד ותפשו אמר ליה ידענא
דלית אנה מהני מינך כלום אלא בוא אראך כמה טובה איבדתה כך הראה להן
כמה דורות איבדו

---

75   Christine Hayes wisely cautions against the tendency to reduce all differences between Babylonian and Palestinian rulings to distinctions in historical and socio-economic forces alone.(Hayes, *Between the Babylonian and Palestinian Talmuds*, 3–24.) The approach I take here is far less reductive.
76   Aldrete, *Daily Life*, 36.
77   Sperber, *The City in Roman Palestine*, 12. In Rome, the practice of placing merchandise outside shops persisted until Domitian (81–96 CE) issued an edict prohibiting it.
78   Saul Lieberman, *Talmuda Shel Kesarin*, 12–13.
79   Following the text of ed. Theodor-Albeck based on MS Vatican Biblioteca Apostolica ebr., 30 (considered the best MS). Other versions contain לעורוני (excerpt in *Midrash Hakhamim*,

'The eyes of both (Adam and Eve) were opened' (Genesis 3:7). And were they blind? R. Judan (Judah) in the name of R. Yohanan son of Zakkai, [cited] R. Berehiah in the name of R. Aqiva: [It can be compared] to a villager[80] who was passing before a glass-vendor's shop [in the city]. In front of him was a box filled with cups and *diatreta* (cut or engraved glass vessels); he swung his stick and broke them. [The vendor] stood up and grabbed him, saying to him: 'I know that I cannot get anything out of you, but come, I will show you how much you have destroyed.' Thus [God] showed them (Adam and Eve) how many generations they destroyed.[81]

This parable explains that the opening of Adam and Eve's eyes was figurative, comparing it to a country fellow who breaks a box of glassware, unaware of their value. The store owner grabs him and, though unable to sue him for damages, shows him the contents, thereby "enlightening" him as to the loss he caused.[82] Taken together with the Yerushalmi passages above, this scenario may well reflect prevailing legal norms in Roman Palestine which release pedestrians from responsibility for damage to wares placed in crowded marketplaces in which collisions were unavoidable. Indeed, the Digest of Justinian expressively concerns itself with protecting the rights of passersby and in ensuring that public places remain passable.[83]

More generally, the adoption of a system of fault by the Amoraim of the Land of Israel parallels the trajectory of Roman law, which gradually came to base liability on fault and negligence. As I will describe in more detail in the concluding chapter, Roman jurists from the second to third centuries transitioned away from a system of strict liability and introduced the idea of negligence and subjective factors across several areas of civil law.[84] The Yerushalmi's

---

Vienna) or סומא (Genesis Rabbati and MS Parma), both meaning a blind person. Albeck prefers עורוני, a blind person, since it conforms to the scenario of one purposely swinging his stick (see his editor's note, p. 175). Sperber (ibid.) follows this in his translation of the passage. However, the change in other MSS to עורוני/סומא might have resulted from the question leading up to the parable asking "were they blind (סומין)?". In light of our discussion of the system of fault espoused by the Amoraim of the Land of Israel, it is likely that this exemption for intentional damage would extend to any pedestrian.

80 See previous note.
81 *Genesis Rabbah* 19.5 (ed. Theodor-Albeck), MS Vatican Biblioteca Apostolica ebr., 30.
82 According to text witnesses in which the person is blind (*supra* n. 79), this correlates with R. Judah's general exemption of blind people from civil liability, among other laws (See B. Bava Qama 86b-87a, Marx, *Disability in Jewish Law*, 96–103.) However, as noted above, this reading is likely incorrect.
83 E.g. *Digest of Justinian,* Book IX, 3:2, Watson, *The Digest of Justinian,* 1:294.
84 Daube, *Roman Law,* 146–47.

preference for a system of fault may thus reflect the legal thought of the jurists who shaped the laws of the Roman Empire.

5 Contextualizing Tort Liability in the Bavli

The progression of legal developments in the laws of Sasanian Persia is less clear. The limited evidence we have comes from discrete passages from Zoroastrian legal/religious texts. Yaakov Elman has examined several passages in the *Hērbedestān,* a sixth-century Zoroastrian work dealing with priestly apprenticeship and the study of sacred texts, which suggest a line of development that may parallel the Bavli's shift from strict liability to negligence.[85] In a section discussing the case of a guardian who accompanies a child en route to priestly training, Sōšāns and Kay Ādur Bozēd, jurisconsults from the late fourth to early fifth centuries, rule that the escort is liable for injury to the child, irrespective of the circumstances (*Hērbedestān* 9.5 and 9.7).[86] By contrast, Sōšāns's student, Abarg (first half of the fifth century), considers the level of fault and negligence, requiring evidence of improper guardianship (*Hērbedestān* 9.8). Even if there is no injury to the child but there is evidence that the guardian acted unlawfully, the matter "is to be tested;"[87] whereas if the child dies through no fault of the escort, he is exonerated. Statements by Rōšn and Wehdōst that follow Abarg's ruling similarly require both injury and evidence of unlawful guardianship for liability. Thus, the later generation did not consider outcome alone as sufficient, but required that the guardian's conduct had been improper.

---

85   Elman, "Toward an Intellectual History of Sasanian Law," 21–35.
     The *Hērbedestān* is one of twenty-one writings that comprised the *Avesta*, the Zoroastrian holy text. This book was initially an oral composition in Young Avestan and was transcribed for written transmission circa 500 CE. See Bailey, *Zoroastrian Problems*, 172; Skjærvø, "Counter-Manichaean Elements in Kerdīr's Inscriptions, Irano-Manichaica II," 320–21. During the Sasanian period, the *Zand* was composed, the Middle Persian translation and commentary on the *Hērbedestān*, which also preserves the opinions of various jurisconsults who are mentioned by name.
86   Reading the passages together, Elman formulates their opinions as follows: "Sōšāns allows the escort to lead the child as far as he may do so safely, while Kay Ādur Bozēd allows him to lead the child in a different manner so long as he adheres to the guidelines regarding distance laid down by the family." Elman, "Toward an Intellectual History of Sasanian Law," 25. In the Middle Persian commentary on the Avestan text of the Nērangestān 1.4, Sōšāns issues a ruling which takes the intention of an offender into account. See Elman, "Scripture Versus Contemporary Needs," 158–60.
87   Elman notes that the test may include either a re-examination of the case or perhaps an ordeal. Elman, "Toward an Intellectual History of Sasanian Law," 26.

In another text, the intention of an actor determines whether his action causes impurity and is hence sinful, or whether it imparts no impurity and is considered meritorious. Though the word used to characterize mindset, *menišn,* usually means thought, in this context it is clear that it specifically refers to intention. The passage in question discusses a case where one finds a corpse in a body of water—a serious problem in Zoroastrian law since it is forbidden to defile water—necessitating its removal. However, since such activity entails the prohibition against becoming impure from contact with dead matter, the proper course of action is unclear. The ancient Avestan text of the *Vidēvdād* (6.28–9) resolves this conundrum by obligating one to remove the dead matter from the water, stating that one who does so will not become impure and hence incur no sin.

> 6.28 O Creator ... ! If this corpse is decomposing and rotting how should these Mazdayasnians behave [with respect to that sin, so that it may not come about]?
> 6.29 Ohrmazd answered: He shall take out of the water as much of (the corpse) as he can hold together with his hands and put it on dry earth. Then he will not incur sins against the waters by leaving the bones or hair about, or (throwing) saliva or vomit, or excrement, or the flow of blood.[88]

The Avestan text obligates passersby to remove a dead body from water while protecting them from incurring any impurities. It further creates an exemption if some parts of the dead body are scattered in the process. It is not stated explicitly whether these parts accidentally fall or if the actors intentionally toss them into the water. Based on the nature of these items, especially the blood which is described as flowing, it would seem that they fall due to the natural decomposition of the dead body. However, the use of the verb "throwing" may imply that the act is intentional—though they still may not intend to contaminate the water.

The *Pahlavi Vidēvdād* (PV), the Middle Persian translation/commentary to the Avestan *Vidēvdād*, clarifies the case.[89]

> Sōšāns said that which Kay-Ādur-Bōzēd said: He will not incur sins by (the corpse) falling again into water, owing to his innocence.[90]

---

88   Moazami, *Wrestling With the Demons*, 173.
89   Although we cannot date the PV text precisely, based on the named sages cited, it can be dated to no later than the early sixth century. Cantera, *Studien Zur Pahlavi-Übersetzung Des Avesta*, 207–29.
90   Moazami, *Wrestling With the Demons*, 173.

Sōšāns and Kay Ādur Bozēd clarify the ambiguous Avestan text, maintaining that the dead matter in question *falls* into the water and that the person acts innocently, indicating that he had neither intention to throw the dead matter nor the ability to prevent it. Their interpretation can be characterized as describing a case of coercion, (in rabbinic parlance, *ones,* as discussed on page 22), and only in such an instance do they exempt a person who defiles water. Sōšāns and Kay Ādur Bozēd's interpretation seems to correlate with their rulings cited in *Hērbedestān*, where they based liability only on injurious outcome. As such, they limit the exemption granted by the Avesta to a case where the dead matter falls unintentionally.

After describing the reward one receives for removing the dead matter, or punishment for failing to do so, PV continues:

(A) When he goes in, he will go in with this thought: "I will bring out as much as there is."

(B) For when he does not go in with this thought, "I will bring out as much as there is"—if one other (corpse) lies there and he strikes with it, then he is impure.

(C) When he shall leave that which he has held (with this intention:) "I will not bring it out"—even if he will afterward return to bring it out, still he is impure.

(D) Whatsoever he can bring out well, he is authorized to seize, lie down, and bring out/pull out, except the water, which he is not authorized to carry, and rain is also water.[91]

(E) When he can so bring that out, he shall cut piece by piece, then he shall cleanse his hands and the knife of moisture after cutting each piece. For each piece a tanāpuhl good deed will be on his account: one for carrying, and one for bringing (out the corpse). It is authorized to carry the whole from the fear of (falling into) the water.[92]

In the anonymous discussion cited in (A), intention is determinative: As long as he intends to pull out however much dead matter there is in the water, irrespective of what he is currently aware of, then he will not incur impurity. In other words, he should pull out as much of the decomposed corpse as possible, but there is a concern that some of the dead matter will fall back into the water

---

[91] Moazami, 173, n. 2. She suggests that this line means "that he is not authorized to carry or use the polluted water."

[92] Moazami, 175.

and pollute it again, and he will have been the cause. One is therefore exempt if he enters the water with the intention of removing *any* dead matter that is present, and whatever dead matter falls or is subsequently discovered will be no fault of his own.[93] In this case, he incurs no impurity and even performs a good deed.

Section (B) continues this line of reasoning, but discusses the reverse; if he only intends to extract the dead matter that he is aware of, then his exemption extends only to that dead matter while anything else he comes into contact with will make him impure. In (C), intention continues to define the action: if one does not intend to go back and retrieve (presumably) that which he left, he is liable for contaminating the water even if he ultimately removes it. As opposed to Sōšāns and Kay Ādur Bozēd, whose primary concern is whether the action is voluntary or not, the later anonymous sections consider the intentions of the actor.

The fact that we find a similar line of development in Zoroastrian and Babylonian rabbinic jurisprudence may be less indicative of lines of influence, and instead reflect that some common factors tend to underlie such shifts in legal thinking more generally. We will return to this in the final chapter. However, the Persian context of the Bavli may help to explain why it was that the early Babylonian Amoraim departed from the Yerushalmi's approach to tort law and turned to strict liability, when, as we will discuss in detail later, the trend within legal systems tends to be the opposite.

David Daube suggests that transitions from objective standards like strict liability to more subjective standards like negligence are features of maturing legal systems. In their early phases, weak mechanisms and a lack of authority make objective standards easier to implement and earn the trust of potential litigants. Only once a judicial system has broad authority and reliable procedures does it have the ability to consider subjective factors in determining guilt and liability.[94] The political realities of Sasanian Persia during this period may therefore be relevant. The Sasanian dynasty seized power from the Parthian regime in the early third century, which coincides with the inception of the amoraic period. Although our knowledge of Parthian law is scant, it is apparent that the Sasanians gradually implemented an extensive and sophisticated system of courts and law enforcement.[95] The new Sasanian regime

---

93 This consideration is much like a ruling on B. Bava Qama 26b which we discuss in the next chapter; where one has the intention when throwing a stone that he will be pleased with any place that it lands, he violates the Sabbath if it lands beyond a distance of four cubits.
94 Daube, *The Deed and the Doer*, 33–34.
95 For a survey of the Parthian and Sasanian legal systems see, Shaki, "Judicial and Legal Systems Ii. Parthian and Sasanian Judicial Systems."

under which the early generations of Babylonian Amoraim lived may therefore have been operating in an early phase of legal development compared to Roman Palestine. At the same time, so far as we can tell, the first generations of Babylonian Amoraim were in fact among the earliest rabbinic sages active in Babylonia, and may have been attempting to establish rabbinic authority among the Babylonian Jewish communities.[96] The early generations of Babylonian sages were therefore not operating with the same social standing as their Palestinian counterparts and hence may have tended toward modes of jurisprudential reasoning appropriate to these circumstances.[97] Admittedly, without further evidence, these suggestions remain speculative.

Ultimately, this initial fissure between Babylonian and Palestinian legal principles is reconciled by fourth- and fifth-generation Babylonian Amoraim. Intention becomes the primary measure for determining culpability. While no other *sugya* presents the views of each generation in the explicit linear progression displayed by B. Bava Qama 27b, in the remainder of this study, I will demonstrate that the developments illustrated here ramify throughout the Bavli.

---

96 Cohen, "In Quest of Babylonian Tannaitic Traditions"; Cohen, *For Out of Babylonia Shall Come Torah*.

97 In a related manner, Cohen describes the earliest Babylonian amoraic activity found in statements of the father of Samuel, R. Shila, and *baraitot* termed "Tanna of the House of Samuel," as dealing with concrete and practical matters, as opposed to the analytic learning characteristic of the Babylonian Amoraim, due to the lack of developed centers of learning at that early period. Cohen, *For Out of Babylonia Shall Come Torah*, 26–27.

CHAPTER 2

The Third Generation of Babylonian Amoraim
A Period of Transition

1 Overview: The Emergence of Competing Schools of Thought in Pumbedita and Mahoza

Thus far we have seen that the first two generations of Babylonian Amoraim adhered to a system of strict liability without exceptions for fault, and that in the third generation, Rabbah (late third and first half of the fourth century) predominantly followed in this vein. During the third generation, however, considerations of subjective factors do begin to enter discussions in matters of civil and religious jurisprudence. In tort law, we see the emergence of several principles that relate to intention, foresight, and the capacity to anticipate harm. The technical term for basic negligence (*peshi'ah*) first appears in rulings attributed to other third-generation sages, R. Nahman b. Jacob and R. Sheshet.[1] Moreover, as Aharon Shemesh has discussed, Rabbah introduces the notion of gross or willful negligence, meaning reckless disregard of a legal responsibility and its consequences for another party, coining the term *shogeg qarov le-meizid* (an inadvertent act that is nearly a malicious one).[2] By introducing the concept that inadvertent acts may be placed on a graduated scale determined by degree of negligence, Rabbah effectively invents a new category in the laws of manslaughter. In the laws of Sabbath, the earliest mentions of *melekhet mahshevet* (a planned action) and *melakhah she-eina tzerikha le-gufa* (labor that is not performed for its intrinsic purpose) — principles that require intention for an activity that violates the Sabbath — also appear in statements that are credited to third-generation Babylonian Amoraim, R. Nahman, Rabbah, and R. Judah b. Iziqiel.[3] Third-generation Amoraim are also among the first to discuss the concept of *ye'ush,* an owner's despair in reclaiming lost or stolen

---

1 B. Bava Qama 107b, B. Bava Metzia 6a.
2 B. Bava Qama 32b, B. Makot 7b. See Shemesh, "Shogeg Karov Le-Mezid."
3 B. Bava Qama 26b, B. Keritut 19b-20b, B. Sanhedrin 62b, B. Shabbat 107b.
   Perhaps relatedly, Rabbah also is seemingly the first to require that every divorce document (*get*) be written and signed for a specific couple (B. Gittin 2a).

property.[4] The seeming dissonance between Rabbah's decisions — he takes a strict position on negligence in the case of the stone (B. Bava Qama 26b, detailed in Chapter 1), but at times factors in negligence as evidenced by his innovation of *shogeg qarov le-meizid* — suggests that the third generation was a transitional point between two legal paradigms for determining liability: one more objective and one more subjective.

Rulings from this period also signal the establishment of two distinct schools of thought regarding the criteria for intentionality associated with the centers of learning of Pumbedita and Mahoza. Statements attributed to rabbis of the Pumbeditan school, starting with Rabbah and R. Joseph (and, as we will see in Chapter 3, their student Abaye), reflect a consequentialist approach which focuses on actions and their outcomes.[5] Where intention is necessary to determine liability, they focus on the performance of a specific deed, irrespective of motivation. By contrast, the rabbis of the Mahozan School, including R. Nahman and R. Sheshet (and exemplified in the next generation by Rava), consider the intention of an actor — both motive and purpose — to assess culpability. Indeed, as David Brodsky has described, R. Nahman regards sinful thoughts as worse than sinful acts, articulated in his dictum "thoughts of sin are more harmful than sin" (B. Yoma 28b-29a).[6] R. Hisda, another third-generation sage of the Mahozan School, introduces a similar condition for purposeful behavior in several laws that regulate ritual observance.

2 Pumbedita: Negligence and Deliberate Action in the Rulings of Rabbah

As detailed in Chapter 1, Rabbah typically echoes Babylonian Amoraim from the first two generations, who prescribed a system of strict liability that did

---

4 R. Joseph (B. Bava Qama 66a), R. Nahman and R. Sheshet (B. Bava Qama 68a), R. Hisda (B. Bava Qama 111b). It is also attributed to Rav (and commented on by R. Sheshet) in B. Bava Qama 67b.

While the term connoting an owner's feeling of despair appears in the Yerushalmi (Y. Bava Metzia 8b 2:1, Y. Gittin 45d 4:4), in several other instances it may indicate a property's state of ownerlessness (e.g. Y. Ma'asrot 52a 5:3; Y. Hallah 58a 1:5; Y. Sanhedrin 23b 6:2; Y. Kilaim 31a 7:4). Moreover, Urbach points out that while it appears in the Bavli attributed to earlier Amoraim, including R. Yohanan, Resh Laqish, and Ulla, based on parallel statements found in the Yerushalmi which lack reference to *ye'ush*, it seems to have been added to these statements by the Bavli's redactors. Urbach, *The Halakhah*, 182–85.

5 See Quinn, "Actions, Intentions, and Consequences."
6 Brodsky, "Thought is Akin to Action," 152.

not account for fault.[7] This approach is corroborated by several other traditions attributed to him. For instance, Rabbah affirms to his student Abaye a tannaitic position which imposed liability even in cases of *ones*, where damages result from forced behavior.[8] He thus upholds the possibility of a tannaitic opinion that imposes liability simply for having been the immediate physical cause of an event that resulted in damage. Yet, other statements attributed to Rabbah consider either negligence or intentional (by contrast with inadvertent) action to determine liability. The lack of consistency in Rabbah's stance seems to indicate that his perspective represents a transitional point between approaches in legal thought.

2.1   B. Bava Qama 26b-27a: Strict Liability and Negligence

Rabbah's dichotomous tendency is evidenced in the collection of rulings attributed to him in B. Bava Qama 26b-27a (these do not appear in the Yerushalmi),[9] which surveys an array of subjects. As detailed above, following Hezeqiah's teaching on M. Bava Qama 2:6 ("a person is always forewarned") and a related discussion, the Bavli presents several cases cited in the name of Rabbah,[10] which support Hezeqiah's reading and impose liability for damages, even in the absence of intentional or premeditated harm. However, in the other areas addressed in these decisions — the five types of compensation

---

7   See sections 2.2 and 3.2.
8   B. Bava Qama 29b. I cite and discuss this *sugya* in Chapter 3.
9   Rabbah and R. Joseph are generally absent from Y. Neziqin. Sussman, "Ve-shuv Liyerushalmi Neziqin," 131, n. 179.
10 A number of manuscripts attribute some or all of these cases to the fourth-generation Amora, Rava: MS Munich 95 regarding the first case (A); MS Escorial G-I-3 regarding (E) and (I); MSS Vatican 116 and Florence II 1 7–9 ascribe this entire group of cases to Rava.

   The Tosafists (*ad loc.* s.v. *ve-amar*) note that the attribution of (E) to Rava is incorrect since, on B. Bava Qama 17b, Rava inquires about a similar case and the redactors responded by citing a case in the name of Rabbah that is discussed on 26b, without indicating that Rava was revisiting his own ruling. In a similar vein, on B. Bava Qama 27a, Rava is cited arguing that the resolution of two cases (L and M) stated by Rabbah are explicit in the Mishnah. (MSS Escorial G-I-3 and Munich 95 attribute this statement to Rabbah. However, the majority of manuscripts and printed editions mention Rava; given the evidence that these cases are accurately attributed to Rabbah, it seems likely that the ascription of the comment that follows the (ambiguous) previous case to Rava is correct.)

   As the analysis in this chapter demonstrates, most of the cases recorded in B. Bava Qama 26b-27a (excepting cases C-D, addressed below) are consistent with other rulings that can reliably be attributed to Rabbah—such as the passages that present him engaging in dialogue with his student Abaye. Kalmin, *Sages, Stories*, 176–80.

levied on one who inflicts bodily injury (i.e. damages, pain, medical expenses, loss of income, and humiliation); violating the Sabbath; manslaughter that prompts flight to a city of refuge; injuring the tooth or eye of a slave who would then be released; and levirate marriage — the presence (or absence) of negligence and intention play a significant role.

Cases A-D and I-K all address varying levels of intentional and negligent behavior (E-H are omitted):[11]

(A) אמ' רבה היתה אבן מונחת לו בחיקו ולא הכיר בה מעולם ועמד ונפלה לענין נזקין חייב לענין ארבעה דברים פטור לענין שבת פטור מלאכת מחשבת אסרה תורה לענין גלות פטור לענין עבד פלוגתא[12] דרבן שמע' בן גמל' ורבנן

(B) הכיר בה ושכחה ועמד ונפלה לענין נזקין חייב לענין ארבעה דברים פטור לענין גלות חייב בשגגה מכלל דהוה לה ידיעה לענין שבת מלאכת מחשבת אסרה תורה לענין עבד פלוגתא דרבן שמעון בן גמל' ורבנן

(C) נתכוון לזרוק שתים וזרק ארבע לענין נזקין חייב לענין ארבעה דברים פטור לענין שבת מלאכת מחשבת אסרה תורה לענין גלות ואשר לא צדה פרט למתכוין לזרוק שתים וזרק ארבע לענין עבד פלוגתא דרבן שמ' בן גמל' ורבנן

(D) נתכוון לזרוק ארבע וזרק שמונה לענין נזקין חייב לענין ארבעה דברים פטור לענין שבת אי אמ' כל מקום שתרצה תנוח אין אי לא לא לענין גלות ואשר לא צדה פרט למתכוין לזרוק ארבע וזרק שמונה לענין עבד פלוגתא דרבן שמע' בן גמל' ורבנן

[E-H]

(I) ואמ' רבה היה ישן בראש הגג ונפל מראש הגג ונתקע באשה חייב בארבעה דברים וביבמתו לא קנה חייב בנזק בצער ברפוי בשבת אבל בבשת לא דתנן אינו חייב על הבשת עד שיהא מתכוין

---

[11] I have omitted cases (E-H) since they do not address issues of negligence and intention but discuss whether liability is incurred by an actor who hastens an injury that would have occurred even without his actions. Cases (E) and (F) discuss instances where the second party is of no consequence and, therefore, bears no culpability. These two cases suggest that guilt is determined by the physical circumstances of an action when it is performed; intention is seemingly of no consequence. The latter two cases, (G) and (H), both consider a murder where multiple actors are involved, and seek to identify who is liable. Both were subject to tannaitic debates and ultimately ruled inconclusive by Rabbah. This series of cases concludes with two more scenarios, which I have also omitted since they do not relate to the theme of intention regarding torts; rather, they evaluate instances where an action leads to death and consider whether the victim would have been expected to take precautionary measures. These cases likewise originate in tannaitic material (M. Sanhedrin 9:1).

[12] The switch from Hebrew to Aramaic might indicate that this was added by the redactors. The same could be said for all of the Aramaic portions scattered throughout the passage.

(J) ואמ' רבה נפל מן הגג ברוח שאינה מצויה והזיק ובייש חייב על הנזק ופטור מארבעה דברים

(K) ברוח מצויה חייב בארבעה דברים ופטור על הבשת ואם נתהפך חייב אף על הבשת ממשמע שנ' ושלחה ידה במבושיו איני יודע שהחזיקה מה ת"ל והחזיקה כיון שנתכוון להזיק אע"פ שלא נתכוון לבייש

(A) Rabbah[13] said: If one had a stone resting on his lap, and he had never been aware of it, and he rose and [the stone] fell; with regard to damages, he is liable; with regard to the [other] four things (i.e. the four forms of compensation), he is exempt; with regard to the Sabbath, he is exempt [since] Scripture prohibits 'planned work' (Exodus 35:33);[14] with regard to exile [to a city of refuge, for inadvertent murder], he is exempt; with regard to [the release of his] slave, this is disputed between R. Simeon b. Gamliel and the Rabbis ...

(B) If he had [at some point] been aware [of the stone in his lap], but forgot about it, then [lit. and] stood up and it fell, with regard to damages, he is liable; with regard to the [other] four things, he is exempt; with regard to exile, he is liable, [for Scripture says,] 'inadvertence' (Numbers 35:11) which implies that there was awareness; with regard to the Sabbath, Scripture prohibits 'planned work'; with regard to a slave — this is disputed between R. Simeon b. Gamliel and the Rabbis.

(C) Where one intended to throw [a stone the distance of] two [cubits], [but instead] threw it [a distance of] four, with regard to damages he is liable; with regard to the [other] four things, he is exempt; with regard to the Sabbath, Scripture prohibits 'planned work'; with regard to exile, 'if he did not entrap' (Exodus 21:13), excluding where he intended to throw two [cubits] but instead threw four; with regard to a slave, this is disputed between R. Simeon b. Gamliel and the Rabbis.

(D) Where one intended to throw [the stone a distance of] four [cubits] but threw it [a distance of] eight, with regard to damages, he is liable; with regard to the [other] four things, he is exempt; with regard to the Sabbath, if he said 'any place it wants it will rest', there is [liability, but] if not, [there is] no [offense]; with regard to exile, 'if he did not entrap', excluding a case where he intended to throw four [cubits] but threw eight; with regard

---

13 Rava, according to MSS Munich, 95, Vatican 116, Florence II I 7–9. *Supra* Chapter 1, n. 31.
14 *Infra* note 59 in this chapter.

to a slave, this is disputed between R. Simeon b. Gamliel and the Rabbis.

[E-H]
(I) And Rabbah said: [In a case where] one is sleeping on a rooftop, and he falls from that rooftop and penetrates a woman, he is liable for four [of] the things, and where she is his deceased brother's widow, he does not acquire her [in levirate marriage]. [The four things] he is liable for [are] damages, pain, medical expenses, and loss of income, but not for humiliation, for it is taught (M. Bava Qama 8:1): 'one is not liable for [causing] humiliation unless he intends'.
(J) And Rabbah said: [In a case where] one falls from a roof due to an exceptional wind and causes damage and humiliation, he is liable for damages, but [he is] exempt from the [other] four things.
(K) [If he falls] via a typical wind, he is liable for four things and exempt from [compensation for] humiliation. If he turns over, he is even liable for humiliation: from what it states [in Scripture]: 'She sends out her hand ... to his genitals' (Deuteronomy 25:11). Do I not know that she seized? What does Scripture mean [when it says], 'and she seizes'? [To tell you] that, as long as one intended to injure, [he is liable for humiliation,] even though he did not intend to humiliate.

The first of these cases (A), analyzed in Chapter 1,[15] considers an individual who causes damage when he stands up, having been unaware of a stone on his lap and imposes liability for damages despite this lack of knowledge or intent to harm. In the second case (B), the tortfeasor also lacks intent to inflict damage or knowledge that his action might cause harm; however, he had prior awareness of having a potentially dangerous object on his person. Under strict liability he would a fortiori be liable. But here, the actor bears a degree of negligence since he had known about the stone on his lap at some point and could have taken precautions to prevent harm. For Rabbah, this level of negligence is sufficient to warrant exile to a city of refuge if death results; however, where there is only bodily injury, it does not warrant payment of the other four compensations. It seems that Rabbah requires this only in cases of gross negligence.

Cases C-D provide definitions of intention with respect to the laws of Sabbath yet, they diverge from the other cases in this passage. In these

---

15   Section 2.2.

rulings though the actor intentionally throws a stone, this is not considered sufficiently negligent to warrant payment for the four additional compensations, as the ruling in (B) would imply. These two cases also appear in B. Shabbat 72b-73a and, although not definitive, that *sugya* strongly suggests an attribution to the fourth-generation sage Rava.[16] It is noteworthy that (C) and (D) appear without attribution, a feature that further distinguishes them from the rest of this passage, whose rulings are explicitly ascribed to Rabbah. These factors seem to suggest that cases C and D were added by the redactors based on Rava's rulings in B. Shabbat, since, like the cases in (A) and (B,) they discuss scenarios that involve a stone and unexpected outcomes, but as applied to Sabbath observance. Thus, these cases and their rulings are out of place and inconsistent with other material in this passage attributed to Rabbah.

After four cases (E-H) that focus on one who hastens injury that would have occurred notwithstanding his interventions, cases I, J, and K return to addressing additional aspects of Rabbah's application of strict liability. All three consider harm that occurs when a person falls from a roof — undoubtedly an unintentional event — with variations on the causes and types of injury inflicted. In each instance, Rabbah imposes liability for damages, irrespective of the circumstances leading to this fall, though he distinguishes between an unusual, and thus unforeseeable, wind (J), and a common wind (K) which can be anticipated with respect to the five compensations. His rulings in these scenarios are congruent with his opinion in case B: the added forms of recompense are only levied in the presence of gross negligence (K).

It may again be argued that the presence of negligence motivates Rabbah's opinions in these three cases. The tortfeasor engages in what could be deemed reckless behavior since the probability of falling from a roof and causing damage is far higher than for more routine activities. The decision to place oneself in such a situation requires adequate precautions to prevent an accident. However, if an unusual gust of wind caused his fall, he is only required to pay for damage since a high degree of negligence is not indicated. Conversely, if a typical wind causes the tortfeasor to fall, this indicates carelessness on his part; he is considered to have been highly negligent and must pay for damages plus the extra compensations save for humiliation (K).[17] This is because M. Bava Qama 8:1 explicitly links liability for humiliation to the intention of the tortfeasor:

---

16   We will return to these cases in the next chapter in discussing rulings attributed to Rava.

17   Tos. R. Perez (*ad loc.* s.v. *ve-amar*), in explaining the logic of Rabbah's position writes: "even though he was coerced, nevertheless he should have been careful not to go up [upon a roof]" (as opposed to the thirteenth-century commentary, the Rashba by R. Shlomo b. Aderet (*ad loc.* s.v. *nafal*) who considered this case one of "total coercion"). Haut likewise explains that strict liability may be applied where one engages in "unusual,

THE THIRD GENERATION OF BABYLONIAN AMORAIM 55

נפל מן הגג והיזיק ובייש חייב על הנזק ופטור על הבושת שני ושלחה ידה
והחזיקה במבושיו אינו חייב על הבושת עד שיהא מתכוון

> ... One who falls from a roof and caused injury and inflicted humiliation: he is liable for the damage but exempt for the humiliation, as it states: 'She sends out her hand and she seizes his genitals' (Deuteronomy 25:11), one is not liable for [causing] humiliation unless he intends.

This mishnah ostensibly indicates that such conduct is aimed at causing humiliation. Rabbah, however, expands the ruling to include the intent to perform an action that ended in an injury, irrespective of whether the actor set out to inflict physical harm or embarrassment upon the victim. Hence, Rabbah rules (K) that an actor is exempt from paying for humiliation if he falls off a roof due to a normal wind and harms another person as a result. Only if the falling man adjusts his position during his descent, does Rabbah impose liability for the embarrassment that he may cause another. By changing his orientation in mid-air, it seems that he is no longer a passive being, but an agent who actively attempts to alter the outcome of his inadvertent stumble; thus, his intentional movement triggers accountability for the shame that he inflicted on the victim. To garner support for this claim, Rabbah cites an alternative (to the Mishnah's) reading of Deuteronomy 25:11, which states that intent to inflict injury, even without an aim to embarrass per se, is sufficient for incurring legal responsibility for humiliation. Although this teaching is presented as a *baraita*, it has no parallel in extant rabbinic texts.

By comparison, in case I, even if a man falls from a roof and lands on his widowed sister-in-law such that he penetrates her sexually, this action does not

---

abnormal, or dangerous activities ... such as clambering about upon a roof." Haut, "Some Aspects," 54.

This is consistent with what Weinrib describes of common law, where liability for unusually perilous conduct is an extension of the system of fault. He states that "the singling out of abnormally dangerous activities for a more stringent liability rule carries on the negligence idea that the requisite degree of care is proportionate to the magnitude of the risk ... the injury would not have occurred unless the defendant had failed to live up to the heightened standard that the riskiness of the activity imposes. ... When injury occurs, unless the defendant can point to a clearly external or idiosyncratic force, fault can be imputed to the activity." He also notes that "strict liability for abnormally dangerous activities is not at odds with fault-based liability or corrective justice. Although the activity is not itself wrongful, its extraordinary riskiness carries with it the obligation to be extraordinarily careful. Materialization of the risk is taken as conclusively showing that the defendant did not fulfill that obligation. The occurrence of injury triggers a liability that extends, rather than denies, the fault principle." Weinrib, *Private Law*, 187–90.

constitute the initiation of a levirate marriage. Rabbah renders this judgment despite an explicit ruling in M. Yebamot 6:1: "... if one has intercourse with his deceased brother's widow, whether [it occurred] inadvertently or advertently, [whether it occurred] under coercion or willingly ... he acquires her [in levirate marriage] ..." In B. Yebamot 54a, the redactors remark on this discrepancy between Rabbah's opinion and the mishnah,[18] and interpret the coercion mentioned in M. Yebamot 6:1 as the case of a man who intended to engage in intercourse with his wife but is forced by his sister-in-law to sleep with her instead. The mishnaic ruling that marriage has taken place, even if through coercion, is thus limited to circumstances that encompass minimal intent to perform a sexual act. These passages therefore indicate that Rabbah requires at least some basic level of intention to engage sexually for a levirate marriage to commence. Since the man on a roof had no plan to participate in intercourse, his involuntary fall could only be a physical action. Levirate marriage does not result from this contact because the act was not sexual in any sense, not even under duress.

It emerges from these decisions that Rabbah imposes liability for damages even in the absence of fault or negligence (A, B), whereas he requires payment of the other four compensations only where gross negligence was evident (I, K). In a case of manslaughter, the guilty party is punished with exile only if his action entailed a minimal degree of negligence (B). This is consistent with another statement attributed to Rabbah (B. Bava Qama 32b and B. Makot 7b), in which he categorizes a case involving a high degree of negligence as *shogeg qarov le-meizid.* In that instance, he rules that exile is inapplicable as the act is considered to be murder.[19]

Irrespective of whether Rabbah actually taught this group of related cases in B. Bava Qama as a single study session,[20] or whether the redactors compiled them from independent contexts, the systematic presentation of these cases with their ramifications across multiple realms of law, may have been constructed, to some extent, to introduce the concept of negligence. Indeed, the differentiating factor among many of these rulings seems to be the role of negligence. However, with the exception of his decision concerning levirate marriage, Rabbah's views of intention are hardly original; rather, they are

---

18   MSS Oxford Opp. 248 (367), Munich 95, Munich 141, ed. Pesaro 1508–1509 attribute this to Rava. However, most scholars (including Friedman) agree that Rabbah is the correct attribution in B. Bava Qama 27b.
19   See Shemesh, "Shogeg Karov Le-Mezid," 399–342.
20   In private conversation, Yaakov Elman remarked on this phenomenon, as illustrated by similar passages attributed to Rava cited in B. Bava Qama 5a-b, 54a and B. Bava Metzia 27a, in which selections from one lecture are transmitted together.

drawn from biblical or tannaitic sources.[21] Similarly, the notion that one is only liable for violating the Sabbath by committing an act that constitutes *melekhet mahshevet* also appears in a teaching attributed to Rabbah's contemporary R. Nahman in the name of Samuel.[22] The innovation presented in this cluster of cases seems to be its association of otherwise unrelated laws, which demonstrates their applicability to other cases and, in some instances, delineates the requirement of intention that is articulated in tannaitic sources to conform to Rabbah's general position. Nevertheless, although Rabbah's rulings share an affinity with his predecessors' decisions, his concern for negligence—however subtle—introduces distance from a purely strict approach.

2.2   B. Bava Qama 56a: Liability for Negligence

Rabbah's attention to negligence is further demonstrated in his interpretation of M. Bava Qama 6:1 describing the case of a barrier built to restrain sheep which fails on its own or is breached by a thief, freeing them to roam unchecked. Although it exempts the owner of this flock for the damages that his sheep cause, Rabbah is credited with qualifying this ruling:

אמר רבה והוא שחתרה אבל לא חתרה מאי חייב

Rabbah[23] said: This [exemption in the case where the wall breaks] is where [the sheep] broke it. But if [the sheep] did not break it what is [the law]? He is liable.

---

21   Drawing from Deuteronomy 25:11, M. Bava Qama 8.1 states that one who causes bodily harm to another person is required to pay for the humiliation suffered by the victim only if the defendant intended to inflict harm. Analogously, Mekhilta de-Rabbi Ishmael, *Neziqin Mishpatim* 8 s.v. *ayin* cites an opinion by R. Isaac that one is only liable for pain inflicted on another person where the injury was caused with intention.

The Bible explicitly states that intention is required for the imposition of liability in the case of murder: Exodus 21:12–14 and Numbers 35:9–34 both discuss the consequences of premeditated and inadvertent murder. The Mishnah elaborates on these concepts in detail (M. Sanhedrin 9:2, M. Bava Qama 5:4, and M. Makot 2:1–3). The ruling on manslaughter in a case where one intends to throw a rock a distance of two cubits but instead it reaches four cubits (Case C) appears in a *baraita* cited in B. Makot 7b.

On the issue of injuries that lead to a slave's manumission, Rabbah (or the redactors, as suggested by the change to Aramaic) states that the requirement for intent by the master appears in a tannaitic debate between R. Simon b. Gamliel and the Sages on the meaning of Exodus 21:26 (B. Bava Qama 26b). This is echoed in Mekhilta de-Rabbi Ishmael, *Neziqin* 9.

22   B. Sanhedrin 62b and B. Keritut 19b. More on this below.

23   MS Vatican 116, Piskei Ha-Rosh M. Bava Qama 6:3, *Hiddushei Ra'avad ad loc.* s.v. *ve-hi* credit this teaching to Rava, but all other manuscripts ascribe it to Rabbah.

According to this reading, the exemption issued in the mishnah is restricted to a case in which the sheep rupture the walls of their pen, seemingly identifying this as the sole instance where the owner is free from fault. The redactors infer from this ruling that an owner is liable for any resulting damages if the barrier fails.[24]

As in the previous series of rulings ascribed to Rabbah, negligence appears to inform his reasoning. A wall that falls on its own indicates that the owner did not sufficiently guard his animals by maintaining a sturdy barrier. Here too, intent to harm does not determine the liability; rather, culpability depends on exercising adequate measures to prevent damages.[25]

In the continuation of the sugya (not quoted), the redactors are troubled by Rabbah's ruling since it implies that liability may even be imposed upon an owner who erected a wall that was strong enough to ensure that his animals would be contained. They reason that if Rabbah were referring to an owner who took proper precautions, then he should be exempt from paying for any damages. Conversely, in the case of a faulty enclosure, how could the owner be exempt if his animals broke through? Such a person is negligent and should be held responsible.

Rabbah's statement is then amended slightly and applied to M. Bava Qama 6:2 which rules that one who leaves his sheep exposed to the sun is liable for whatever damages that they cause, irrespective of whether they are well guarded.[26] Rabbah's succinct comment is now understood as a clarification that the owner of a herd is liable "even" if his sheep breach a protective wall. This is viewed as negligence too, for under such conditions animals in distress will strive to escape the scorching heat. In his discussion of this passage, Halivni argues that the redactors were aware that Rabbah stated "*hatra*" but, being unsure of its context, they offered two possibilities, with a preference for the latter.[27] Regardless of the original meaning of Rabbah's terse

---

24   Its redactorial provenance is indicated by the change from Hebrew to Aramaic.
25   This criterion for negligence is also reflected in modern English and Commonwealth law, which considers whether the risk was "reasonably foreseeable" and, if so, how a reasonable person would respond to this threat. Such rational action would be based on the probability of the danger. In American law, negligence is defined similarly, together with the economic incentives for lowering the level of risk. Wright, "The Standard of Care in Negligence Law," 249; Kelley, "Restating Duty," 1061; Weinrib, *Private Law*, 148–49.
26   Or, as the latter segment of this mishnah discusses, if the flock is placed in the care of one who is mute, cognitively impaired, or a minor. However, the redactors do not seem to be discussing this part of the mishnah.
27   Halivni notes that although the redactors commonly cite an amoraic comment on one passage from a mishnah or *baraita*, then apply it to another clause, it is unusual for them to revise an amoraic quotation. He thus considers this passage an example of

statement, both of these renderings are compatible with his position in B. Bava Qama 26b-27a, which holds parties liable for damages if they have been negligent, notwithstanding the intent to cause harm.

2.3 B. Bava Qama 28b-29b: Intent to Act

Rabbah's interpretation of the opinion ascribed to the third-generation Tanna R. Judah, in M. Bava Qama 3:1, limiting liability based on intention, also narrows the parameters of what counts as an intentional act. Following the case of the pedestrian who accidentally breaks a jug (analyzed in Chapter 1), the second half of the mishnah discusses the following scenario:

נשברה כדו ברשות הרבים והחליק בה אחר במים או שלקה בחרסיה חייב רבי
יהודה אומר במתכוין חייב באינו מתכון פטור

> If one's jug broke in the public domain, and another slipped on the water or was injured by the shards, he (the owner of the jug) is liable. R. Judah says: If he intended, he is liable. If he did not intend, he is exempt.

The first opinion in this mishnah rules that if someone breaks his jug in the public domain and another person is injured as a result, the owner of the jug is liable for all damages incurred. R. Judah counters that the owner is liable only if he acted with intention. Given the ambiguity of this opinion, multiple readings have been presented to clarify his comment. According to its apparent meaning, which appears in the Yerushalmi's discussion of this mishnah,[28] the jug

---

אלא אי איתמר הכי איתמר (if you will say it, so shall you say it), which commonly prompts the modification of amoraic statements. In such cases, the question that motivates an emendation is not particularly compelling; rather, the redactors had two versions of an amoraic statement and they were attempting to determine which one was accurate. Halivni, *Mekorot U-Mesorot: Bava Kama*, 228.

28 Y. Bava Qama 3c cites the opinions of R. El'azar and R. Yohanan, who debate the positions held by the Sages and R. Judah with regard to the second case in M. Bava Qama 3:1: "[R. El'azar said: their (R. Judah and the Sages) dispute was [only regarding] while the jug is falling, but after it falls, all agree that [the owner of the jug] is liable.]* R. Yohanan challenged R. El'azar: if [R. Judah deemed the owner of the jug] exempt while [his jug] is falling, should he not *a fortiori* be exempt after it falls [as well]? R. Yohanan said: The dispute is regarding both during the fall and after the fall ... according to the opinion of R. Yohanan [R. Judah's requirement of intention refers to] where one intends the shards. According to the view of R. El'azar [intention refers to] where one intends to damage."

*This line is missing from MS Escorial, but is found in MS Leiden and the printed edition.

was broken with the goal of causing damage;[29] R. Judah thereby reasons that if the jug breaks accidentally its owner is blameless. An alternate understanding is offered in Tosefta Bava Qama 2:4, which bases R. Judah's decision on the concept: שאין שמירתן עליו, "because guarding [the jug] is not his obligation."[30] Like the Sages, R. Judah only imposes liability on a person who leaves property in the public domain causing a pedestrian to be injured. R. Judah qualifies, however, that ownership is defined by the intent to retain possession of that item.[31] This tosefta's opinion appears in both Talmuds: the Bavli presents it as the view of R. Joseph (likely R. Joseph II)[32] and R. Ashi,[33] and the Yerushalmi attributes it to R. Yohanan.[34] Rabbah offers an unprecedented interpretation:

היכי דמי מתכוין אמ' רבה במתכוין להורידה למטה מכתפו

> How is it like (what are the circumstances of the case), 'when he intends' [according to R. Judah]? Rabbah[35] said: where he intends to lower it down from his shoulder.[36]

For R. El'azar, intention is related to a desire to incur damage. R. Yohanan maintains that it refers to the owner's intention to retain possession of the resultant shards.

29 Albeck, "Is there a Category of Intention in Talmudic Criminal Law?," 461; Eilberg-Schwartz, *The Human Will in Judaism*, 204; Neusner, *A History of the Mishnaic Law of Damages, Part I*, 35.

30 See Moscovitz, *Talmudic Reasoning*, 220. He references this tosefta as an example of enthymematic explanations, since it does not specify the circumstances that require owners to guard their property.

31 R. Judah's position in this tosefta comports with the interpretation attributed to R. Joseph in the Bavli that, if the owner did not intend to retain ownership of the jug after it fell, he is exempt. The tosefta elaborates that his responsibility is negated because he is no longer obligated to guard the jug. Goldberg, *Tosefta Bava Kamma*, 61.

32 Halivni, *Mekorot U-Mesorot: Bava Kama*, 111. R. Joseph II, one of the later Saboraim, as opposed to the first R. Joseph (the teacher of Abaye), since an explanation of Abaye's opinion is ascribed to R. Joseph here.

33 B. Bava Qama 29a.

Neither MMS Escorial nor Munich 95 mentions R. Ashi. However, in passages where two identical statements are presented in sequence, the omission of one is often due to a scribal error.

34 *Supra* n. 28.

35 MS Escorial G-I-3 attributes this to Rava; however, the ascription to Rabbah appears in all other manuscripts and is confirmed by Abaye's query to Rabbah concerning this ruling. Kalmin has noted that in-person contact between Rava and Abaye was rare and, in most instances, Abaye was rather in the presence of his teacher Rabbah, discussing Rabbah's own opinion. Kalmin, *Sages, Stories*, 176–80.

36 B. Bava Qama 28b.

The first ruling of the mishnah follows the notion that the process of lifting or lowering a heavy object entails an inherent risk that it might fall and if it does, it must be removed in a timely manner to avert another accident; failure to exercise such care is deemed negligent. In accordance with R. Judah, Rabbah also considers intention, but defines it as intent to lower a jug as opposed to lifting it. Rabbah does not probe whether the harmful act is premeditated; rather, he reasons based on whether the damages resulted from an intentional action. From this perspective, liability is assigned only when the object is being purposefully lowered and its breakage was therefore a direct result of that intended action.

In this case, Rabbah defines intent in relation to the purpose of the physical action. When one begins to lower an object and it continues along that trajectory and breaks, the damage incurred directly results from the deliberate act. As Herbert Hart has conceptualized this type of scenario, the shattering of that object is immediately and invariably tied to the strictly intentional effort to lower it, rendering the two events inextricable.[37] By comparison, when raising an object, the intention is for it to move in the opposite direction of its subsequent fall. If it drops, intentionality has been disrupted; therefore, the resultant injuries are deemed unintentional.[38] Rabbah once again directs the tannaitic standard of intention toward action, without regard for motive.

When assessing the mishnaic decisions on damages, Rabbah seems to identify notions of absolute liability as well as alternatives that take intentional action and negligence into consideration. In his rulings on the payment of extra compensation in cases of bodily injury and culpability for manslaughter, Rabbah moves away from the implementation of strict liability by factoring negligence into account, albeit to varying degrees. Analyzed in the aggregate, these passages suggest that Rabbah accepted the stringent view

---

37 Hart, "Intention and Punishment," 120. Hart makes this distinction when describing cases of double effect.

38 A similar distinction is made with regard to accidental killing in M. Makot 2:1, זה הכלל כל שבדרך ירידתו גולה ושלא בדרך ירידתו אינו גולה, "This is the general rule: [When one inadvertently kills] on his way going down (i.e. a ladder), he is exiled (as this would be considered manslaughter, whose punishment is exile); but [when one inadvertently kills when he is] not on his way going down [but going up] he is not exiled (rather he is exonerated)."

An accidental killing is defined as a death that has been caused by a lawful act performed with the reasonable belief that no harm would likely result. This is as opposed to involuntary manslaughter, where death is caused either by an unlawful act or a lawful action that was carried out in an unlawful or negligent manner. See Garner, *Black's Law Dictionary*, 547, s.v. manslaughter.

of his predecessors while beginning to weigh the significance of negligence. Specifically, in contrast to the rulings attributed to prior generations, Rabbah applies a standard of strict liability only in cases where the action has been performed intentionally, without reference to motivation. For Rabbah, to be deemed negligent and held liable for damages, one must have engaged intentionally in an activity that, intended or not, caused harm.

3   Mahoza: Negligence and Purposeful Action

Rulings that are attributed to sages from the city of Mahoza,[39] including R. Nahman b. Jacob, R. Sheshet, and R. Hisda demonstrate a more decisive break with a doctrine of strict liability and a greater interest in concepts relating to intention. Like their contemporary, Rabbah, R. Nahman and R. Sheshet base responsibility on negligence and, as noted above, they even appear to coin a precise legal term for this concept, *peshi'ah*, drawing from the biblical root פשע, (likely from Exodus 22:8 "in all charges of misappropriation").[40] These sages require three oaths to verify the testimony of an unpaid custodian who claims that property under his care was stolen; in one, he swears "an oath that I was not negligent with it" (שבועה שלא פשעתי בה).[41] By affirming that he had not been negligent, the custodian is granted an exemption from compensating the owner for his missing property. In a related manner, R. Sheshet explains a tannaitic ruling which grants an exemption to a shepherd who abandons his flock which is subsequently attacked by a lion or a wolf. R. Sheshet reasons that we evaluate the shepherd based on whether he would have been able to save them had he been there.[42] R. Sheshet considers the subjective capabilities of the shepherd and not merely the presence of an ostensibly negligent act or

---

39   Yaakov Elman has written at length about the cultural exposure of Mahozan rabbis, which he attributes to their proximity to the (albeit seasonal) urban center of Ctesiphon, by contrast with the more culturally isolated community of Pumbedita, which was located on the Euphrates and relatively far from the capital. See for example Elman, "Acculturation to Elite Persian Norms in the Babylonian Jewish Community of Late Antiquity."

40   David Daube describes the etymology of this rabbinic term from its biblical source as follows: "The main route leading from liability for 'treachery' to that for 'fault' was via an extension of the former category—more and more careless conduct was assigned to it, till at last the need for a fresh thought related, more comprehensive criterion was recognized." Daube, *The Deed and the Doer*, 118.

41   B. Bava Qama 107b, B. Bava Metzia 6a. See Elman, "Toward an Intellectual History of Sasanian Law," 60; Daube, "Negligence in the Early Talmudic Law of Contract: Talmudic Law."

42   B. Bava Metzia 106a; *baraita* also reported in B. Bava Metzia 41a.

injurious consequences. But the interest in intentionality expressed by these Amoraim is not limited to monetary law. Rulings ascribed to R. Nahman in particular demonstrate similar concern for intention when determining guilt in other matters.[43] Analogously, another third-generation Mahozan Amora, R. Hisda, introduces a need for intention when performing various religious acts where no such requirement had previously been stated.

3.1 R. Nahman: Purpose Defines the Prohibition

In several instances, R. Nahman limits the scope of forbidden behavior by delineating a need for intentionality. For example, he is cited as explaining that the ban against doing laundry during the week of the Ninth of Av is contingent on one's purpose:[44]

> שבת שחל תשעה באב להיות בתוכה אסורין לספר ולכבס אמ' רב נחמן לא שנו אלא לכבס וללבוש אבל לכבס ולהניח מותר

> [During the] week in which the Ninth of Av falls, it is prohibited to cut hair and to launder clothes. R. Nahman said: This was taught only with respect to launder and to then wear [immediately], but it is permitted to launder and to lay aside.[45]

For R. Nahman, the prohibition against laundering clothes is only applicable to one who plans to wear the freshly washed garments immediately. However, no violation has been committed where one washes these items for a future date (presumably after the Ninth of Av).[46] Here R. Nahman considers the purpose and motive for this action to determine whether a transgression has been committed.

---

43 I found only one such ruling attributed to R. Sheshet: In B. Keritut 11a-b, he determines whether one is guilty of having engaged in a prohibited sexual relationship on the basis of intention in response to a *baraita* which, among other topics, asserts that one who knowingly engages in sexual intercourse with a halakhically impermissible partner is treated as one who does so unintentionally. R. Sheshet rejects this *baraita* on the grounds that a man is only blameless for illicit sexual relations in the absence of intention; where there is intention, however, he is certainly guilty. He therefore interprets the *baraita* as exempting non-vaginal intercourse even if performed purposely, similar to one who unintentionally engages in illicit vaginal intercourse.

44 See Cohen, "Rav Nahman and Rav Sheshet," 17–19.

45 B. Taanit 29b. Text cited from the critical edition of b. Taanit by Malter, *Ta'anit*, 455.

46 Rashi *ad loc.* s.v. *afilu.*

In similar manner, whereas Rabin in the name of R. Yohanan states that a divorcée or widow who waits ten years to remarry will be unable to bear children, R. Nahman counters that this harsh consequence is dependent on the woman's motive:

> כי אתא רבין א"ר יוחנן כל ששהתה אחר בעלה עשר שנים ונשאת שוב אינה יולדת אמר רב נחמן לא שנו אלא שאין דעתה להנשא, אבל דעתה להנשא מתעברת.

> When Rabin came (to Babylonia from the Land of Israel), he stated in the name of R. Yohanan: A woman who waited ten years after [separation from] her husband, and then remarried, would bear children no more. R. Nahman said: This was taught only [in respect to one who] had no intention of remarrying. If, however, her intention was to marry again she may conceive.[47]

According to R. Nahman, she would become infertile only if she had no intention to remarry; whereas, if she wished to marry again, she would certainly be able to conceive.

3.2 *Mitasseq and Melakhah She-eina Tzerikha Le-gufa*: Exemptions in the Laws of the Sabbath

Several principles related to intentionality in the laws of the Sabbath also first appear in statements attributed to sages from this period. R. Nahman, in the name of his teacher Samuel, refers to the category of *mitasseq*, the inadvertent performance of a prohibited action due to being involved in, and therefore distracted by, another task:[48]

> אמר רב נחמן אמר שמואל מתעסק בחלבים ועריות חייב שכן נהנה מתעסק בשבת פטור מלאכת מחשבת אסרה תורה

> R. Nahman said: Samuel said: One who is occupied (*mitasseq*) with [one act and unwittingly engages in eating forbidden] fats[49] or illicit

---

47 B. Yebamot 34b.
48 Samuel discusses a case of *mitasseq* in regard to positive acts. Namely, he rules *mitasseq be-Qodashim pasul;* one who inadvertently brings a sacrifice is invalid. (B. Zebahim 47a; B. Menahot 110a; B. Hullin 13a). This is raised as a question to R. Huna regarding the biblical source for this ruling.
49 Rashi B. Keritut 19b s.v. *mitasseq be-halavim* explains this as a reference to a case where non-kosher and kosher fats are placed before a person who, despite intending to eat the kosher one, mistakenly consumes the former.

relations,[50] he is liable since he derived benefit [from his act].[51] One who is occupied [and unwittingly violates] the Sabbath[52] is exempt; [for] the Torah prohibits 'planned work' (*melekhet mahshevet*).[53]

Through this usage of *mitasseq*, R. Nahman invokes a category that factors the absence of intention into account when determining liability. Although the term *mitasseq* appears in tannaitic rulings,[54] in those instances, it is unclear whether it denotes a principle or simply serves as a descriptor for actions in specific contexts. Several tannaitic passages support the case-specific interpretation.[55]

R. Nahman in this rule follows tannaitic texts which state that the status of *mitasseq* frees one from a violation of the Sabbath but not from illicit sexual relations or consuming prohibited foods.[56] However, they offer no justification for these rules. It is R. Nahman who offers a reason, which underscores that in the latter two the experience of immediate physical benefit negates the inadvertence of *mitasseq*.[57] Thus, participating in a visceral sensory experience, even without the motivation to perform a forbidden act, indicates cognizance, which excludes the release from responsibility.[58]

Regarding the Sabbath, by contrast, R. Nahman is among the first to be credited with stating in the name of Samuel that one who violates the Sabbath in a case of *mitasseq* is exempt since, one must engage in a planned act, *melekhet mahshevet*, to be liable.[59] It seems that this principle was unknown to earlier

---

50 E.g. one who engages in sexual intercourse with his menstruant wife believing her to be ritually pure, or with his sister on the assumption that she is his wife (Rashi ibid. s.v. *mitasseq be-arayot*).

51 The idea that liability is limited to situations where one acts with the intention of receiving a tangible benefit also appears in laws that discuss the exchange of secular objects for sacred ones. See Tosefta Me'ilah 2:6.

52 In B. Sanhedrin 62b, the case presented as an example of *mitasseq* on the Sabbath is where one intends to lift an object that is not moored in the ground but instead cuts something that was attached to the ground, which is prohibited on the Sabbath. Since a permitted act was intended, no guilt is incurred. See Tosafot, B. Sanhedrin 62b s.v. *le-hagbeiyah*.

53 B. Keritut 19b-20b, B. Sanhedrin 62b.

54 E.g. M. Sheqalim 6:2; M. Rosh Hashana 4:8; M. Eduyot 2:5; M. Keritut 4:3, T. Shabbat 9:15–16, 10:19; T. Rosh Hashana 2:6; T. Taharot 4:8.

55 E.g. T. Shabbat 10:19; T. Shabbat 9:15-16. On the use of verbs as conceptual terms in tannaitic literature, see Moscovitz, *Talmudic Reasoning*, 353.

56 T. Shabbat 10:19 mentions the exemption with regard to the Sabbath; Y. Shabbat 11:6, 13b adds that it does not apply to forbidden fats and illicit relations. See Chapter 3, section 3.2.

57 See Rashi, B. Sanhedrin 62b s.v. *she-khein*.

58 Albeck, "Is there a Category of Intention in Talmudic Criminal Law?", 465.

59 The thirty-nine types of labor that are prohibited on the Sabbath are derived from activities that were performed to build the Tabernacle, based on the juxtaposition of the

sages. In M. Keritut 4:2, the exemption for *mitasseq* is derived from Leviticus 4:23, "that of which he is guilty" (אשר חטא בה). The redactors in B. Keritut 19b attempt to resolve the discrepancy between the use of the concept of *melekhet mahshevet* by R. Nahman and its absence from tannaitic rulings,[60] but in B. Sanhedrin 62b it appears that *melekhet mahshevet* had already become a widely accepted principle and understood as the reasoning behind the exemption for *mitasseq*.[61] Rabbah similarly refers to *melekhet mahshevet* in his cluster of rulings reported in B. Bava Qama 26b (analyzed earlier in this chapter).

In a similar vein, another third-generation Pumbeditan sage, R. Judah b. Yehezqel,[62] introduces a related principle regarding the laws of Shabbat in the name of Rav, Samuel's contemporary. R. Judah teaches that labor which is not performed for its intrinsic purpose (*melakhah she-eina tzerikha le-gufa*) does not constitute a biblical violation of the Sabbath.[63] He reports Rav as stating that this concept undergirds the opinion of the prominent third-generation Tanna, R. Simeon bar Yohai, who exempts one who transports a bed that has a corpse on it from one domain to another on the Sabbath (M. Shabbat 10:5). Since the corpse-bearer is not interested in carrying the corpse or the bed per se, but is concerned with removing and disposing of the body, carrying between domains is not being performed for its intrinsic purpose where one seeks possession or use of the object being transferred.[64]

---

biblical verses that describe its construction (Exodus 31:1–11) with those which prohibit labor on the Sabbath (vv. 12–17) following the opinion of Rashi B. Shabbat 49b. (According to the view advanced by R. Hai Gaon, the forms of labor that violate Shabbat may encompass any activity associated with the Tabernacle service. See this interpretation, cited at the beginning of *Sefer Maaseh Rokeah*). R. Nahman (and Rabbah) ostensibly derived the principle of *melekhet mahshevet* from Exodus 35:33: וּבַחֲרֹשֶׁת אֶבֶן לְמַלֹּאת וּבַחֲרֹשֶׁת עֵץ לַעֲשׂוֹת בְּכָל מְלֶאכֶת מַחֲשָׁבֶת, "to cut stones for setting and to carve wood—to work in every kind of designer's craft [lit. in every work of thought]," regarding the labor being executed. See Cassuto, *A Commentary on the Book of Exodus*, 459.

60 Several Talmudic commentators discuss this lack of consistency: e.g. *Sfat Emet*, ad loc. s.v. *be-gemara*, suggests that R. Eliezer's definition of *mitasseq* describes cases that demonstrate minimal intention, whereas R. Nahman's absolution of *mitasseq*, based on the concept of a planned action, is applied in the absence of intention. Rashi, by contrast, cites the same cases to describe the *mitasseq* for both R. Nahman and R. Eliezer, (which leads *Sfat Emet* (ibid.) to reason that for Rashi, R. Eliezer was unaware of R. Nahman's principle of 'a planned act'). See also Tosafot B. Sanhedrin 62b s.v. *le-hagbeiyah*.

61 As evidenced in a ruling by Abaye, the fourth-generation Amora cited there.

62 R. Judah b. Yehezqel is associated with the Pumbeditan School. See B. Qiddushin 70a, where he strongly disapproves of R. Nahman's Persian ways. Elman, "The Socioeconomics of Babylonian Heresy," 85.

63 B. Shabbat 107b.

64 Following Rashi B. Shabbat 93b s.v. *ve-Rabbi Shimon poter*. However, other commentators debate what constitutes the intrinsic purpose of forbidden labor. The Tosafists argue that

Third-generation Amoraim thus begin to integrate intentionality into the laws of the Sabbath by introducing concepts that evaluate desecration of the Sabbath with respect to an agent's intention. However, these notions remain primarily focused on the action. In Chapter 3 we will see that fourth-generation sages coin more precise terminology that explicitly underscores intention and purpose as fundamental conditions for an action to be deemed a violation of the Sabbath.

3.3   R. Hisda: Intention in the Fulfillment of Religious Precepts

In addition to their emphasis on intention as a factor in determining culpability, third-generation sages also discuss intentionality in fulfilling religious obligations. This concept is already evident in early rabbinic law. The Mishnah consistently rules that intention is necessary for the performance of particular ritual obligations (*mitzvot*): the requirement to "direct his heart" is stated in regard to reciting the daily *Shema*, hearing the *shofar* on Rosh Hashanah, and listening to or reading the Book of Esther on Purim.[65] M. Berakhot 5:1 similarly details the devotional practices of those who dedicated extensive time to mentally prepare for prayer. This mishnaic perspective is furthered in decisions attributed to R. Hisda[66] who, at several points in the Talmud, issues rulings that stress the importance of intention vis-à-vis various rituals, specifically regarding circumcision, constructing a valid *sukkah*, and nullifying leavened bread before Passover. R. Hisda's positions on the significance of intention in these observances are discussed in the remainder of this section.

With regard to circumcision, the prevailing position evidenced in ancient Israel and in early rabbinic texts validates a circumcision under nearly any circumstance, irrespective of how it took place, who performed the ritual, or the presence of intention.[67] As Shaye Cohen has summarized: "Intention was

---

the actor's goal must accord with those who performed the same labor when constructing the Tabernacle. See Tosafot B. Shabbat 94a *s.v. Rabbi Shimon poter*.

65   M. Berakhot 2:1; M. Rosh Hashana 3:7; M. Megillah 2:2.

66   R. Hisda, an elder among fourth-generation Babylonian sages, was the pre-eminent teacher in Sura until his death in 309 CE. See B. Moed Qatan 28a, *Iggeret Rab Sherira Gaon*, ed. Lewin, Frankfurt (1920), 85, Strack and Stemberger, *Introduction to the Talmud and Midrash*, 92. R. Hisda is reported to have been both the father-in-law and primary teacher of Rava. See B. Berakhot 56a, B. Shabbat 129a, and B. Yebamot 34b and Henshke, "Abaye and Rava," 190–91.

67   For example, in T. Avoda Zara 3:12, R. Meir bans non-Jews from performing circumcisions on Jews only from a concern that they might endanger the infant. The Sages counter that if a Jew is present and can ensure the safety of the child it is permitted; both views

irrelevant; involuntary circumcision was fine, too."[68] Even as this position is strongly advanced by R. Yose, a third-generation Tanna who lived in the mid-second century, it is contested by R. Judah,[69] who maintains that a Cuthean (Samaritan) was not permitted to circumcise a Jew, lest he have inappropriate thoughts during this ritual.[70]

Several generations later, R. Hisda addresses and expands on this subject, on the basis of R. Judah's ruling:

אמר רב חסדא מאי טעמא דרבי יהודה דכתיב לה' המול

> R. Hisda said: What is the reason for R. Judah['s ruling]? For it is written: 'for the Lord — he shall circumcise' (Exodus 12:48).[71]

Although R. Judah introduces the notion that intention is pertinent, he asserts this only to avert the possibility of idolatrous thoughts during the ritual; he makes no claim for the necessity of positive intentions. However, in his explanation of R. Judah's position, R. Hisda reworks the syntax of a verse (Exodus 12:48) that describes the Passover offering, by combining two separate clauses ("If a stranger who dwells with you would offer the Passover **to the Lord — all his males must be circumcised**; then he shall be admitted to offer it; he shall then be as a citizen of the country. But no uncircumcised person may eat of it"),[72] to suggest that specific intent is necessary to perform a circumcision as commanded by God. By introducing this requirement, R. Hisda assigns new significance to the ritual act itself, which had previously focused on the acquisition of a physical mark.[73]

---

affirming that intention is not required. See also Josephus, *Jewish Antiquities* 13:257–58, 13:318–19; B. Menahot 42a.

68 Cohen, *Jewish Women*, 21–22.
69 In B. Avoda Zara 27a, this is identified as R. Judah the Prince by the redactors. Another *baraita* (B. Avoda Zara 26b-27a), which discusses a scenario of a city that lacks a Jewish physician, reports that R. Judah allowed a Samaritan physician to perform a circumcision but not an idolater. The redactors identify this R. Judah as the third generation Tanna, R. Judah b. Ila'i and hence not in conflict with the R. Judah in the baraita who invalidates a Samaritan. See Rubin, *Beginning of Life*, 90–91.
70 T. Avoda Zara 3:13 B. Avoda Zara 27a; Y. Yebamot 9a 8:1. Cohen has noted the affinities between R. Judah's view and that expressed by Origen in *Against Celsus* 5:47. Cohen, *Jewish Women*, 22, nt. 47.
71 B. Avoda Zara 27a.
72 JPS translation from Sarna, *JPS: Exodus*.
73 My thanks to Dov Linzer, who raised this point in a lecture.

Intention is also incorporated into two rulings regarding *skhakh*, the covering placed on top of a *sukkah*, the temporary dwelling erected for Sukkot. In the Mishnah, the School of Shammai requires that a *sukkah* be constructed specifically for use on the festival and hence disqualifies one built too early; however, according to the accepted opinion, of the House of Hillel, the structure must simply conform to an objective set of specifications to be valid.[74] In the Talmud, R. Hisda qualifies that this standard is only applicable if the *skhakh* has been put in place with the intention that it provide shade, rather than, for instance, privacy.[75] On a related theme, a Mishnah-era ruling invalidates a *sukkah* if a sheet has been hung underneath the *skhakh* to catch any leaves that might fall; R. Hisda clarifies that the *sukkah* remains valid if the intention for placing this sheet is purely decorative.[76] In both of these cases, R. Hisda promotes the idea that this structure cannot be evaluated on objective criteria alone; rather, its validity is also contingent on intentionality.

Similarly, in B. Pesahim 31b, R. Hisda is among the first sages to contend that one may nullify *hametz*, leavened bread, before Passover solely by means of an intentional mental effort in circumstances where it is physically impossible to eliminate it.[77] According to rulings from the Land of Israel, *hametz* must be disposed of physically.[78]

---

74 M. Sukkah 1:1. The Bavli's anonymous discussion (ibid. 9a) both understands Beit Shammai's opinion as being motivated by a requirement of intention when constructing a *sukkah* and initially offers the same form of Scriptural proof text that R. Hisda provided with respect to circumcision: "... the festival of Sukkot, seven days for the Lord" (Leviticus 23:34).

75 B. Sukkah 8b-9a.

76 Ibid. 10a.

77 Shamma Friedman remarks that mental nullification is a Babylonian concept that was applied to M. Pesahim 3:7 and two *baraitot* (cited in B. Pesahim 7a, 8a) based on their interpretations in the Bavli. Moreover, this notion is absent from the parallel tosefta (T. Pesahim 3:12); Friedman, *Tosefta Atikta*, 333–47 (Chapter Fifteen).

The earliest sages to mention this concept are: Rav, who obligates one searching his home for *hametz* to also "nullify it" (*tzarikh she-yivatel*)(B. Pesahim 6b, quoted in Y. Pesahim 28d), and R. Hisda, who stipulates that one must nullify inaccessible *hametz* in his heart (*ve'tzarikh she-yivatel be-libo*). Although Friedman argues that both Rav and R. Hisda's requirements for nullification are mere formalities which are not legally effective, R. Hisda's instruction is more rigorous, for it maintains that inaccessible *hametz* is only considered out of one's possession if the owner nullifies what he cannot physically destroy. Rav, by contrast, obligates mental nullification only for hypothetical *hametz* that one may have inadvertently missed.

78 See e.g. *Mekhilta de-Rabbi Ishmael, Pesah* 8; M. Temurah 7:5. Friedman further demonstrates that the notion of *bitul be-leiv*, mental nullification which is presented in the Yerushalmi's discussion of M. Pesahim 3:7 only pertains to a scenario where disposal of *hametz* is not required, since other commandments take precedent (Y. Pesahim 30b). Friedman, 340.

Admittedly, related ideas with respect to intention are developed in earlier rulings, such as Samuel's requirement that ritual fringes be spun *"le-shmah"*[79] along with similar tannaitic opinions regarding phylacteries and slaughtering animals.[80] However, R. Hisda is notable for having introduced intentionality as a requirement for festival and life-cycle observances, extending beyond the criteria that the Mishnah seems to indicate, to define the status of a ritual action or object.[81] In Chapter 4, I examine R. Nahman's position and several other passages that touch on ritual law, and I explore in depth the role of intention in relation to the status of ritual as a public enactment of religious faith.

4 Summary

Whereas the early Babylonian Amoraim consistently apply strict liability in tort law, the rulings examined here attributed to third-generation sages indicate a modification of this standard, as evidenced by the inclusion of negligence, intention, and limitations on the scope of personal liability in cases of damage and in certain ritual transgressions. This change may be related to the growing influence of Palestinian teachings on sages during this period.[82] In Chapter 1 we saw that the dominant approach in the Land of Israel, as demonstrated in the Mishnah and Yerushalmi, advocates the determination of liability based on fault, with particular attention to an actor's intention. The preference for intention may also reflect what David Kraemer has described as the growing self-awareness evinced in rulings attributed to this generation of Babylonian sages, a point I will return to in the concluding chapter.[83]

---

[79] B. Menahot 42b.
[80] Chapters One and Two in M. Zebahim.
[81] See also B. Nazir 32a, which further demonstrates the interest in intention among third-generation Amoraim and its ramifications for ritual observance. This passage records a debate between R. Nahman, R. Hisda, and Rabbah b. R. Huna regarding a case where an error was intentionally committed while separating the tenth animal for tithes. R. Nahman maintains that the tithe is invalid so the animal improperly counted as the tenth is not consecrated, whereas R. Hisda and Rabbah b. R. Huna counter that the outcome is the same, whether or not he acted intentionally; even an intentional error may result in a tithed animal. Similarly in B. Berakhot 20b R. Hisda, R. El'azar, and R. Ada b. Ahava all rule that thinking the words of *Shema* does not fulfill one's obligation, but it is nevertheless preferable to doing nothing. See Brodsky, "Thought is Akin to Action," 155–56.
[82] Elman demonstrates that select Palestinian teachings gained currency specifically in the schools of Pumbedita. Elman, "Two Cities," 5. Zvi Dor, by contrast, argues for Palestinian influence on Rava and his students from Mahoza. Dor, *The Teachings of Eretz Israel in Babylon*.
[83] Kraemer, *The Mind of the Talmud*, 36.

During this transitional phase, however, concepts relating to intentionality were not consistently applied. As the analysis in this chapter shows, Rabbah is aligned with the strict positions of M. Bava Qama 2:6 and 3:1, yet he also voices dissent from them under certain conditions by taking negligence and intention into consideration. In Mahoza, R. Nahman, R. Sheshet, and R. Hisda more reliably demonstrate concern for motivating factors. Among third-generation sages, intention also becomes a condition for liability for desecrating the Sabbath.

In the next chapter, we will consider additional statements attributed to third-generation sages that comport with this description and which are recurrently contrasted with opinions of fourth-generation sages. In the fourth generation of Babylonian Amoraim, a picture emerges of an increasingly consistent tendency toward emphasizing intentionality in a variety of legal spheres, and the growing distinctions between the schools of Pumbedita and Mahoza also become more readily apparent.

CHAPTER 3

The Fourth Generation of Babylonian Amoraim
A Period of Innovation

1   Overview

The fourth century was a period of significant innovation in the history of Talmudic jurisprudence and legal conceptualization. Much of this may be attributed to two outstanding fourth-generation sages: Abaye (from Pumbedita) and Rava (from Mahoza).[1] Aside from issuing many rulings, Rava in particular ushered in a distinctly new era of legal thought by introducing a number of key legal principles that continued to ramify throughout the later amoraic and redactional periods. As I will show, the concept of intention was a key factor underlying a variety of these principles and rulings.

Abaye and Rava both consider the intention of an actor in a range of cases. In tort law, they reject strict liability and rather look to subjective causal factors. With regard to the laws of the Sabbath, they formulate the principle *davar she-ein mitkavvein,* an unintended effect, which exempts unintended violations. They are also attributed with discussing the subject of *ye'ush,* a person's feeling of despair that he will not regain ownership of his property that allows another to take possession of it, with more frequency than previous generations.[2] However, significant differences between the two sages become apparent. Rulings attributed to Abaye tend to require only volition—intent to perform an action itself—in determining liability. Rava, by contrast, consistently determines liability based on the specific intention of an actor to violate a norm, and not simply the action and its consequences. In tort law, he posits that one must act with the distinct purpose of causing harm in order to be held liable. In the category of religious offenses, Rava similarly looks to an actor's intention to commit the specific offense. Taken together, these contrasting views indicate an increased focus on the role of intention among these preeminent fourth-generation sages, and the emergence of two main approaches as

---

1   It has long been established that Abaye and Rava ushered in a new era of thinking and conceptualization which distinguishes them from earlier Amoraim. See Tosafot B. Qiddushin 45b s.v. *hava,* Sussman, "Ve-shuv Li-yerushalmi Neziqin," 101, n. 188; Moscovitz, *Talmudic Reasoning,* chap. nine.
2   B. Gittin 37b; B. Qiddushin 52b; B. Bava Qama 66b, 67b; B. Bava Metzia 21b.

to what constitutes intentional behavior. As we might expect, these correlate with the distinction between the Pumbeditan and Mahozan sages of the previous generation, discussed in the previous chapter. Ultimately, however, it is Rava, arguably the most creative and important Amora of the Bavli, whose unmistakable influence on subsequent generations of Babylonian Amoraim is evident throughout the Bavli's redactional strata.

In order to better understand Rava's legal thought, we will conclude by considering an analogue to Rava's consistent emphasis on intentionality: Aristotle's discussion of corrective justice in the *Nicomachean Ethics*. The theory of justice and moral blame laid out by Aristotle overlaps in significant ways with a range of Rava's rulings, and may therefore shed light on what underlies his novel approach to intentionality.

2   Pumbedita: Abaye

We begin by looking at those rulings in which Abaye challenges his teacher, Rabbah.[3] As we saw in the previous chapter, Rabbah both follows the standard of strict liability advanced by early Babylonian Amoraim, and at the same time begins to distance himself from it by considering negligence and whether one acted with volition. Although Abaye follows Rabbah in rulings based on action and intent to act, in several passages Abaye questions Rabbah's strict rulings, maintaining that there is no liability in the absence of purposeful action. This constitutes a further distancing from the standard of strict liability of the early generations.

2.1   *Challenge to Rabbah's Strict Liability*

Abaye and Rabbah are presented as debating the tannaitic position of R. Eliezer, which essentially forbids one from owning an animal which has acted aggressively on three consecutive occasions:

ר' אליעזר או' אין לו שמירה אלא סכין
אמ' רבה מאי טע' דר' אליעזר דאמ' קרא ולא ישמרנו בעליו שוב אין לו שמירה לזה
אמ' ליה אביי אלא מעתה כי יכרה איש בור ולא יכסנו הכי נמי שוב אין לו כסוי לזה ... והתנן כיסהו כראוי ... פטור

---

3   According to gaonic sources, Abaye was also his nephew. Strack and Stemberger, *Introduction to the Talmud and Midrash*, 94–95.

אלא היינו טע' דר' אליעזר כדתניא ר' נתן או' מניין שלא יגדל אדם כלב רע
בתוך ביתו ולא יעמיד סולם רעוע בתוך ביתו ת"ל ולא תשים דמים בביתך

> R. Eliezer said: there is no [effective] guarding [for the *mu'ad* animal] except the knife.
>
> Rabbah[4] said: what is R. Eliezer's reason? For Scripture states (Exodus 21:36): 'its owner did not guard it,' there is no guarding for it anymore.
>
> Abaye said to him: But now, [when the verse states] (Exodus 21:33) 'if a person digs a pit and does not cover it', here too [infer]: there should be no covering for it anymore ... But it has been taught (M. Bava Qama 5:6): 'if one properly covers it ... he is exempt'?
>
> Rather, the reason for R. Eliezer is, as it has been taught [in a *baraita*]: R. Nathan said: From where do we know that one should not raise a bad tempered dog in his house and he should not put up a rickety ladder in his house? Scripture says (Deuteronomy 22:8): 'and do not place blood in your house'.[5]

Rabbah supports R. Eliezer's position by citing a biblical proof text, "its owner did not guard it" (Exodus 21:36), understood to mean "there is no guarding for it anymore." In other words, once an animal is proven to be dangerous, its owner is responsible for all damages it causes, irrespective of whether preventative measures are taken. This echoes Rabbah's rulings in B. Bava Qama 27a where he imposes liability for one who causes damages when falling from a roof. When there is a possibility that damages could result from risky behavior (sleeping/walking on a roof, owning an aggressive animal), the tortfeasor is responsible for the harmful outcome. Abaye counters that, although R. Eliezer disapproves of keeping a vicious animal, its owner may still guard it properly and thereby release himself from liability as doing so does not automatically constitute negligence. While Rabbah's position finds parallel in the Yerushalmi,[6] Abaye's is unprecedented.

---

4   Following MSS Florence II I 7-9, Munich 95 and the Vilna and Soncino editions. MSS Hamburg, Vatican 116, and Escorial G-1-3 attribute this to Rava. However, as noted by Kalmin, it is more likely that Abaye posed a question directly to his teacher Rabbah, than to his younger contemporary, Rava—with who he was rarely in direct contact. Kalmin, *Sages, Stories*, 174–90.

5   B. Bava Qama 45b-46a. On the different versions of the mishnah under discussion, M. Bava Qama 4:9 and which version Rabbah and Abaye seem to have had, see Halivni, *Mekorot U-Mesorot: Baba Kama*, 178–79.

6   Y. Bava Qama 4:9, 4c: אמ' ר' לעזר. והלא שמור הוא והתורה חייבתו. אמ' ר' לעזר. כל שמירה שאמרה תורה אפי' הקיפו חומת ברזל אין משערין אותו אלא בגופו. לפיכך רואין אותו אם ראוי לשמירה פטור ואם לאו חייב.

Abaye rejects another strict ruling of Rabbah in the context of a *baraita* discussing exile for accidental killing:

תנו רבנן בשגגה פרט למזיד בבלי דעת פרט למתכוין
מזיד פשיטא בר קטלא הוא (אלא) אמר רבה אימא פרט לאומר מותר
א"ל אביי[7] אי אומר מותר אנוס הוא
אמר ליה שאני אומר האומר מותר קרוב למזיד הוא

> Our rabbis taught: 'Inadvertently' (Numbers 35:11): excluding [one who kills] maliciously. 'Without knowledge' (Deuteronomy 19:4): excluding one who has intent.
>
> [That the verse excludes a case where one kills] maliciously is obvious, he is worthy of death! Rabbah[8] said: I would say it excludes one who says (i.e. believes) it is permitted.
>
> Abaye said to him: If [it is a case where] one says it is permitted, [it is a case of] coercion [and he should be exempt]!
>
> [Rabbah] said to him: for I say that one who says it is permitted is close to [one who acts] maliciously.[9]

The teacher and student debate why one who mistakenly thinks that murder is permitted is denied exile to a city of refuge.[10] For Rabbah it is nearly

---

R. Lazar said: but it was guarded and [yet] the Torah makes him liable? R. Lazar said: all [things that require] guarding that the Torah mentions, even if he surrounds it with a metal wall [are not effective, rather] we only calculate it with its body (i.e. it is to be killed). Therefore, we look at it, if it is worthy for guarding, one is exempt [if it gets out]. If not, one is liable.

This also seems the more likely understanding of R. Eliezer's position from its original context in M. Bava Qama 4:9. (See *Rif*'s commentary on this passage, and S. Atlas' notes on *Hiddushei HaRa'avad ad loc.*, 117–119 note 42.)

7   The attribution to Abaye is absent from ed. Venice, but is present in all other textual witnesses.
8   Though most of the MSS as well as ed. Vilna attribute this ruling to Rava, the attribution to Rabbah seems more likely. *Hiddushei Ritva ad loc.* s.v. *amar* has the attribution of Rabbah citing the passage as follows: א"ל אביי לרבה. A Genizah fragment (National Library of Israel's Institute of Microfilmed Hebrew Manuscripts, F12577) of its parallel passage, B. Makot 9a, likewise attributes the question to Rabbah, as does *Hiddushei Ramban* (*ad loc.* s.v. *ha*). Aharon Shemesh maintains that the correct attribution is Rabbah. Shemesh, "Shogeg Karov Le-Mezid," 406. As noted previously, it is also more likely that Abaye was engaged in a dialogue with his teacher Rabbah, than his contemporary, Rava. *Supra* n. 4.
9   B. Makot 7b; parallel in B. Makot 9a. Of the two, 7b is likely the original setting since in 9a it is embedded in the redactional strata. Furthermore, Rabbah's statement copies the phrasing of the *baraita* which he comments on in 7b.
10 Either the actor thought that there is no prohibition against killing (Rashi *ad loc.* s.v. *be-omer*), or that the victim was one whom there is no command against killing, such as an animal (*Hiddushei Ritva ad loc.* s.v. *eima*).

equivalent to deliberate murder, characterized as *qarov le-meizid,* an inadvertent act which is closer to a malicious one, presumably because he should have known better,[11] making exile inadequate. This complements Rabbah's rulings in B. Bava Qama 26b in which cases of manslaughter characterized by small degrees of negligence still qualify for exile. Abaye, by contrast, maintains that one who acts under a mistaken impression is characterized as *be-ones,* under coercion, and is therefore necessarily exempt from punishment.[12]

Abaye expresses a similar concern in another challenge directed at Rabbah. Following the latter's interpretation of R. Judah's requirement of intent as referring to intent to lower a jug leading it to its accidental fall (see Chapter 2, 2.3), Abaye raises an objection given the dissenting opinion of R. Meir. R. Meir's opinion appears in a *baraita* discussing a scenario where a pitcher breaks or a camel falls and the owner fails to remove the hazard. R. Meir ruled that one is responsible for damages that occur as a result of the broken shards or the fallen camel, while the Sages ruled that he is exempt, though liable in the eyes of the "heavenly court." R. Meir, however, concurred with the Sages that the owner is exempt in a case where he places jugs on a roof in order to dry them and they fall due to an unusual wind. Based on this *baraita,* Abaye raises the following challenge to Rabbah:

ר' יהודה או' במתכוין חייב בשאין מתכוין פטור
היכי דמי מתכוין אמ' רבה במתכוין להורידה למטה מכתפו
אמ' ליה [אביי] מכלל דמחייב ר' מאיר אפלו נפשרה
אמ' ליה אין מחייב היה ר' מאיר אפלו אוזנו בידו
אמאי אנוס הוא ואונס רחמ' פטריה דכת' ולנערה לא תעשה דבר אין לנערה חטא
מות וג'

> R. Judah says: If he intended, he is liable. If he did not intend, he is exempt.
> How is it like (what are the circumstances of the case) 'when he intends'?
> Rabbah said: where he intends to lower it down from his shoulder.[13]
> Abaye said to him (Rabbah): this implies that R. Meir imposes liability even if it falls apart?
> [Rabbah] said to him: yes, R. Meir imposes liability even where its handle is in his hand.

---

11 See *Hiddushei Ramban ad loc.* s.v. *aval:* "He should have learnt [the laws] and he did not."
12 For further analysis of this passage, see Shemesh, "Shogeg Karov Le-Mezid," 406–9.
13 See Chapter 2, 2.3 for a discussion of Rabbah's opinion.

But why, he is coerced and [in a case of] coercion the Merciful One absolved, for it is written (Deuteronomy 22:26): 'And to the girl you shall do nothing, the girl does not have a mortal sin'?[14]

Abaye questions Rabbah's interpretation of R. Meir as imposing liability even where a jug breaks through no voluntary action of the custodian. It seems he could not accept the imposition of liability in an instance where damages are caused without a direct or purposeful action, even within his understanding of the rejected view of R. Meir.[15]

Similarly, in B. Bava Batra 22b-23a, Abaye challenges his other teacher, R. Joseph, another third-generation Pumbeditan sage, by introducing the concept of *gerama*, indirect causation, and arguing that indirect damages do not carry the same level of culpability as direct damage. Abaye's challenges to Rabbah and R. Joseph thus indicate a further move away from strict liability by focusing on the causes and circumstances of damages as well as the intent of actors.[16] In the following section we will see similar exchanges between these sages on issues of ritual law.

2.2 Challenges Regarding the Laws of the Sabbath

Abaye challenges Rabbah and R. Joseph in several cases regarding the laws of the Sabbath based on various concepts relating to intentionality which he introduces. In each instance he argues that these concepts underlie tannaitic rulings.

For example, as Ephraim Urbach pointed out, Abaye is the first to be attributed with using the term *muqtzah* in the laws of the Sabbath and festivals as referring to a category of items which are not intended to be used.[17] Previously, *muqtzah* designated places and concrete objects alone.[18]

---

14   B. Bava Qama 28b-29b.
15   Although most Talmudic commentators assume that the question, "but why, he is coerced" was also raised by Abaye (Tosafot R. Perez *ad loc.*, Shita Mequbetzet *ad loc.* s.v. *ve-zeh*), Halivni maintains that it is redactional. Halivni, *Mekorot U-Mesorot: Baba Kama*, 109, n. 2; page 114. If so, it may have been drawn from Abaye's challenge raised against Rabbah in B. Makot 7b.
    Halivni further remarks that Abaye's understanding of the mishnah which appears later in this passage was not stated in response to the question raised against Rabbah's position, but was an independent interpretation of M. Bava Qama 3:2. See also *Pnei Yehoshua* (*ad loc.* s.v. *ella*) which makes this point as well.
16   An exchange between Abaye and R. Joseph in B. Yebamot 52b regarding acquisitions likewise hinges on a question of intent.
17   B. Shabbat 44a, 46b. Urbach, *The Halakhah*, 179–82. Where it is attributed to earlier Amoraim (B. Shabbat 45a, 128a; B. Beitzah 6a), Urbach argues that they are later redactional additions.
18   See Rubenstein, "Abstract Concepts," 51–58.

In another case Abaye again questions Rabbah based on his (and Rava's, as we will see below) assumption that the Sabbath can only be violated via an intentional action. Consequently, he differs with Rabbah and R. Joseph regarding cutting grass on the Sabbath:

תנו רבנן התולש עולשין והמזרד זרדין ... אם לייפות את הקרקע כל שהן
אטו כולהו לאו ליפות את הקרקע נינהו
רבה ורב יוסף דאמרי תרויהו באגם שנו
אביי אמר אפילו תימא בשדה דלאו אגם כגון דלא[19] קמיכוין

> Our rabbis taught: 'One who plucks endives or prunes reeds ... if [he does so in order] to improve the ground, [he is liable to bring a sin offering for] any amount'.
> Do they not all [serve] to improve the ground?
> Rabbah[20] and R. Joseph both said: They taught [this only with regards to] a swamp.[21]
> Abaye said: You can even say [this law applies to] a field that is not a swamp, [in] a case where he does not intend [to improve the land].[22]

Rabbah and R. Joseph rule that irrespective of an individual's intention, an action which results in an improvement to the ground constitutes a violation of the Sabbath. Because they consider the action and its consequences alone, they exempt one from bringing a sin offering for pruning only in a place where doing so does not improve the soil. Abaye counters that engaging in such actions may not entail a sin offering as long as one does not intend to improve the condition of the soil.[23]

Abaye similarly questions R. Joseph concerning the ruling of R. Simeon (b. Yohai) permitting one to drag a chair on the Sabbath even though this will

---

19 מיכוין שרי] MS Oxford Opp. Add. fol. 23 (366).
20 Ed. Soncino cites Rava and R. Joseph; however, the majority of MSS cite Rabbah. Furthermore, as Rabbah and R. Joseph were contemporaries and are often cited together, it is almost certain that Rabbah is the correct attribution.
21 A swamp has no need or use for improvement. Rashi *ad loc.* s.v. *be-agam*.
22 B. Shabbat 103a.
23 It is unclear whether the last clause regarding intention is part of Abaye's statement or a redactional elaboration of his ruling. The fact that it appears with many variants in the MSS indicates the latter. Nevertheless, it seems to be implicit in Abaye's ruling since there does not appear to be any other reason readily available to explain Abaye's leniency. If not, the redactors may have been influenced by Rava, which we will see was often the case.

THE FOURTH GENERATION OF BABYLONIAN AMORAIM

create furrows in the ground, violating the prohibition of plowing. His challenge is based on the principle of *davar she-ein mitkavvein,* an unintended effect:

(A) רמי ליה אביי לרב יוסף מי אמ' ר' שמעון כבתה מותר לטלטל' כבתה אין לא כבתה לא מאי טעמא דילמא בהדי דנקיט לה כבתה הא שמעינ' ליה לר' שמעון דאמ' דבר שאין מתכוין מותר דתניא ר' שמעון או' גורר אדם כסא ... ובלבד שלא יתכוין לעשות חריץ[24]

(B) כל היכא דכי מיכוין איכ' איסורא דאורית' כי לא מיכוין גזר ר' שמעון מדרבנן כל היכ' דכי מיכוין ואיכא איסורא דרבנן כי לא מיכוין שרי ר' שמעון לכתחילה

(C) מיתיב רבא מוכרי כסות מוכרין כדרכן ובלבד שלא יתכוין בחמה מפני החמה ובגשמים מפני הגשמים והצנועין מפשילין במקל לאחוריהן והא הכא דכי מיכוין איסורא דאוריתא איכא כי לא מיכוין שרי ר' שמעון לכתחילה

(D) אלא אמ' רבא הנח לנר שמן ופתילה הואיל דנעשה בסיס לדבר האסור

(A) Abaye raised a contradiction to R. Joseph: Did not R. Simeon say, 'if [a lamp] is extinguished, it may be carried'? If it is extinguished, yes [it may be carried, which implies] if it is not extinguished, no [it may not be carried]. What is the reason? Perhaps through his handling it, he will extinguish it. But we have heard that R. Simeon said an unintentional act is permitted, for it was taught: 'R. Simeon says: a person may drag a chair ... [on the Sabbath] so long as he does not intend to make a furrow'?

(B) In all cases where if one had intent there would be a biblical violation,[25] R. Simeon made a rabbinic decree [against doing so even]

---

24 Although in the Bavli's version R. Simeon's ruling hinges on one's intention, other citations of this *baraita* omit this condition.

T. Beitzah 2:12 (Lieberman): רבי שמעון אומר גורר אדם מטה כסא וספסל וקתדרה אצלו בשבת ואין צריך לומר ביום טוב

Y. Shabbat 6a, 5:1; Y. Kilaim 27b, 2:9: לא יגרר אדם את המטה ואת הכסא ואת הספסל ואת הקתידרה מפני שהוא עושה חריץ ורבי שמעון מתיר

Albeck therefore concludes that R. Simeon's original ruling was not concerned with one's intention but rather with permitted modes of carrying. (Albeck, *The Mishna: Seder Zeraim,* 370 in his notes to M.Kilaim 9:5.) In his examination of this term in tannaitic texts, Kalcheim demonstrates the inconsistency of this term's appearance in text witnesses and how it evolved from its original meaning of intention to do an action, to its later iteration of intention to violate a prohibition. Kalcheim, "Davar Sh'ain Mitkaven," 53–64.

25 Hence, extinguishing a fire on the Sabbath, which is one of the thirty-nine prime categories of prohibited actions on the Sabbath and a biblical prohibition, falls under the rabbinic decree (Rashi *ad loc.* s.v. *issura*).

where one does not have intent. In all cases where if one had intent there would [only] be a rabbinic violation,[26] when one did not have intent, R. Simeon permitted it *ab initio*.

(C) Rava objected: (M. Kilaim 9:5 states:) 'A garment seller may sell [garments containing mixed fibers] in the usual manner (by donning his wares) so long as he does not intend in the sun [to wear them as protection] from the sun and in the rain [as protection] from the rain. The modest ones hang [them] on a stick behind them'. And here, where [the merchant] intends [to derive benefit from the garment] there is a biblical prohibition, yet where he does not intend [to derive benefit], R. Simeon permits [wearing the garment] *ab initio*![27]

(D) Rather Rava said: Leave aside [the case of] a lamp, oil, and wick since they become a base[28] for that which is prohibited.[29]

Abaye questions the consistency of R. Simeon's positions: On the one hand, his ruling suggests that it is prohibited to carry a lit lamp on the Sabbath since the fire may inadvertently become extinguished. Yet, R. Simeon permits one to drag a chair on the Sabbath even though a furrow may be created, because it is not what the actor intends. This implies that R. Simeon maintains that an unintended effect (*davar she-ein mitkavvein*) is permitted on the Sabbath. Although this principle is ascribed to R. Simeon, Abaye and Rava are actually the first to be attributed with stating it explicitly.[30]

R. Joseph, or the redactors answering on his behalf, responds to Abaye's query by positing that R. Simeon's putative leniency of *davar she-ein mitkavvein* is limited to rabbinic prohibitions (B). By contrast, Rava, (section C)

    Many of the medieval commentators note the contradiction between this ruling and another principle pertaining to the laws of Sabbath, מלאכה שאינה צריכה לגופה "labor that is not performed for its intrinsic purpose," discussed in the previous chapter (see Tosafot *ad loc.* s.v. *de-kol*; *Hiddushei Ha-Ramban ad loc.* s.v. *kol*; *Hiddushei Ha-Rashba ad loc.* s.v. *kol*, *Hiddushei Ha-Ritva ad loc.* s.v. *kol*). However, as already explained, these are amoraic concepts and thus do not reflect R. Simeon's original rulings. See Kalcheim, "Davar Sh'ain Mitkaven."

26 Digging an indentation does not violate biblical law since it is considered an irregular form of plowing (Rashi ibid.).

27 It is unclear whether this mishnah was actually cited by Rava or by the redactors.

28 I.e. the flame is prohibited to carry, and the oil and lamp become secondary to it and thus forbidden to be carried.

29 B. Shabbat 46b–47a. For another version of this discussion see B. Shabbat 29b.

30 See discussion below in section 3.2.

Abaye's contemporary and possible author of the principle, applies it to rabbinic and biblical prohibitions alike. Rather than limit his leniency regarding unintended acts to rabbinic violations, Rava invokes another principle to explain why R. Simeon forbade one from carrying a lit candle on the Sabbath; it becomes a base for a forbidden object (section D).[31] It is unclear whether Abaye accepts Rava's broad application.

This *sugya* represents an important development in the laws of Sabbath in which the fourth-generation Amoraim Rava and Abaye apply (and elsewhere coin) a specific principle which exempts unintentional violations of the Sabbath, thus emphasizing the necessity of intentional behavior in determining guilt. At the same time, it offers a glimpse into their distinct approaches which reflect broader differences between them and their respective schools. Abaye questions his Pumbeditan predecessors concerning strict rulings where an actor's intention is at stake and which undermine the exemption that lack of intention should entail. Yet the position which the *sugya* presents as the Pumbeditan one—as placed in the mouth of R. Joseph and possibly accepted by Abaye—ultimately limits the exemption resulting from *davar she-ein mitkavvein* to rabbinic prohibitions. Rava, by contrast, is presented as applying *davar she-ein mitkavvein* to all prohibitions, viewing lack of intention as a uniformly applicable exemption.

As we will see in the section that follows, this aligns with what appears to be a more general approach of Rava, evidenced in a broad range of his rulings in which intention consistently plays a key role.

3   Mahoza: Rava[32]

3.1   *Tort Law*

Rava was a student of R. Nahman of Mahoza, whose rulings, as discussed in the previous chapter, consider negligence as well as the specific purpose of the agent performing an act. Rava continues in this vein, but far more expansively, introducing a requirement of intentional action in areas where it had not before been applied. He often rules based on a very strict definition of intention, requiring intent to violate a prohibition.

---

31   On the development of *basis le-davar assur* with regard to the laws of the Sabbath and how it draws from purity laws, see Kretzmer-Raziel, "The Impact of Purity Laws on Amoraic Laws Concerning Handling on the Sabbath," 185–88.

32   Portions of this section appeared in *JLAS*, Strauch Schick, "Reading Aristotle in Mahoza."

Rava's focus on intentionality is evidenced in several cases involving torts discussed in tractates Bava Qama and Bava Metzia. In each of these cases Rava considers the subjective intentions of individuals whose actions result in harm. Additionally, whereas his predecessors, including R. Nahman, introduced the term for negligence into Babylonian amoraic law (*peshi'ah*) and based rulings on its presence,[33] Rava makes a clear distinction between negligent conduct and purposely harmful acts. Accordingly, he decreases the amount of liability imposed on a tortfeasor in cases of negligence, but imposes full liability upon one who willfully and directly causes harm.

3.1.1 B. Bava Qama 27b: Rights of Pedestrians

As discussed in Chapter 1, the earlier amoraic understanding of M. Bava Qama 3.1 ("a person is always forewarned") deems an accidental tortfeasor liable under most circumstances. Rava, in contrast, goes so far as to sanction even the intentional destruction of property by a pedestrian when he has no malicious intent and the injurious act is either unavoidable or is necessary to allow pedestrians to exercise their right of way in public thoroughfares.[34] As opposed to the early amoraic view reported in that *sugya*, Rava does not deem causing damage alone sufficient grounds to confer liability.

3.1.2 B. Bava Metzia 96b: Borrower's Rights

Rava's insistence on taking into account factors beyond the bare outcome of an action is also evident in a case where he exempts a borrower from compensating a lender for damage to tools or work animals. B. Bava Metzia 96b reports:

(A) איבעיא להו כחש בשר מחמת מלאכה מהו אמ' להו ההוא מרבנן ורב חלקיה בר רב אויא שמיה מה לי קטלה פלגא מה לי קטלה כולה

(B) אמ' רבא מכלל דכי מתה מחמת מלאכה חייב ולימא ליה לאו לאוקמה בכילתא שאלתה אלא אמ' רבא הי מיבעיא כחש בשר מחמת מלאכה דפטור אלא אפלו מתה מחמת מלאכה נמי פטור דאמ' ליה לאו לאוקומה בכילתא שאלתה

(C) ההוא גברא דשאיל נרגא מחבריה איתבר אתא לקמיה דרבא אמ' ליה זיל איתי שהדי דלא שנית ביה ואיפטר

(D) ואי ליכא סהדי מאי

(E) תא שמא דההוא גברא דשאיל נרגא מחבריה ואיתבר אתא לקמיה דרב אמר ליה זיל שלים ליה נרגא מעיילא אמר ליה רב כהנא ורב אסי לרב דינא הכי ושתיק רב

---

33 See Chapter 2, text by n. 41.
34 See Owen, "Philosophical Foundations of Fault in Tort Law," 220.

THE FOURTH GENERATION OF BABYLONIAN AMORAIM 83

(A) It was asked of them: What is [the law if a borrowed animal] became emaciated because of work? One of the rabbis, and R. Hilqiah the son of R. Avia is his name, said: What [is the difference] to me if he killed part of it or if he killed all of it (he should be required to pay)![35]

(B) Rava[36] said: This implies that if it dies because of its work, [the borrower] is liable. But let him say to him 'I did not borrow it to put it in an enclosure'! Rather Rava said: It goes without saying that he is exempt where it becomes emaciated from the work, but even if it dies as a result of the work, [the borrower] is also exempt, because he can say to him, 'I did not borrow it to put it in an enclosure'.

(C) [There was] a certain man who borrowed an axe from his friend [and] it broke. He came before Rava. (Rava) said to him: Go bring witnesses that you did not deviate [from how it is usually used.] And he exempted him.

(D) And what if there are no witnesses?

(E) Come and hear, there was a man who borrowed an axe from his neighbor and it broke. He came before Rav [who] said to him: Go and pay him an axe in good condition. R. Kahana and R. Assi said to Rav: Is this the law? And Rav was silent.[37]

The previously accepted ruling, cited in the names of Rav and his student R. Hilqiah, is that a borrower must pay compensation for damage to an item in his care—regardless of how it is used (A, E). Rava introduces a novel standard for liability: so long as a borrower uses an object in its usual manner, he need not compensate the lender for damage sustained in the course of its use (B, C). Here too, Rava issues an exemption due to the lack of intent to damage the item and/or the right conferred to a borrower to use the property in a normal fashion.[38]

The redactors, presumably influenced by Rava's ruling, try to harmonize Rav's position with that of Rava, by limiting the former's ruling to a case in which there are no witnesses to testify how the borrower used the item in

---

35   Following MS Hamburg. The majority of manuscripts and both printed editions lack this question. R. Hilqiah states what is attributed to Rava in MS Hamburg, in which case Rava and R. Hilqiah do not present opposing views; rather, R. Hilqiah raises a question which Rava resolves. MS Hamburg seems to have a superior reading: It is easy to account for a missing sentence; the scribe could have mistakenly skipped from the statement of R. Hilqiah to after the first 'אמר רבא', and then conflated the first half of Rava's statement with R. Hilqiah's. It is less likely that a whole sentence that was not previously there would be added.

36   All text witnesses contain attributions to Rava.

37   B. Bava Metzia 96b–97a.

38   *Hiddushei HaRashba* (ad loc. s.v. *afilu*) explains that one who lends his animal in order to perform work anticipates that it might grow thin or die.

question (D). Nevertheless, it is clear that Rav maintained that a borrower is liable, no matter how damages occur, as is evidenced by R. Kahana and R. Assi's question to him regarding his strict decision. Only Rava factors the specific circumstances which led to the loss, as opposed to the objective fact that the borrower damaged the lender's property.[39]

3.1.3   B. Bava Metzia 83a: Borrower's Oath

Rava also makes a distinction between unintentional and intentional harm in explaining M. Bava Metzia 2:8, which addresses a case in which a custodian breaks a barrel under his care while moving it. R. Meir rules that irrespective of whether the custodian is being paid for services, he must take an oath to exempt himself from liability. In the Bavli's discussion, surprise is expressed at this ruling, since elsewhere the redactors infer that R. Meir maintains '*nitqal posheï'a*', one who stumbles is considered negligent and hence responsible to compensate the plaintiff;[40] an oath should therefore be insufficient. Rava is subsequently cited as clarifying the nature of the oath:

היכי משתבע אמ' רבא שבועה שלא בכונה שברתיה

> How does (the custodian) take an oath? Rava[41] said: An oath that I did not break it intentionally.[42]

---

39 See also B. Bava Qama 112a where Rava lessens liability for heirs who eat an animal that their father had bequeathed to them which, unbeknownst to them, was on loan.

40 B. Bava Qama 28b-29a. R. Meir did not state *nitqal posheï'a*, but rules that one is liable to compensate anyone who is injured by broken shards or his camel that has fallen in the public domain that he does not remove. The redactors interpret the underlying rationale as reflecting the general principle of *nitqal posheï'a*, one who stumbles is considered negligent and thus legally liable. Such abstract conceptualization is typical of the redactional strata. Moscovitz, *Talmudic Reasoning*. This understanding of R. Meir's opinion is taken as a given in subsequent *sugyot* (e.g. B. Bava Qama 31a, 99b).

However, it is possible that R. Meir distinguishes between pedestrians and custodians who cause accidental damage, and only exempts the latter from remitting compensation by taking the oath that biblical law allows (Exodus 22:10). Nevertheless, the redactors equate a custodian with other tortfeasors and conclude that a paid custodian should not be able to free himself from liability with an oath.

41 Rabbah] MS Hamburg, *Hiddushei Ha-Ritva ad loc.* s.v. *ve-ha*, making the attribution to Rava in this case suspect due to the superiority of this manuscript. I have nevertheless included it in my discussion of Rava's rulings because all other MSS and printed editions attribute this to Rava and it contradicts Rabbah's rulings cited on B. Bava Qama 26b. This is also Rava's opinion in a case which is reported as being brought before him cited further on in this *sugya* where he frees a defendant from liability if he brings witnesses to verify that the damage was unintentional. Nevertheless, if MS Hamburg is correct and Rabbah is the attribution, it would corroborate with his rulings in which he makes inroads into the prior strict approach.

42 B. Bava Metzia 83a.

A custodian is able to escape liability despite the fact that he is considered negligent per R. Meir (per the redactors); by taking an oath that he did not cause damage *be-khavvanah,* "intentionally." A negligent act is inadequate grounds to make one liable; an oath affirming that he did not purposefully cause damage is therefore sufficient to exempt the custodian. While it could be argued that the distinction between intentional and negligent acts is limited to a case of custodianship (though this is clearly not the view of the redactors),[43] this constitutes the first instance where such a distinction is used to determine the level of liability.

3.1.4   B. Bava Qama 62a: Guarding a Golden Dinar

In B. Bava Qama 62a, Rava offers another ruling that hinges on the distinction between damages resulting from negligence rather than intentional actions:

אמ' רבא הנותן דינר זהב לאשה ואמ' לה הזהרי בו של כסף הוא הזיקתהו משלמת של זהב דאמ'[44] לה מאי הוה ליך גביה דאזיקתיה פשעה בו משלמת של כסף דאמרה[45] ליה נטירותא דכספ' קבילי עלי דדהבא לא קבילי עלאי

> Rava[46] said: One who gives a golden *dinar* to a woman[47] and says to her, 'be careful with it, as it is a silver [*dinar*]'. If she damages it, she must pay for a golden [*dinar*] since he can say[48] to her, 'What did you have against it that you damaged it'! If she is negligent with it, she [only] has to pay for a silver [*dinar*], because she can say[49] to him, 'I accepted upon myself the custodianship of a silver [*dinar*]; I did not accept upon myself that of a golden [*dinar*]'.[50]

In this case when damage results from negligence, Rava makes the custodian liable only to the subjective level of knowledge and responsibility she accepted. Conversely, when damage is done intentionally, he deems the custodian responsible for the full value of the coin regardless of her ignorance of the object's true value and the implicit contractual obligation.[51] Since the

---

43 *Supra* n. 40.
44 The switch to Aramaic is very well an indication that this is a redactional elaboration.
45 See previous note.
46 "Rava" appears in every text witness.
47 The unusual specification of a woman in this ruling is explained by R. Joseph b. Habib (fourteenth-century) as a scenario common in betrothals. The law would be the same had the *dinar* been given to a man. *Nimmuqei Yoseph* on *Rif* B. Bava Qama (25b) s.v. *hai*.
48 The passage switches to Aramaic, indicating that this is a later redactional elaboration.
49 See previous note.
50 B. Bava Qama 62a.
51 See also B. Bava Metzia, 96b-97a; B. Bava Qama 40b, 58a.

custodian intentionally damaged the particular coin under her care, ignorance of the *dinar's* value is irrelevant.

Like the preceding case, this too concerns a custodian, yet Rava's distinction between intentional harm and negligence in cases of ignorance of the object damaged is not limited to the particularities of the contractual obligations between a bailor and bailee. The same distinction is made in the *sugya* immediately preceding this one regarding one who lights a fire in another's haystack (an intentionally harmful act) and one who lights a fire in his own field but allows it to spread to another's haystack (a negligent act). In the former case, Rava requires compensation for all of the property destroyed; in the latter, he requires compensation only for objects normally found in haystacks.[52] The distinction between intentional and negligent actions reappears in several other rulings attributed to Rava in B. Bava Qama. For instance, in 58a he imposes a smaller penalty when animals damage property due to a shepherd's seemingly negligent behavior. Rulings attributed to Rava even consider the imputed intentions of animals that damage property.[53]

What emerges from these cases is that Rava bases his rulings on a strict understanding of intentional actions,[54] assigning liability only when one acts with the specific intent to cause the resulting damages. Where one is negligent he is exempt from full compensation, and where he damages another's property in an instance where he has a right to use it, he is completely released from liability, even though he performed the action which led to the damages with complete volition.

3.2 *Religious Law: Intention in the Laws of the Sabbath*

Rulings attributed to Rava throughout the Bavli also consider intention to be a key factor in culpability for religious violations. As we discussed in the previous chapter, R. Nahman, citing his teacher Samuel, rules that *mitasseq* (the inadvertent performance of a prohibited action due to being involved in, and therefore distracted by, another task) exempts one from violations of the Sabbath.[55] Rava seemingly accepts R. Nahman's notion of *mitasseq*, but gives explicit expression to the role of intention as a mitigating factor. In explaining the exemption for one who intends to perform a permitted act on the Sabbath but instead commits

---

52 The conceptual link between the *sugyot* was noted by R. Jacob Joshua Falk in his commentary, *Pnei Yehoshua* Bava Qama 61b s.v. *be-pheirush Rashi R. Judah*. I have omitted this *sugya* due to its complexity. Those interested may see Strauch Schick, "Intention," 134.
53 B. Bava Qama 40b.
54 See Masek, "Intentions."
55 B. Keritut 19b; B. Sanhedrin 62b. See Chapter 2, 3.2.

THE FOURTH GENERATION OF BABYLONIAN AMORAIM 87

a violation,[56] Rava[57] cites a tradition which exempts a case of שגג בלא מתכוין, "[one who performs an act] inadvertently without intention," on the Sabbath. Although this tradition draws on tannaitic texts, T. Shabbat 10:19 and a *baraita* in Y. Shabbat 13b, the specific terminology which explicitly relates to intention, *shagag be-lo mitkavvein*, is unique to this tradition cited by Rava.[58] Shaul Kalcheim therefore argues that this is the original formulation of the principle *davar she'ein mitkavvein*,[59] which Rava along with Abaye subsequently employ in a range of cases.[60] As we saw above, in B. Shabbat 46b–47a Rava even extends it to areas unrelated to the laws of the Sabbath, such as *kilaim*.

Rava also factors intentionality in his understanding of M. Shabbat 10:4, where he links it to accomplishing a desired result. This mishnah states:

המתכוין להוציא לפניו ובא לו לאחריו פטור לאחריו ובא לו לפניו חייב

> One who intends to take [an object] out in front of himself, [but instead] it came behind him, is exempt (from having violated the Sabbath). [If he intends to take out an object] behind him [but instead] it came in front of him, he is liable.

The Bavli records the following discussion:

מאי שנא לפניו ובא לו לאחריו דפטור דלא איתעביד מחשבתו לאחריו ובא לו לפניו נמי הא לא אתעביד מחשבתו
אמר ר' אלעזר תברה מי ששנה זו לא שנה זו
אמר רבא ומאי קושיא דילמא לפניו ובא לו לאחריו היינו טעמא דפטור דנתכוון לשמירה מעולה ועלתה בידו שמירה פחותה לאחריו ובא לו לפניו היינו טעמא דחייב דנתכוון לשמירה פחותה ועלתה בידו שמירה מעולה

> What is the difference if it is in front of him and it came behind him that one is exempt, for he did not carry out his thought (his intention); if it is behind him and it comes in front of him he also did not carry out his thought?

---

56 B. Shabbat 72b. For a discussion of this passage, see section 4.3 below.
57 Halivni argues that it was not stated by Rava, but belongs to the redactional strata transported from B. Sanhedrin 62. Halivni, *Meqorot U-Mesorot: Shabbath*, 209.
58 Stephen Wald demonstrates that the entire tradition, though presented as a *baraita*, is a composite of re-formulated amoraic statements and tannaitic traditions. Wald, *Shabbat, Chapter VII*, 142.
59 Kalcheim, "Davar Sh'ain Mitkaven," 109–10.
60 Rava: B. Shabbat 81b, B. Ketubot 6b; Abaye: B. Shabbat 41b, 103a, B. Yoma 34b; Rava and Abaye: B. Shabbat 133a.

> R. El'azar said: There is a contradiction! Whoever taught this (the first ruling of the mishnah), did not teach this (the second rulings).
>
> Rava[61] said: And what is the question? Perhaps [where he intends to carry] it before him and it comes behind him, the reason he is exempt is because he intended a superior guarding and a diminished guarding came to his hand. [On the other hand, if he intends to carry] behind him and it comes before him, the reason he is liable is because he intended a diminished guarding and a superior guarding came to his hand.[62]

The redactors note that the exemption in the first clause of the mishnah is understandable because the actor has not fulfilled his intention. However, since the same could be said of the second case, why is the actor held accountable for violating the Sabbath? R. El'azar, a third-generation Amora,[63] explains that the two rulings of the mishnah indeed represent opposing positions and are the product of different Tannaim. The parallel Yerushalmi *sugya* (Y. Shabbat 12b) contains a more detailed version of R. El'azar's opinion, explaining that the two clauses reflect rulings by different Tannaim in M. Keritut 4:3, and is therefore a straightforward understanding of M. Shabbat 10:4.[64] Rava, by contrast, devises a logic by which the two clauses do not contradict; they describe different circumstances which reflect whether the intentions of the agent were accomplished. In the first case, the actor intends to carry his item in front to better guard it.

---

61   רב אשי] MS Oxford Opp. Add Fol. 23 (366), though this is likely a scribal error since R. Ashi issues the comment immediately following this one. All other text witnesses contain "Rava."
62   B. Shabbat 92b.
63   In all likelihood, this is referring to R. El'azar b. Pedat. Initially from Babylonia, he later immigrated to the Land of Israel.
64   M. Keritut 4:3 (MS Parma, Biblioteca Palatina, 3137) states: "R. Ishmael Hashezuri and R. Simeon say: [R. Eliezer and R. Joshua in M. Keritut 4:2] do not disagree over transgressions of the same category that he is liable. Concerning what do they disagree? Concerning something of two categories, R. Eliezer holds [one] liable to a sin offering, and R. Joshua exempts [him]. R. Judah said: Even if one intended to pick figs and [instead] picked grapes, [or intended to pick] grapes and picked figs, [or to pick] black and [instead] picked white … R. Eliezer holds [one] liable to a sin offering, and R. Joshua exempts." In the Yerushalmi's discussion in Y. Shabbat 12b, R. El'azar states that the two clauses of M. Shabbat 10:4 reflect the two opinions of M. Keritut 4:3: The second case of M. Shabbat 10:4, deeming one who intends to carry behind him and instead carries in front liable, reflects the position of R. Ishmael Hashezuri and R. Simeon. Even where one does the opposite of what they intended, they violate the prohibition against carrying. By contrast, the case which exempts the actor where the item ends up being carried from behind, follows R. Judah's understanding of R. Joshua, who applies the latter's exemption in all cases where one intends one action and does another, even where they involve the same violation. See Halivni, *Meqorot U-Mesorot: Shabbath*, 260–61."

When it ends up in the back, the item is less guarded, and the actor's intention is not fulfilled; he therefore has not violated the Sabbath. However, in the second case, despite the original intent to carry the object from behind, because it ends up being carried in front the item is being better protected, such that the result fulfills the purpose of the intended action.[65] Rava's solution no doubt results from a desire to maintain the internal harmony of M. Shabbat 10:4 as opposed to attributing it to different authors, an approach commonly taken by Rava in his dealings with conflicting tannaitic texts;[66] nevertheless, it is consistent with his general position which deems intention decisive in determining liability.

4 Rava in Contrast to Abaye in Religious Law

Rava's focus on intention in religious violations is especially apparent where his position is contrasted with that of Abaye.[67] An ongoing and consistent divide between these two sages emerges as to what constitutes intent sufficient to render one guilty: Rava focuses on specific purpose and Abaye requires a more general intent to act.

4.1 B. Sanhedrin 61b: Idol Worship out of Love and Fear

Contrasting rulings attributed to Abaye and Rava are reported regarding a case of one who performs idol worship out of "love and fear," presumably of another person,[68] rather than to accept the idol as a deity:

איתמ' העובד ע"ז מאהבה ומיראה אביי אמ' חייב רבא אמ' פטור אביי א' חייב
דהא פלחה רבא אמ' פטור אי קבליה עליה באלוה אין אי לא לא

> It was said: if one worships idolatry out of love and fear, Abaye said: He is liable; Rava said: He is absolved. Abaye said: 'He is liable'- because he has worshipped it. Rava said: 'He is absolved'- if he accepted it as a deity he is [liable], if not, he is not [liable].[69]

---

65 It is not certain whether the whole explanation was stated by Rava or was a later elaboration by the redactors. Even if this is a redactional interpretation of Rava's opinion, it is still noteworthy that this is how the redactors understood the position of Rava.

66 Henshke, "Abaye and Rava," 187–90.

67 This is not to say that they were actually engaged in a discussion. See Kalmin, *Sages, Stories*, 176–84.

68 Rashi (*ad loc.* s.v. *me-ahavah*). Alternatively, Maimonides suggests it is "love and fear" of the idolatry or its form of worship (*Mishneh Torah: Hilkhot Avoda Zara* 3:6) R. Joseph Karo (*Keseph Mishneh ad loc.*) and R. Aqiva Eiger (*ad loc.* s.v. *heikhi*) argue that fear of a person qualifies as a case of coercion for which Abaye should absolve the offender.

69 B. Sanhedrin 61b.

Rava absolves a person for idol worship out of "love and fear," while Abaye maintains that one is liable. The Bavli's redactors explain each of their respective rulings as follows: Abaye's strict ruling is based on the *act* of idol worship, no matter the motivation for doing so, whereas Rava's exemption is understood to be based on the *motive* for performing an act.[70] Absent a specific intention to worship an idol as a deity, Rava exempts the individual.

4.2   B. Sanhedrin 74a-b: Martyrdom

This distinction also underlies Rava and Abaye's differing explanations as to how the biblical personality Esther could have publicly engaged in a sexual relationship with Ahasuerus, a non-Jew, rather than choose martyrdom, as mandated by tannaitic law.[71] Their contrasting opinions follow R. Yohanan's famous decision obligating martyrdom when confronted with idol worship, illicit sexual relations, or murder. Although R. Ishmael (a second-generation Tanna) maintains that one may worship idolatry to save one's life, the redactors limit this to private violations. In public, however, one is required to choose martyrdom rather than violate even the most minor offense. The redactors then bring up the case of Esther and cite Rava and Abaye to resolve the difficulty:

(A) והא אסתר פרהסיא הואי אמ' אביי אסתר קרקע עולם היתה רבא אמ' הנאת עצמן שאני

(B) דאי לא תימ' הכי הני קוואקי ודימוניקי היכי יהבינן להו אלא הנאת עצמן שאני הכא נמי הנאת עצמן שאני

(C) ואזדא רבא לטעמיה דאמ' רבא גוי דאמ' ליה להאי ישראל קטול אספסתא ושדי לחיותאי ואי לא קטילנא לך ליקטול ולא לקטלוה שדי לנהרא ליקטליה ולא ליקטול מאי טעמ' לעבורי מלת' קא בעי

    (A) But Esther [marrying Ahasuerus] was public? Abaye[72] said: Esther was like the ground of the earth.[73] Rava said: [When they demand it for] their own benefit/pleasure [it] is different.

---

70 Relatedly, Rava states that the Jews of Shushan were justifiably angry at Mordechai for not bowing to Haman, thereby instigating his anger against them (B. Megillah 12b–13a). See Elman, "Rava as Mara De-Atra of Mahoza," 65–66.

71 B. Sanhedrin 74a-b. See T. Shabbat 15:17.

72 While ed. Barko cites R. Yohanan as the author of this ruling, most MSS as well as the Vilna edition attribute it to Abaye (this page is missing from MS Florence II I 7–9). Since the majority of textual witnesses attribute this position to Abaye and moreover, Rava and Abaye's conflicting rulings appear together throughout the Bavli, it seems likely that Abaye is the correct attribution. Perhaps R. Yohanan was mistakenly inserted since his name appears throughout the passage in question.

     Nevertheless, attributing this ruling to R. Yohanan is consistent with the ruling of R. Yohanan that appears in B. Bava Qama 27b (see Chapter 1): Both are cases of coercion in which the wrongdoer is absolved.

73 I.e. she did not engage in any action, rather she was like a passive object upon which an action was performed (Rashi ibid. s.v. *qarqa*).

(B) For if you do not say so, how can we give them (i.e. the magian priests) these braziers[74] and bellows?[75] Rather [since their intention is for] their own benefit, [it] is different. Here also [in Esther's case, since it was for] their own benefit, [the law] is different.

(C) And Rava follows his reasoning, for Rava said: a non-Jew who says to a Jew [on the Sabbath] 'cut this alfalfa and throw it to an animal, and if not, I will kill you', let him cut it and not be slain. [But if the non-Jew tells him on the Sabbath, 'cut the alfalfa and] throw it into the river', let [the Jew allow himself to] be killed and not cut. What is the reason? He wanted to make him violate a prohibition.

To explain why Esther could have publicly engaged in a sexual relationship with a non-Jewish king and not choose the path of martyrdom,[76] (A) Abaye states that Esther was *qarqa olam,* a passive participant in the act as opposed to an active subject. Rava's rationale is that since Ahasuerus's intent was sexual gratification, not having Esther violate her religion, she was permitted to comply. For Rava, the obligation of martyrdom over publicly violating a prohibition depends on the intention of the coercer. A support for Rava's ruling is brought, either by Rava himself or by the redactors, based on the "braziers and bellows" given by Jews to the Zoroastrian temples under coercion of the Persian authorities (B).[77] In donating these objects, Babylonian Jews publicly contributed to an idolatrous practice, which would ostensibly fall under the obligation of martyrdom as ruled by R. Ishmael. However, since the intention of the *magi* in soliciting them was not aimed at having Jews violate their religion, rather to make use of these vessels for their own purposes, there was no prohibition in complying.[78] The actual practice of his day thus correlates with Rava's position.

---

74 Sokoloff, *Babylonian Aramaic,* 990a, s.v. kevv'akei.
   kevv'akei ve- deimonikei likewise appear in the Vilna edition. However, these terms appear in a variety of spellings in the MSS: קווקי ודמונקי :MS Munich 95; קאווקי ודמוניאקי: MS Herzog; קורקי ודמונ(י)קי :MS Karlsreuhe Reuchlin 2. קוקני :MS of the Rif cited by Rabbinovicz, 210, (דקדוקי סופרים י' (מינכן, תרכ"ח-תרפ"ו).

75 Sokoloff, 343a, s.v. deminka. Rashi (*ad loc.* s.v. *hani*) explains these terms as tall brass vessels in which coals were placed in order to be used as heaters.

76 According to the Tosafists (*ad loc. ve-ha*), she was already married to Mordechai and hence guilty of adultery, which warrants martyrdom.

77 דימוניקי is a Middle Persian loanword, *damēnag* Mackenzie, *A Concise Pahlavi Dictionary,* 24, s.v. damēnag [dmynk] fan; Mackenzie, 343; Rosenthal, 341.

78 Rashi explains the braziers and bellows as relating to a service performed during a Zoroastrian holiday for which Jews were among those forced to contribute. Ad loc. s.v. *heikhi yahovinon lehu.* In gaonic responsum this is identified as a holiday which occurs at night called *Sadag,* in which fire was taken to display outside. See *Teshuvot ha-Ge'onim,* ed. A. Y. Harkavy, 144.

The redactors also note that Rava's ruling accords with another ruling of his, in which the intent of the non-Jew defines the permissibility of a prohibited action (C). Rava maintains that if one is compelled by a non-Jew to cut vegetables on the Sabbath, he may do so depending on why the non-Jew orders him to. If it is to feed an animal, it is permitted, since the non-Jew's command is clearly aimed solely at satisfying his own needs. Conversely, if the non-Jew orders him to discard what he picked into a river, it is prohibited, since his motive is evidently to force a violation.[79] Rava sees intent as determinative of the nature of an act. In this case it is not the agent's, but the coercer's intent which defines whether the act falls under the obligation to be killed rather than violate the law. In contrast, Abaye, who focuses on actions, exempts Esther only because he maintains that she was passive, "like the ground of the earth,"[80] rendering her an object that is acted upon rather than an agent.

4.3 B. Shabbat 72b-73a: Davar She-ein Mitkavvein

Further differences between Rava and Abaye's approaches to intentionality emerge regarding what constitutes intentional behavior with regard to violations of the Sabbath. As discussed previously, Rava and Abaye are the first to employ the principle of *davar she-ein mitkavvein*, and hence give explicit expression to the role of intention in the laws of Sabbath. In B. Shabbat 72b-73a they argue about what constitutes an intentional violation of the Sabbath:

Rosenthal counters that this alleged Persian holiday was based on later sources dating from the Muslim period, and that there is no evidence of it in texts from the Sasanian period. The bellows and braziers were rather taken by zealous Zoroastrians who wanted to rescue fires that had been contaminated by non-Zoroastrians by bringing them to a *dādihā gāh*, religious place. The fire was not used for worship, but to lend an air of festivity. Rosenthal, 39–42.

79 In B. Avoda Zara 54a, Rava issues a similar ruling regarding idolatrous acts performed under coercion. As in B. Sanhedrin, Leviticus 18:5 is explicated to mean that one who is forced to commit idolatry under threat of death may do so. Although Rava's statement seemingly continues with an exposition of Leviticus 22:32, "and you shall not desecrate my holy name," that one is prohibited from committing idolatry even under threat of death, this may be a redactional addition (which its opening Aramaic *hadar katav* may indicate) in order to introduce the distinction between public versus private offenses, as in B. Sanhedrin 74a-b. Alternatively, if both expositions are part of Rava's statement, it could refer to an instance where the non-Jew forces the Jew in order to have him violate his religion and thus consistent with B. Sanhedrin. (See Tosafot *ad loc.* s.v. *matqif; ha*).

80 The term *qarqa olam* is used in a similar manner in tort law to indicate a passive contributing factor (such as impact with the ground) which absolves the tortfeasor. Thus in B. Bava Qama 30a, Rav exempts a tortfeasor from compensating one who is injured due to water that the tortfeasor has spilled because *qarqa olam hezeqeito*, the ground of the earth has harmed him.

THE FOURTH GENERATION OF BABYLONIAN AMORAIM

> אתמר נתכוון להגביה את התלוש וחתך את המחובר פטור לחתוך את התלוש
> וחתך את המחובר רבא אמר פטור אביי אמר חייב רבא אמר פטור הא לא
> נתכוון לחתיכה דאיסורא אביי אמר חייב דהא קמיכוין לחתיכה בעלמא

> It was said: if one intends to pick up [that which is] detached [from the ground on the Sabbath], and [instead] cuts that which is attached he is exempt. [If he intends] to cut that which is detached and cuts that which is attached: Rava[81] said: he is exempt. Abaye said: he is liable. Rava said 'he is exempt'- because he did not intend a prohibited cutting. Abaye said 'he is liable'- because he intended a cutting generally.[82]

Where one intends to cut that which is detached from the ground, an act which on its own is permitted on the Sabbath, but it turns out to still be attached, Abaye deems the actor liable because he intended to perform a cutting action which ultimately violated the Sabbath. Again, in Abaye's jurisprudence, so long as one performs an intended action, the requirement of intentional behavior has been met. Rava, in contrast, requires specific intention to perform a prohibited action that violates the Sabbath. Consequently, if one merely intends to cut an object which he believes to be detached from the ground, there is no liability.

Later in this *sugya*, two more cases are cited which further demonstrate their differing approaches:

> איתמר נתכוון לזרוק שתים וזרק ארבע רבא אמר פטור אביי אמר חייב
> רבא אמר פטור דלא קמיכוין לזריקה דארבע אביי אמר חייב דהא קמיכוון
> לזריקה בעלמא
>
> כסבור רשות היחיד ונמצאת רשות הרבים רבא אמר פטור ואביי אמר חייב
> רבא אמר פטור דהא דלא מיכויין לזריקה דאיסורא ואביי אמר חייב דהא קא
> מיכוין לזריקה בעלמא

> It was said: Where one intended to throw [a distance of] two [cubits], [but instead] threw it [a distance of] four [on the Sabbath]; Rava[83]

---

81 Although Rava's position appears before Abaye's, which is usually not the case (following the general rule cited by R. Joseph Ibn Aknin, and established by the medieval Tosafist, R. Isaiah b. Mali d'Trani in his *Tosafot RI"D*, that Rabbah is generally cited before his student Abaye, and Abaye before Rava, his contemporary, see Friedman, "Writing of the Names."), Rava appears in every text witness.

82 B. Shabbat 72b. The discussion that follows ('Rava said: From where do I say this? For it was taught …') was discussed above in section 3.2.

83 Following MSS Vatican 108, Munich 95 and the printed editions. MS Oxford Opp. Add Fol. 23 (366) attributes these two cases to Rabbah.

said: he is exempt. Abaye said: he is liable. Rava[84] said, 'he is exempt'- since he did not intend a four [cubit] throw;[85] Abaye said, 'he is liable'- since he intended to throw generally.

[In a case where] someone thought [he was throwing in] a private domain and it was found to be a public domain; Rava[86] said: he is exempt and Abaye said: he is liable. Rava[87] said, 'he is exempt'- since he did not intend a prohibited throw; and Abaye said, 'he is liable'- since he intended to throw generally.[88]

Here too, Rava requires precise intention and maintains that one is guilty only if he intends to throw in such a way as to violate the Sabbath. Conversely, Abaye rules that where there is intention to act, one is liable for violating the Sabbath despite the lack of intention to do so in a prohibited way.[89]

4.4   B. Menahot 64a: Action versus Intention

The different parameters for what constitute intentional behavior that emerge from these rulings of Abaye and Rava concerning the Sabbath are consistent with those of their respective teachers, Rabbah and R. Nahman. As described in the previous chapter, where intentional behavior is required, Rabbah of Pumbedita limits such intention to intent to act, while R. Nahman of Mahoza introduces a concern for one's purpose in acting and assigns liability only

---

It is unclear which attribution is correct. As discussed in the previous chapter, these two rulings appear in B. Bava Qama 26b-27a among a list of cases attributed to Rabbah (which I labeled cases (C, D), and while there it would appear that these are rulings of Rabbah, as already noted above (see Chapter 2 and text by note 16), this seems unlikely since they contradict Rabbah's other rulings and are the only traditions there to appear without attribution. An (incorrect) attribution to Rabbah in B. Bava Qama might have led the scribe of MS Oxford to attribute these two cases in B. Shabbat to Rabbah. Although, as in the previous case, the fact that Abaye is cited second might indicate that 'Rabbah' is the correct attribution (*Supra* note 81); nevertheless as noted, all extant MSS attest to an attribution of Rava making the order not determinative.

84   See previous note.
85   If one tosses an object to a distance of less than four cubits, it does not constitute a sufficient throw to make one guilty for violating the Sabbath. Rashi *ad loc.* s.v. *de-lo*.
86   See note 83.
87   See note 83.
88   B. Shabbat 73a.
89   Michael Higger understood the debate between Rava and Abaye to be regarding what constitutes intention to sin, but both agreed that there must be intention to sin in order to be held liable (Higger, "Intention in Talmudic Law," 55.) However, Higger based this on the redactorial understanding of Rava and Abaye's rulings in B. Hagigah 19b.

THE FOURTH GENERATION OF BABYLONIAN AMORAIM   95

when one intends to commit a wrong. This bifurcation between Mahoza and Pumbedita regarding whether to emphasize intention or action comes to the fore in a set of contrasting rulings attributed to Rava and Rabbah. In the first scenario, one needlessly slaughters two animals for the same sin offering on the Sabbath, but later discovers that the first animal was unfit to be offered.[90] Though it was initially prohibited to slaughter the second animal, this *sugya* probes whether there is a violation of the Sabbath if it was ultimately warranted. To clarify the issue, the *sugya* then turns to a case which in modern terms would be characterized as one of 'double effect'.[91]

(A) אמר ליה רבינא לרב אשי נמצאת הראשונה כחושה בבני מעיין מהו בתר מחשבתו אזלינן וגברא לאיסורא קא מיכוון או דילמא בתר מעשיו אזלינן

(B) א"ל לאו היינו דרבא ורבה דאיתמר שמע שטבע תינוק בים ופרש מצודה לעלות דגים והעלה דגים לעלות דגים והעלה דגים ותינוק רבא אמר חייב ורבה אמר פטור

(C) ועד כאן רבה לא קא פטר אלא כיון דשמע אמרינן נמי דעתיה אתינוק אבל לא שמע לא

(D) ואיכא דאמרי אמר ליה היינו פלוגתא דרבה ורבא דאיתמר לא שמע שטבע תינוק בים ופרש מצודה להעלות דגים והעלה דגים חייב להעלות דגים והעלה תינוק ודגים רבה אמר פטור ורבא אמר חייב רבה אמר פטור זיל בתר מעשיו ורבא אמר חייב זיל בתר מחשבתו

   (A) Ravina said to R. Ashi: If it is found that the first [animal that was slaughtered] was internally lean (and therefore unfit to be brought as a sacrifice), what is [the law]? Do we go according to his thought and the man intended [to violate] a prohibition, or perhaps we go according to his action (since the second slaughter turned out to be necessary, is he exempt from violating the Sabbath)?

   (B) [R. Ashi] said to [Ravina]: Is this not [the rulings] of Rava and Rabbah? As it was said: If one heard that a child was drowning in the sea and he spread out a net to bring up fish, and he brought up [only] fish, he is liable [for violating the Sabbath]. [If he intended]

---

90   Earlier in this *sugya*, Rabbah rules that if the first animal was emaciated and the second animal was fat and thus preferable to be brought as a sin offering, one does not violate the Sabbath upon slaughtering the second animal; rather, the second animal should be slaughtered.

91   For a discussion on the doctrine of double effect, see Quinn, "Actions, Intentions, and Consequences."

to bring up fish, and he brought up fish and the child,[92] Rava said: He is liable. Rabbah said: He is exempt.

(C) And until now, Rabbah only exempted him because he heard [that a child was drowning], we [therefore] say that his mind was also on the child, but if he had not heard [that a child was drowning], he is not [exempt].

(D) And there are those who say [that R. Ashi's response was as follows: R. Ashi] said to [Ravina]: this is the dispute between Rabbah and Rava. As it was said: If he had not heard that a child was drowning in the sea and he spread out his net to bring up fish and he brought up fish, he is liable; [if he spread out his net] to bring up fish and he brought up the child and fish, Rabbah said: he is exempt and Rava said: he is liable. Rabbah said 'he is exempt'—[we] go according to his deeds. And Rava said 'he is liable'—[we] go according to his thought (i.e. his intent).[93]

In response to Ravina's query (A), R. Ashi[94] reports a dispute between Rabbah and Rava regarding a case where a net which had been aimed at catching fish—an action which is forbidden on the Sabbath—saves a drowning child. Rava held that the fisher is guilty of violating the Sabbath, while Rabbah maintained that he is absolved. Two traditions of R. Ashi's understanding of their debate follow (B, C, and D), both of which understand Rabbah as focusing on the consequences of the action, and Rava on the agent's intention.

R. Ashi is first reported as explaining the case as one in which the fisher hears about a drowning child and is absolved by Rabbah because he is assumed to have intended to save it as well as go fishing (C). According to this tradition, R. Ashi posits no fundamental debate between Rava and Rabbah regarding whether action or intention is preferred, since both agreed that the individual's

---

92   Y. Shabbat 14b records a similar case which states:

ר' יוסי בי ר' בון בשם רב חונא ראה תינוק מבעבע בנהר ונתכוון להעלותו ולהעלות נחיל של דגים עמו מותר

R. Yose son of R. Bun (said) in the name of R. Huna: If one sees a child gurgling in the river, and he intends to bring (the child) up and to bring up a basket of fish with it, it is permitted.

This statement appears along with two other rulings which pertain to instances where one engages in one activity which brings about another result. However, in the Yerushalmi's case, there is no violation because the actor intends to do a permitted action.

93   B. Menahot 64a.
94   Sixth-generation Babylonian Amora, second half of the fourth century to fifth century.

intention determines guilt. Their debate is rather understood as whether one's intention may be redefined by their later action.

While this may seem counter to Rabbah's view, it need not reflect Rabbah's actual ruling, but rather as it was interpreted by R. Ashi, a student of Rava. As we have already seen in B. Bava Qama 27b, it is not unusual for Rava's student to interpret a dissenting approach—particularly that of Rabbah—to accord with a Mahozan position with respect to determining guilt. There, R. Papa similarly interprets a strict ruling reported in the name of Rabbah.[95] Nevertheless, even if this is R. Ashi's understanding of Rabbah, the focus on action remains. In this version, Rabbah's notion of intention is based on the final result of the action. Rabbah only assumes there was a (secondary) intention to rescue the child if later actions appear to testify to it.

The second tradition (D) both better addresses the original case of Ravina's question and gives explicit expression to what we have demonstrated to be the Pumbedita-Mahoza bifurcation. In this version, the person is unaware of the drowning child when fishing: Rabbah absolves the fisher because he considers the action and its consequence when determining liability. Rava, by contrast, deems him culpable because he stresses the agent's motive. Though his actions saved the child, Rava considers the intention of the violator paramount and determinative of guilt, even if the result contradicts a moral intuition that he should be absolved. For Rabbah, the agent's motive is irrelevant as is the total unforseeablility of the good consequence that resulted; the objective outcome of saving the child retroactively justifies a violation of the Sabbath, as it would in a regular case of saving a life.[96]

5 Rava's Emphasis on Intention: Precedents and Parallels

The cases surveyed in this chapter yield a consistent picture of Rava's approach to liability and guilt which regularly contrasts with the views of Pumbeditan sages. In civil law, Rava distinguishes between damages caused through negligence and those resulting from intentional actions, assigning corresponding degrees of liability. Lacking malicious intent, even if one acts negligently, he is absolved from full compensation. In the realm of religious law, he exempts

---

95 See Chapter 1, 3.2.
96 B. Shabbat 102a records another debate between Rava and Rabbah regarding one who throws an object forgetting it is the Sabbath, remembers, and forgets again before the action is completed. Rabbah deems this minimal awareness adequate to be considered a purposeful violation of the Sabbath, while Rava does not.

certain offenses where there is no specific intent to transgress a commandment. However, as we just saw, where one's intentions are malign, even if the outcome is positive, Rava considers the person guilty. Abaye likewise considers an actor's intention, but he sees it as inexorably linked with one's actions. Where one acts with intention, irrespective of the specific purpose, he is liable. As such, though Abaye clearly places more weight on intent than his Pumbeditan teachers, he maintains a lax criterion of what counts as an intentional action, which aligns with his predecessors. Rava, on the other hand, though he mirrors R. Nahman in some respects, forges a unique path in downplaying negligence and making specific intention a pivotal condition across a broad range of rulings.

5.1   Land of Israel Precedents

It is possible that Rava's stance reflects his tendency to position himself with teachings from the Land of Israel.[97] Many have noted that Babylonian Amoraim, from the generation of Rava and on, were highly receptive to the teachings of Palestinian Amoraim,[98] and in some of the cases discussed above, Rava's rulings parallel earlier Palestinian traditions. His decision in the case of the pedestrian who breaks a jug (B. Bava Qama 27b) directly parallels the final interpretation cited in the corresponding Yerushalmi passage (Y. Bava Qama 3b). His ruling that martyrdom is not required in a case of religious coercion when the non-Jew's intention is aimed at satisfying his own desires (B. Sanhedrin 74a) likewise finds precedent in Y. Shebiit 10a-b, which records a similar teaching in the name of the third-century (third-generation) Palestinian Amora R. Abbahu, a generation before Rava. In response to a question concerning R. Yannai's decision to permit plowing during the Sabbatical year, R. Abbahu explains: "the [non-Jew's] intention is not to force [Jews] to violate [their religion]; rather their intention is to collect taxes."[99] Both Rava and R. Abbahu base the obligation of martyrdom on the intention of the coercer; where they have their own self interests in mind, martyrdom is not warranted. His exemption of one

---

97   As noted above Rava demonstrates a tendency to apply Palestinian interpretations of the Mishnah. Elman, "Rava Ve-Darkei Ha-Iyyun Ha-Eretz Yisraeliyyot Be-Midrash Ha-Halakhah"; Fraade, "Rabbinic Polysemy and Pluralism Revisited: Between Praxis and Thematization"; Zellentin, *Rabbinic Parodies*.

98   Dor, *The Teachings of Eretz Israel in Babylon*; Kalmin, *Jewish Babylonia*, 4, 249 n. 6, and Chapter 3. There he cites an extensive bibliography of the scholarly discussion of the topic, noting the "influx of Palestinian traditions" in Babylonia during the fourth century.

99   In the Yerushalmi, Rava's younger contemporary, R. Yonah, similarly sanctions baking bread for the Roman general Ursicinas on the Sabbath because the latter's intention is aimed at having warm bread and not at having Jews violate the Sabbath.

who intends a permitted action on the Sabbath but ends up committing a violation (B. Shabbat 72b-73a) parallels Palestinian traditions cited in Y. Shabbat 13b.[100] Rava's rulings in these cases may primarily reflect earlier traditions. Nevertheless, the central role that intention consistently plays in Rava's jurisprudence is remarkable.

5.2   Parallels in Zoroastrian Literature

Some of Rava's rulings have parallels in Zoroastrian literature (as do various other statements of Rava on a range of subjects).[101] As far as we can tell, the relevant developments in Zoroastrian law occurred after Rava's time. Nonetheless, it is helpful to note where such parallels exist, as they may point to similar patterns of thought occurring in Sasanian Persia.

Yishai Kiel has highlighted the affinity between the Talmudic and Zoroastrian conceptions of intentionality and unwitting transgressions, particularly in the rulings of Rava.[102] Not only do both the Bavli and Middle Persian literature address the same question of whether ignorance of the punishment reduces the severity of the transgression, they handle it in similar ways. This may help to situate a few of Rava's rulings (e.g. B. Shabbat 72b-73a), but the Pahlavi texts that Kiel examines likely post-date Rava.[103] David Brodsky describes parallels between the Zoroastrian ideology of sinful thoughts and the views of Babylonian sages, notably Rava and R. Nahman.[104] As was mentioned in Chapter 1, the similar move in Zoroastrian civil law from strict liability based on outcome to one that factors intent and negligence also helps to contextualize the Bavli's development.

Although the precedents in the Yerushalmi and parallels in Zoroastrian law help to situate Rava's unique approach to intention, in the final part of this chapter I propose that a more comprehensive doctrine, one with close analogues in Aristotle's philosophy of corrective justice, may form the conceptual underpinning of Rava's body of jurisprudence.

---

100 Wald, *Shabbat, Chapter VII*, 143–44.
101 For example, Rava attributed long life, children, and wealth as consequences of astrological fate rather than religious merit (B. Mo'ed Qatan 28a), which Elman notes has direct parallels in Middle Persian teachings. Elman, "Acculturation to Elite Persian Norms in the Babylonian Jewish Community of Late Antiquity," 43–51. Rubenstein however argues that this was not anomalous among the general rabbinic view. Rubenstein, "Talmudic Astrology: Bavli Šabbat 156a-b," 143.
102 Kiel, "Cognizance of Sin and Penalty in the Babylonian Talmud and Pahlavi Literature: A Comparative Analysis," n. 59.
103 For the dating of the Sasanian jurists and texts see Chapter 1, section 5.
104 Brodsky, "Thought is Akin to Action."

6 Rava's Jurisprudence and Aristotelian Corrective Justice

Aristotle's *Nicomachean Ethics* has had a profound and lasting influence on Western philosophy and jurisprudence, serving as a foundational text for tort law. The text is primarily a treatise on the attainment of human goodness or happiness through living a life in which human potential is realized. This flourishing is accomplished through the perfection of character and virtuous living, by exercising the human capacity for reason, guiding oneself by reason, and engaging in activities that actualize the virtues of the rational soul. Among these virtues is justice, the idea that each person receives their proper due; this includes corrective justice, which aims to rectify unfairly imposed losses.[105] Aristotle linked legal liability to moral blame, which is determined by whether one acts intentionally and maliciously. One who acts with the intent to do harm displays an unvirtuous character and is therefore responsible for compensating their victim.

6.1 *Aristotle on Corrective Justice*

Book five of the *Ethics* centers on acts of justice and injustice. A loss or injury wrongfully imposed on another creates an injustice which can only be rectified by the perpetrator compensating the victim, thus restoring equality between the two parties.[106] Liability is fixed to moral responsibility, determined by whether the actor engages in a voluntary and intentionally harmful action.

> One does injustice or does justice whenever one does them willingly. Whenever one does them unwillingly, one does neither justice nor injustice, except coincidentally, since the actions he does coincidentally are coincidentally just or unjust.
>
> An act of injustice and a just act are defined by the voluntary and the involuntary. For when the action is voluntary, the agent is blamed, and thereby also it is an act of injustice. And so something will be unjust without thereby being an act of injustice, if it is not also voluntary.[107]

---

105 Medieval and early modern scholars term it 'commutative justice', while modern tort theorists refer to it as 'corrective justice'. Gordley, "Tort Law in the Aristotelian Tradition," 132, n. 4.

106 The beginning of book five explains how justice is served through monetary restitution and exchange. "For [not only when one steals from another but] also when one is wounded and the other wounds him, or one kills and the other is killed, the action and the suffering are unequally divided [with profit for the offender and loss for the victim]; and the judge tries to restore the [profit and] loss to a position of equality … " Aristotle, *Nichomachean Ethics*, Translated by Terence Irwin (Second Ed.), 72 at 1132a. All quotes are taken from this edition.

107 Aristotle, 79 at 1135a.

Where one acts without intent to cause injury, even though harm results, the agent is not considered to have committed an injustice and is accordingly exempt from liability.[108] In Aristotelian ethics, it is not the outcome which determines responsibility, but the character of the person and the nature of the decisions which guide one to act.

Legal responsibility is also based on whether the agent acts voluntarily, with knowledge of the victim, instrument and means by which he will injure him,[109] and without the influence of external forces or circumstances.[110] Actions committed in ignorance or by accident are considered involuntary acts which do not generate moral or legal guilt.[111]

Further on, Aristotle makes a distinction between different types of injury:[112]

(A) Actions done with ignorance are errors if someone does neither the action he supposed ... but coincidentally the result that was achieved was not what he thought (for instance [he hit him] to graze, not to wound) ... If, then, the infliction of harm violates reasonable expectation, the action is a misfortune. If it does not violate reasonable expectation, but is done without vice, it is an error. For someone is in error if the principle of the cause is in him, and unfortunate when it is outside.[113]

(B) If he does it in knowledge, but without previous deliberation, it is an act of injustice; this is true, for instance, of actions caused by spirit and other feelings that are natural or necessary for human beings ...; but he is not thereby unjust or wicked, since it is not vice that causes him to inflict the harm.

(C) But when his decision is the cause, he is unjust and vicious.

Section (A) describes instances in which damages arise from ignorance of the particulars of a case. Where the harm occurs unexpectedly and is due to

---

108 Aristotle, 79 at 1135a.
109 Aristotle, 79 at 1136a.
110 Aristotle, 79 at 1135a.
111 Aristotle, 79–80 at 1135a.
112 Aristotle, 80 at 1135b. Labeling is my own.
113 Many maintain that "misfortune" and "error" are the first two types of injuries and those committed in passion fall under the third category. Daube, however, argues that it is far more likely that "error" and "misfortune" are two subcategories of the first type, followed by wrongs committed in passion, making premeditated wrong the third type—as we have divided it up. Daube, *Roman Law*, 142. Irwin likewise explains: "Misfortunes and errors are two subclasses of the class of errors introduced in b12." Aristotle, *Nichomachean Ethics*, 338 s.v. 1135b 17–18.

circumstances external to the actor, the harmful outcome is characterized as a misfortune. An error is described as a case where the injury is expected and results from an intentional act, yet there is no blame on the part of the actor since his act is based on incorrect information or misperception.[114] This would include a case in which one mistakes his fellow soldier for an enemy. In instances of both misfortunes and errors the offender is exempt from legal responsibility.[115]

Section (B) discusses an individual whom Aristotle elsewhere terms 'incontinent', whose actions result from physical desire and 'passions'; he too is not considered as blameworthy as one who engages in premeditated and intentional harm. Cases of incontinence are distinguished from the first class of injury since they are done willfully and voluntarily by the actor. Book seven of the *Ethics* provides a fuller description of incontinence and differentiates between one who acts impetuously on the one hand and in weakness on the other; the latter being cases where one makes a wrong decision under the influence of a passion after much deliberation. The appetite for pleasure and the emotion of anger are discussed in detail, with the former considered to be the most powerful urge which leads one to act against reason. It is also the more blameworthy since it involves a greater degree of premeditation and plotting than an act performed in anger—especially in the presence of provocation.

The underlying rationale is that passions create a temporary blindness and cognitive incapacity preventing one from making proper decisions. When passion temporarily overcomes one's rational capacities, the resulting actions are comparable to acts committed while drunk or asleep—states in which one has a diminished level of cognitive awareness and intellectual capacity. Although the incontinent person is required to compensate the victim for an act of injustice, since the injury is characterized as having been done willingly and intentionally, nevertheless he is not considered unjust or as possessing a wicked character. One is considered wicked only when the harm is the result of prior deliberation as mentioned in (C). A conscious decision to cause harm reflects directly on the character of the actor, thereby revealing his lack of virtue. In such an instance

---

114 Daube, *Roman Law*, 132, 144. While many have identified a case of error as describing one of negligence in the sense of unreasonable foreseeable risk, Daube demonstrates that Aristotle is not referring to negligence; he rather emphasizes ignorance and lack of information. Daube points out that the *Ethics* makes no mention of negligence nor does it examine the possibility that the wrongdoer could have been more careful, one of the basic criterions of negligence.

115 This is later made clear in 1136a, 80, where it states that all involuntary acts are to be pardoned, which include those performed in and caused by ignorance. Involuntary acts are not pardoned, however, when they violate normal human behavior, such as bestiality.

he is both deemed unjust and must pay compensation. Book five concludes that it is worse to commit an injustice than to suffer one, because "it is blameworthy, involving vice that is either complete and unconditional or close to it."[116] In other words, doing injustice affects the very character of the person, making him morally corrupt—a worse evil than suffering at the hands of others.

6.2   Parallels with Rava

Rava's rulings concerning torts strongly parallel the Aristotelian system of corrective justice. As we have seen, Rava only imposes full liability when one engages in an action intending to cause injury; damages caused through negligence warrant lesser compensation.[117] Rava's focus on, and understanding of, intentional action mirrors Aristotle's conception of liability as requiring the intention to commit an injurious act, which flows from the latter's more general theory of moral responsibility and voluntary actions. These parallels suggest that Rava's rulings may emanate from a similar conception of justice in which intention is strongly determinative of liability.

Although some have understood the *Ethics* to require compensation for negligent acts as it does for intentional ones,[118] the plain meaning of the text argues rather strongly against such an understanding.[119] Indeed, the general consensus among scholars going back to Thomas Aquinas is that Aristotelian justice exempts one who causes injury through negligence from having to provide compensation.[120] David Daube understands Aristotle to view only intentionally inflicted harm as generating legal responsibility because "when his decision is the cause, he is unjust and vicious."[121] Choosing to harm another

---

116   Aristotle, *Nichomachean Ethics*, 85 at 1138b.
117   See B. Bava Qama 58a, 61b, 40b; B. Bava Metzia 96b-97a.
118   See Wright, "Substantive Corrective Justice," 705–6. Wright believes that Aristotle distinguishes between intent, negligence and strict liability in determining grounds for compensation.
119   Gordley, "Tort Law in the Aristotelian Tradition," 140.
120   It is only beginning with the jurists that Roman law imposes liability for harm caused negligently as well as intentionally (see discussion in Chapter 1). Daube, *Roman Law*, 146–47; Cohen, *Jewish and Roman Law: A Comparative Study*, 2:578–609. This was also the view of Thomas Aquinas, who tried to explain liability for negligence according to Aristotelian principles; though he admitted that Aristotle made no such claim. Aquinas, Gillet, and Pirotta, *In decem libros Ethicorum Aristotelis ad Nicomachum expositio*, xiii, n. 1043.1; Gordley, "Tort Law in the Aristotelian Tradition," 140.
121   Aristotle, *Nichomachean Ethics*, 79 at 1135b; Daube, *Roman Law*, 142.

is a paradigmatically immoral act, rendering the perpetrator morally corrupt and legally responsible to compensate their victim in order to correct the injustice.[122]

Although Aristotle states that one who is careless is subject to corrective justice, which seems to be synonymous with liability for negligence,[123] it appears that Aristotle only deems a person who is *habitually* careless as blameworthy for an inattentive act. Here the agent's responsibility stems from allowing oneself to develop a character trait which led to the carelessness; in this he is regarded as having acted willingly.

Rava's rulings concerning religious violations also parallel concepts developed in Aristotle's ethics. As we saw, Rava requires that one act with the intention of violating a specific norm to be considered culpable, and exempts one whose intended action, such as cutting something already detached from the ground, is permitted.[124] This aligns with Aristotle's description of error:

> Someone does neither the action he supposed, nor to the person, nor to the instrument, nor for the result he supposed. For he thought, for instance, that he was not hitting, or not hitting this person, or not for this reason; but coincidently the result that was achieved was not what he thought, (for instance, [he hit him] to graze not to wound) ...[125]

Even if an action is done with volition, if the result of the action is not what was intended, Aristotle deems the injurious act involuntary and hence pardonable. Rava likewise considers one to have violated the Sabbath only if one intends to do an act that one knows is forbidden.[126]

In a remarkable similarity, in several instances Rava exempts one who violates a prohibition resulting from emotional states or appetitive drives and thus differentiates between actions stemming from deliberate decisions and those stemming from passions. Hence, one who worships idolatry out of "love and fear," i.e. based on an emotion not mediated by a decision to accept the idol as one's deity, is not considered an idolater.[127] Similarly, Aristotle claims that:

---

122 Finnis, "Intention in Tort Law."
123 Aristotle, 38 at 1113b.
124 B. Shabbat 72b-73a.
125 Aristotle, *Nichomachean Ethics*, 80 at 1135b. Labeled as (A) above.
126 It is unclear what Rava rules in a case where one intends to kill one person but kills another instead. This is discussed in Chapter 5, n. 18.
127 B. Sanhedrin 61b.

Perhaps it is not the type of action that makes the difference [between merely doing injustice and being unjust]. For someone might lie with a woman and know who she is, but the principle might be feelings rather than decision. In that case he is not unjust, though he does injustice—not a thief, for instance, though he stole, not an adulterer though he committed adultery, and so on in the other cases.[128]

For both, transgressions resulting from passions are considerably less serious than those resulting from deliberation. Similarly, when Rava exempts one from choosing martyrdom where the coercer's motive was to satisfy their own appetites, he effectively places such drives in a different category than those motivated by a decision to cause a Jew to violate religious precepts.[129]

Another ruling of Rava also highlights his distinction between acts done deliberately and those stemming from passions. Although biblical law clearly exempts a woman who is raped from punishment, one rabbinic view nonetheless forbids her from her husband on the possible grounds that she had consented at some point during intercourse.[130] Rava, however, considers her blameless:

אמר אבוה דשמואל אשת ישראל שנאנסה אסורה לבעלה חיישינן שמא תחלתה באונס וסופה ברצון
... ופליגא דרבא דאמר רבא כל שתחלתה באונס וסוף ברצון אפילו היא אומרת הניחו לו שאלמלא לא נזקק לה היא שוכרתו מותרת מאי [טעמא] יצר אלבשה

The father of Samuel said: the wife of a [non-priest] Jew who is raped is prohibited to [resume living with] her husband; we suspect that perhaps initially it was under coercion, but its end was with consent ... And this

---

128 Aristotle, *Nichomachean Ethics*, 77 at 1134a.
129 B. Sanhedrin 74a-b. Abaye's position in this case may parallel another Aristotelian distinction between mixed voluntary/ involuntary acts, and wholly involuntary forced ones. Obviously all situations of potential martyrdom are those in which an agent is coerced to do an action they do not want to do and would regret having done. On Aristotle's account they are 'mixed' in that the reason for acting is coercion but the action itself is volitional. In some cases a person must not do them but rather "suffer the most terrible consequences and accept death" (*Nicomachean Ethics* 1110a27). However, Esther's passivity renders her act as forced; as Aristotle explains "something is forced without qualification whenever its cause is external and the agent contributes nothing" (1110b2). There was therefore in effect no act done by Esther for which she should have chosen martyrdom.
130 A woman who willfully engages in intercourse with a man other than her husband is divorced and deprived of the monetary rights entitled by her marriage contract. Maimonides, *Mishneh Torah: Ishut* 24:6.

conflicts with Rava,[131] for Rava said: All [cases] where the beginning was under coercion and its end was with consent, even if she says 'leave him' for had [the rapist] not cohabited with her, she would have hired him, she is permitted [to continue living with her husband]. [What is the reason?][132] Desire has possessed/overwhelmed her [lit. clothed her].[133]

The reason for Rava's leniency (even in a case where the woman explicitly claims that she wants the intercourse to continue) is explained, ostensibly by the redactors, as *yetzer albeshah*;[134] which seems to mean that once she is involved in a sexual act, the passions aroused are not under her control.[135] Since she did not voluntarily enter into sexual intercourse, all aspects of the subsequent act are deemed coerced. This neatly compliments another ruling of Rava, that if a man is raped by a woman who is a forbidden relation, culminating in full sexual congress, he is guilty. Rava[136] maintains: אין אונס לערוה לפי שאין קישוי אלא לדעת, "there is no [absolution on grounds of] coercion[137] with regard to illicit relations, because an erection only occurs with awareness/consent."[138] In other words, Rava believes that an erection is never involuntary, so the man's arousal indicates some degree of accession to the sexual act.

131   Rabbah] MS Munich 95. However, all other MSS attribute this ruling to Rava, and it accords with his other rulings.
132   This question is absent from MS Vatican 113.
133   B. Ketubot 51b. See B. Ketubot 54a for parallel.
134   If *ma'i taama* is absent from the text, as it is in MS Vatican 113, that might be an indication that *yetzer albeshah*, is part of Rava's ruling and not a later redactional explanation. However, the shift to Aramaic would point to its redactional provenance. See Rosen-Zvi, *Demonic Desires*, 109–10. He explains the connotation affixed to the term 'yetzer' in the stammaitic strata.
135   See B. Qiddushin 81b, for another case in which this phrase is used. Maimonides explains that a woman in this situation is exempt because: "when she begins to cohabitate under duress, it is not in her control to not desire it, since the natural inclination of a person will compel her to desire it." Maimonides *Mishneh Torah: Issurei Bi'ah* 1:9.
      The view that women tend to become compliant even when raped no doubt reflects the androcentric perspective of the Talmud.
136   MS Munich 95 has the attribution of ר' אבא, an understandable scribal error.
137   I.e. others physically overpower and force a man into a forbidden sexual relation by threat of death (Tosafot *ad loc.* s.v. *ein*) or a woman overpowers him (*Hiddushei Ha-Ramban ad loc.* s.v. *ha*).
138   B. Yebamot 53b. This ruling appears with regard to M. Yebamot 6:1 which states that one acquires his deceased brother's widow in levirate marriage—even through an act of intercourse in which there is neither intention nor desire. As discussed in Chapter 2, Rabbah rejects this mishnah and rules it does not result in a levirate marriage. Rava's statement here is cited as a question as to what the case of coercion in the mishnah refers to. However, it is possible that Rava is explaining the position of this mishnah; levirate marriage occurs through any act of intercourse because there is always an assumption that the man consents to it.

Any subsequent sexual act, even if done under coercion, is deemed voluntary. However, because a woman can be forced into a sexual act without being aroused, any subsequent arousal is deemed out of her control.[139]

The contrasting rulings for men and women regarding forced intercourse reflect a further distinction that Aristotle makes between acts and states. An act can be considered involuntary when coerced or when it results from a mental state in which one is not in rational control. However, such states themselves can be voluntary or involuntary depending on the circumstances leading up to them. If one could have prevented himself from entering a state where he lacks control (such as by getting drunk) he is liable on account of voluntarily entering such a state. Rava, it seems, applies similar considerations to a man entering a state of sexual arousal accompanied by an erection, which he always considers to be a state one enters willfully as opposed to a purely automatic physiological response. Liability for whatever follows results from having voluntarily entered the state, even if all subsequent actions are involuntary.[140] A woman who is raped, by contrast, does not enter the state of sexual arousal voluntarily and is therefore blameless for the involuntary actions that result from the state of overwhelming desire.

This distinction between acts and states might also explain a rather puzzling ruling of Rava where, in contrast to Abaye, he implicates one who receives forbidden benefit against his will,[141] though there is no intention on the part of the agent:

איתמר הנאה הבאה לו לאדם בעל כרחו אביי אמר מותרת ורבא אמר אסורה

> It was said: [As to forbidden] benefit that comes to a person against his will:[142] Abaye said: it is permitted; Rava said: it is forbidden ...[143]

---

139 Michael Satlow notes how this conforms to Aristotle's overall view of the gender divide; men are capable of subduing their desires, making one's failure to do so his responsibility. Women, in contrast, possess weaker abilities, which therefore render them blameless. Rosen-Zvi, *Demonic Desires*, 110; Satlow, "'Try to Be a Man': The Rabbinic Construction of Masculinity," 27–28.

140 There are several other cases in which Rava exempts victims of coercion. See B. Nedarim 27a; B. Gittin 72b-73a (Kahana, "Gilui Da'at ve-'Ones be-Gittin.") While Rava's general stance is to absolve one in cases of *ones*, the difference in the case of B. Ketubot 51b is that he exempts the woman even if she ultimately agrees. Hence, the reason of *yetzer albeshah* is necessary.

141 Although some elements of the passage (in some MSS) might indicate that Abaye and Rava were engaged in dialogue, Kalmin suggests that they represent the work of the redactors, speaking on Rava's behalf. Kalmin, *Sages, Stories*, 291.

142 According to medieval commentators the case describes one in the presence of idolatry that emits a fragrant scent, an impossibility to avoid. (Rashi *ad loc.* s.v. *hakhi*, *Hiddushei Ha-Ran ad loc.* s.v. *hana'ah*.)

143 B. Pesahim 25b-26a.

Abaye's ruling correlates with his decisions that exonerate one who acts under compulsion,[144] yet we would also expect Rava to exempt this unintended act. Two possibilities as to the source of their disagreement are offered, which relate to the dispute between the Tannaim R. Simeon and R. Judah (as interpreted by Rava and Abaye) regarding the principle of *davar she-ein mitkavvein*, and whether the prohibited benefit could have been avoided.[145] However several scholars have argued that these explanations do not reflect the opinions of Rava and Abaye, since they are found exclusively in the redactional strata and vary across text witnesses.[146] Furthermore, given that Rava and Abaye discuss *davar she-ein mitkavvein* elsewhere, they would have ostensibly explicated here that the issue was intention as opposed to receiving benefit.[147] It is therefore more likely that Rava and Abaye's rulings turned on the issue of whether receiving pleasure/benefit is prohibited even if one does not desire it. Rava's strict ruling becomes explicable in light of the Aristotelian distinction between acts and states. Once an agent willfully enters the situation where a prohibition will occur, even if he does not intend to benefit at the time, he is liable.

6.3   *Reading Aristotle in Mahoza?*

As noted in the introductory chapter, there is evidence that a fourth-century rabbi living in Sasanian Iran could have been aware of Aristotelian philosophy. Whether Rava's rulings reflect an underlying Aristotelian philosophy, a preference for Palestinian teachings, or some combination of the two, the similarities between Rava's rulings and Aristotle's views on corrective justice and moral responsibility suggest that there is at least a typological relation between the two. We might reasonably propose that underlying Rava's jurisprudence is a larger theory of moral responsibility which shares important features with the *Ethics*. Where one acts without intention, though the act causes injury, the agent is not characterized as unjust and immoral, and therefore is subject to lesser degrees of legal liability. Culpability for the violation of a religious precept similarly depends upon whether one intends to violate it. When the action intended was thought permissible or when one acts out of uncontrollable passion, culpability does not follow, much in the same way

---

144   See B. Bava Qama 28b–29b.
145   See Chapter 5, section 3.1 for an extended discussion of the redactorial understanding of Rava and Abaye's rulings in this case.
146   Kalcheim, "Davar Sh'ain Mitkaven," 131–41; Halivni, *Meqorot U-Mesorot: Erubin and Pesahim*, 345–46.
147   See Chapter 5, n. 28 for further discussion.

that Aristotle assigns moral responsibility on the basis of deliberate intentional action.

There remains one final area with regard to Rava's jurisprudence that is worthy of attention: the role of intention in cases involving the performance of ritual acts and religious obligations. Curiously, unlike his positions regarding the violation of norms, Rava does not require intention when performing a *mitzvah*. In the chapter that follows, we will discuss this anomalous position of Rava's, and how it establishes ritual performance as a distinct area of rabbinic law.

CHAPTER 4

Mitzvot Ein Tzerikhot Kavvanah
Divorcing Ritual Performance from Intention

1   Overview: A Radical Change in Ritual Law[1]

We have seen that in a range of areas Rava consistently requires that one intend to violate a norm to be held culpable, and that in many cases he considers intention as a salient factor where his predecessors and contemporaries do not. Although this is true in civil law as well as in regard to culpability for religious transgressions, Rava breaks from this approach when it comes to the fulfillment of ritual obligations or *mitzvot*, as expressed in the dictum *mitzvot ein tzerikhot kavvanah*, "(the performance of) positive commandments (i.e. ritual obligations) does not require intention." As will become clear, it is the redactors who formulate the principle itself, but it is based on a series of rulings in which Rava maintains that intention is unnecessary to discharge a ritual obligation.

Dispensing with intention in the performance of rituals is a radical innovation, not only in contrast to Rava's rulings regarding civil liability and religious violations, but in the wider context of rabbinic law. In tannaitic and earlier amoraic rulings the position seen consistently is that intention is crucial when performing rituals.[2] *Mitzvot ein tzerikhot kavvanah* is significant not only because it relegates intention in the performance of ritual *mitzvot*, but because it introduces a novel bifurcation between areas of law that had previously seen no such radical division in the rabbinic tradition; effectively placing the fulfillment of religious obligations in its own domain, apart from both tort law and religious violations. The emergence of what we now call 'ritual', as a distinct category, can to a significant degree be linked to this development within rabbinic legal thought.

This first part of this chapter begins with a source-critical analysis demonstrating a chronological progression from the tannaitic position requiring

---

1   Elements of this chapter are drawn from my earlier article appearing in *JSQ*, Strauch Schick, "Mitzvot Eyn Tzerikhot Kavvanah."
2   I.e. intention to do an action for the purpose of fulfilling a specific religious obligation. Gruenwald, *Rituals and Ritual Theory in Ancient Israel*, 165; Albeck, "Is there a Category of Intention in Talmudic Criminal Law?," 461–62. Albeck distinguishes between five different levels of *kavvanah* that one can have when performing a *mitzvah*.

intention in the performance of particular ritual acts to its apparent antithesis beginning with Rava's rulings, and continuing through the anonymous strata of the Bavli. By reconstructing the formation of various *sugyot* discussing the necessity of intention in ritual practice, we will see how this principle evolved from Rava's isolated ruling to an independent legal rule.

In the second half, I examine Middle Persian texts that stress the necessity of intention concerning religious and civil violations without indicating any differentiation between these and ritual fulfillment. Read in this context, *mitzvot ein tzerikhot kavvanah* is remarkable not only in that it breaks with rabbinic precedent, but with prevailing religious attitudes in Sasanian Persia as well. I conclude the chapter by exploring the possibility that the formulation of the principle may anticipate a broader shift in religious thinking beginning in this period, including developments in Christian monastic literature, which similarly relegate the importance of intention and instead underscore the performative element of religious acts.

2   The Development of *Mitzvot Ein Tzerikhot Kavvanah*

2.1   *The Mishnaic View: Shema, Shofar, Megillah*

As noted earlier, the Mishnah evinces great concern for intentional behavior,[3] and it unambiguously requires intention in the performance of three specific rituals: reciting the *Shema*, hearing the *Shofar* on Rosh Hashanah, and listening to/reading the scroll of Esther during Purim:

> היה קורא בתורה והגיע זמן המקרא אם כיון לבו יצא ואם לאו לא יצא
>
> [Where] one was reading the [portion of] Torah [containing *Shema*], and the time of [its] reading arrives: if he directed his heart (*im kivein libo*), he has fulfilled [his obligation]; if not, he has not fulfilled [it]. (M. Berakhot 2:1)

> וכן מי שהיה עובר אחורי בית הכנסת או שהיה ביתו סמוך לבית הכנסת ושמע קול שופר או קול מגילה אם כיון לבו יצא ואם לאו לא יצא אף על פי שזה שמע וזה שמע זה כיון לבו וזה לא כיון לבו
>
> As well, one who was passing behind a synagogue, or his house was near a synagogue, and heard the sound of the *shofar* [on Rosh Hashanah] or the sound of [reading] the scroll [of Esther on Purim], if he directed

---

3   See p. 18.

his heart (*im kivein libo*), he has fulfilled [his obligation]; if not, he has not fulfilled [it]. Even though this one heard and this one heard, one directed his heart and one did not direct his heart. (M. Rosh Hashana 3:7)[4]

כותבה דורשה ומגיהה אם כיון לבו יצא ואם לאו לא יצא

If one was writing [the scroll of Esther on Purim], expounding it, or proofreading it [while reading] if he directed his heart (*im kivein libo*), he has fulfilled [his obligation]; if not, he has not fulfilled [it]. (M. Megillah 2:2)

In three cases discussed in three tractates, the Mishnah rules that one must "direct his heart" to fulfill a ritual obligation.[5] As is customary with mishnaic law, the rulings are confined to specific cases rather than offered as, or subsumed under, general principles. These rulings are corroborated in the Tosefta.[6]

Regarding *Shema* and Megillat Esther, it is possible that *kivein libo* might refer just to attention to the words.[7] However, M. Berakhot 5:1 employs the term regarding prayer, and there it explicitly refers to mental concentration. Furthermore, with respect to the *shofar*, since there are no words, intention must refer to listening carefully or with intent to fulfill the *mitzvah*. The latter interpretation finds support in the mishnah that follows, which contains a homily on a seemingly unrelated scriptural passage:

---

[4] In the Yerushalmi's understanding of this mishnah (Y. Rosh Hashana 59a, 3:5), the reason one has to actively "direct his heart" is because he was passing by a synagogue—implying that had he been standing, "there is a presumption that he intended." In Palestinian rabbinic law, there is an assumption of the need for intention. Lieberman, *Tosefta Kefshuta: Seder Mo'ed*, 3:1045.

[5] In tannaitic literature, K-V-N in the *pi'el* form juxtaposed with *leib/da'at* means "to intend" (M. Menahot 13:11; Sipra *Nedava* 8:9; Sifre 41, 86). Alone, it suggests "to physically direct" (M. 'Arakhim 5:1; M. Parah 4:2). In the ancient view, the heart holds the intellect and ethical reflection (1 Kings 3:12; Proverbs 16:23; Psalms 64:7); see Muffs, *Studies in the Aramaic Legal Papyri from Elephantine*, 176–77. Only in the reflexive *hitpa'el* form does K-V-N by itself imply "to intend" (M. Shabbat 12:5; M. Yebamot 16:5; T. Yadayim 2:3).

[6] T. Berakhot 2:2, 7; 3:18; T. Rosh Hashana 2:6-7. The Tosefta also requires intention when taking tithes (T. Terumah 3:6) and during hand-washing (T. Yadayim 2:3).

[7] See *Hiddushei Ha-Ritva* B. Rosh Hashana 28b, s.v. *be-koreh*; Friedman, *Tosefta Atikta*, 434, n. 52. Y. Berakhot 10b stating "the recitation of *Shema* does not require intention, [whereas] prayer requires intention," clearly refers to concentrating on the words.

Scholars note the Mishnah's novelty in emphasizing intention when performing religious acts; see Balberg, "Recomposed Corporalities," 11–17; Levinson, "From Narrative Practice to Cultural Poetics," 345–68. Ishai Rosen-Zvi counters that the Tannaitic 'intention' disregards the subjective thoughts of individuals, being informed by rabbinic law; Rosen-Zvi, "The Mishnaic Mental Revolution," 47–58; Rosen-Zvi, *Demonic Desires*.

> והיה כאשר ירים משה ידו וגבר ישראל וכאשר יניח ידו וגבר עמלק וכי ידיו
> של משה עושות מלחמה או ידיו [8]שבורות מלחמה אלא כל זמן שהיו ישראל
> מיסתכלים כלפי למעלן ומכוונים את לבם לאביהם שבשמים היו מתגברים ואם
> לאו היו נופלים ...

'And it came to pass, when Moses held up his hand that Israel prevailed and when he put his hand down Amaleq prevailed' (Exodus 17:11). Did the hands of Moses make war or break war? Rather, [it is to tell you that] as long as Israel were looking upward and directing their hearts (*u-mekhavvnim et libam*) to their Father in Heaven they prevailed, but otherwise they fell. (M. Rosh Hashana 3:8)

The connection between 3:7, referring to the obligation of *shofar*, and 3:8, concerning devotion to God lies in their joint use of K-V-N L-B; the use of this phrase appears to be a deliberate alteration for literary purposes—other versions of this homily lack this formulation.[9] We can therefore be fairly confident that in 3:7 *kivein libo* in the context of *shofar* has a related meaning of intention to serve G-d, which in this case is fulfilling a *mitzvah*.[10] Given that all three of the mishnayot use nearly identical formulations containing *im kivein libo*, the meaning regarding Megillah and *Shema* likely also refers to directing one's heart toward the service of God.

2.2 Early Amoraic Views: Accidental Immersion

The tannaitic view requiring intention for *mitzvot* appears to persist through the early generations of Amoraim. As we discussed in Chapter 2, R. Hisda introduced a requirement of intention when performing various rituals. Similarly, with regard to *shofar*, B. Rosh Hashana 29a reports R. Zeira (third-generation Palestinian Amora) ordering his attendant: "Have (the proper) intention and blow [the *shofar*] for me (*i-kavvein ve-taka li*)," consistent with M. Rosh Hashana 3:7.

---

8   MS Kaufman A50 fol. 76v. The text of this mishnah appearing in the printed editions of the Bavli and MSS British Library 400, Oxford 366, Oxford: Heb. d. 58/11–18, Enelow 270, 319 have ומשעבדים את לבם.

9   *Mekhilta de-Rabbi Ishmael, Amaleq* 1 and *Mekhilta de-Rabbi Shimon bar Yohai* 17:11.

10 This is also evidenced from M. Rosh Hashana 4:8. Fraenkel explains this mishnaic unit as presenting ideological discord between *halakhah* and *aggadah*. 3:7, the halakhic imperative, requires one intend to fulfill the precept; 3:8, the *aggadah*, recommends aspiring to direct one's heart to fulfilling God's will. Fraenkel alternatively suggests that the aggadic notion of 'intention' found in 3:8 elaborates on 3:7's halakhic 'intention'; Fraenkel, 662, n. 36.

Change appears in the rulings of the third-generation sage, R. Nahman. He proposes an exception, apparently to Rava, distinguishing between rituals performed for *hullin*, non-sacred purposes, as opposed to sacred ones. This discussion appears in two corresponding *sugyot*, B. Hagigah 18b-19a and B. Hullin 31a-b. (The first sections, A, B, and C differ, while sections D and on are nearly identical in both *sugyot*.)

B. Hullin 31a	B. Hagigah 18b-19a
1A. איתמר נידה שנאנסה וטבלה אמ' רב יהודה אמ' רב טהורה לביתה ואסורה לאכו' בתרומה ור' יוחנן אמ' אף לביתה לא טהרה[11]	A. ת"ר הנוטל ידיו נתכוון ידיו טהורו' לא נתכוון ידיו טמאו' וכן המטביל ידיו נתכוון ידיו טהורות לא נתכוון ידיו טמאות[12]
1B. אמ' ליה רבא לרב נחמן לרב דאמ' טהורה לביתה ואסורה לאכול בתרומה עון כרת הותרה איסור מיתה מיבעיא	B. והתניא בין נתכוון בין לא נתכוון ידיו טהורות[13]
1C. אמר ליה בעלה חולין הוא וחולין לא בעי כוונה	C. אמר רב נחמן לא קשיא כאן לחולין כאן למעשר
1D. ומנא תימר' דתנן ...	D. ומנא תימרא דחולין לא בעו כוונה דתנן ...
	E. איתיביה רבא לרב נחמן טובל לחולין והוחזק לחולין אסור למעשר הוחזק אין לא הוחזק לא
	F. הכי קאמ' אף על פי שנתכוון לחולין אסור למעשר
	G. איתיביה טבל ולא הוחזק כאילו לא טבל מאי לאו כאילו לא טבל כלל
	H. לא כאילו לא טבל למעשר אבל טבל לחולין
	I. הוא סבר דחי קא מדחי ליה נפק דק ואשכח דתניא טבל ולא הוחזק אסור למעשר ומותר לחולין

---

11 אף לביתה אסורה נמי אסורה] MS Vatican 122.
12 Following MSS Cambridge - T-S F2 (1).204, London–BL Harl. 5508 (400), Oxford Opp. Add. fol. 23, Munich Vatican 171, Vatican 134, Ed. Venice, Spanish, Vilna, along with the *baraita* as it appears in T. Yadaim (Zuckermandel) 2:3. Ed. Pesaro, MS Goettingen 3 omits 'his hands' and MS Munich 95 omits the second case of the *baraita* entirely.
13 Following the printed editions and MS Munich 95.
    תניא אידך אחד נוטל ואחד המטביל...] MSS Goettingen 3, BL Harl. 5508 (400), Munich 6, Cambridge - T-S F2 (1).204, Cambridge - T-S F2 (1).207, Cambridge - T-S F3.10.

(A) B. Hagigah: Our rabbis taught: One who washes his hands, if he has intention, his hands are pure. If he does not have intention, his hands are impure. And likewise, one who immerses his hands [in a ritual bath], if he has intention, his hands are pure. If he does not have intention, his hands are impure.

(A1) B. Hullin: It was stated: If a menstruating woman accidentally immerses, R. Judah[14] said Rav said: She is pure to [have sex with] her husband [lit. her house] but forbidden to eat tithes. R. Yohanan said: She is even impure to her husband.

(B) B. Hagigah: But it is taught: 'whether or not he intends, his hands are pure'?

(B1) B. Hullin: Rava said to R. Nahman: According to Rav who said she is pure to her husband [lit. her house] but forbidden to eat tithes;[if] a sin which carries with it the penalty of *kareit* is permitted, is a prohibition [punishable by] death necessary?

(C) B. Hagigah: R. Nahman[15] said: There is no contradiction. This [i.e. where intention is unnecessary, refers] to *hullin*, unconsecrated food; this [i.e. where intention is necessary, refers] to tithes.

(C1) B. Hullin: He said to him: [Sex with] her husband is *hullin*, and *hullin* does not require intention.

(D) And from where do you say that *hullin* does not require intention? For it is taught ...[16]

(D1) And from where do you say [that *hullin* does not require intention]? For it is taught.

(E) Rava[17] asked R Nahman: 'One who immerses [in a ritual bath] for *hullin* and intends [to purify himself] for *hullin*, is prohibited [from eating] tithes'. (M. Hagigah 2:6). If he intends, yes (he may eat ordinary food); if he does not intend, no, (he may not)?

(F) This is what it is saying: Even though he intends for *hullin*, he is prohibited [from eating] tithes.

(G) He (Rava) asked him: 'One who immerses and does not intend [to purify himself] is considered as if he did not immerse'. Is this not

---

14   R. Judah absent from MSS Vatican 121, 122.
15   R. Nahman b. Isaac] MS Oxford Opp. Add Fol. 23 (366). In all textual witnesses of both passages, Rava questions R. Nahman b. Jacob. It is also more likely (and usual) that Rava questioned his teacher, than his disciple, R. Nahman b. Isaac.
16   I have omitted this tannaitic text and its explanation.
17   Printed editions of B. Hagigah attribute this to Rabbah, though all text witnesses of B. Hullin 31a cite Rava, which seems likely, since he was R. Nahman's student.

[to be understood that he is considered] as if he did not immerse at all?

(H) No, [it is to be understood that he is considered] as if he did not immerse for tithes, but he did immerse for *hullin*.

(I) [Rava] thought [R. Nahman] was putting him off, but he went out, investigated and found that it is taught: 'if one immerses without [particular] intent, he is prohibited [to partake of] tithes but permitted to [eat] hullin'.[18]

In Hagigah, R. Nahman distinguishes between *hullin* and sacred (C) to harmonize two contradictory *baraitot* regarding whether intention is necessary when purifying one's hands (A, B),[19] thereby introducing the notion that hand-washing performed for *hullin* does not require intention.[20] This distinction is similarly reported in Hullin following Rava's query (B1) concerning an amoraic debate between the first- and second-generation Amoraim Rav and R. Yohanan regarding the ritual status of a menstruating woman who falls into water (A1). R. Nahman responds by distinguishing between immersions for sacred versus *hullin* purposes (C1): A woman must have intention when immersing vis-à-vis tithes and anything consecrated for temple use, but not in order to resume marital relations, since this is *hullin*. R. Nahman bases his ruling on the case of a woman falling, reflecting that he dispenses with even a minimal intent to act.

Although it is unclear in B. Hullin who states "*hullin* does not require intention" (C1), its Aramaic formulation (as opposed to R. Nahman's Hebrew statement) and the ease with which the two clauses can be divided, suggest that it is a redactional addition.[21] Furthermore, in B.Hagigah it appears in the anonymous question posed to R. Nahman's ruling, likewise suggesting its redactorial origins (D).

Both passages have identically structured endings: Tannaitic support for R. Nahman, challenges by Rava (D, D1 E, G), R. Nahman's responses (F, H) and Rava's concession to R. Nahman upon finding tannaitic proof (I). The parallels suggest that this unit was likely grafted from one *sugya* onto the other. Several

---

18 For a reading on the gender politics underlying this *sugya*, see Ilan, "A Menstruant 'Forced and Immersed.'"

19 Hands retain a constant state of (low-grade) impurity because of the notion: *ha-yadayim asqaniyot*, the hands are always busy, i.e. touching or doing things irrespective of the person's awareness. (M. Taharot 7:8). See Furstenberg, "The Purity of Hands"; Balberg, *Purity*, 59–61, for a discussion regarding the idea of hand impurity.

20 For an alternate explanation, see Halivni, *Meqorot U-Mesorot: Erubin and Pesahim*, 600.

21 Friedman, "A Critical Study."

indications point to B. Hullin as the original version. In B. Hullin, R. Nahman's opinion responds to Rava's initial inquiries, thereby anticipating Rava's challenges, while in B. Hagigah, R. Nahman's interpretation appears independently. Furthermore, in Hullin, R. Nahman introduces his distinction into a case concerning immersion, which parallels Rava's challenges.[22] The *sugya* in Hagigah may therefore have initially contained R. Nahman's reconciliation of the *baraitot* alone, and later incorporated Rava's challenges due to the similarity with his response to Rava in B. Hullin.[23]

It emerges from both passages that R. Nahman distinguishes between sacred and secular rituals, requiring intention only in cases of the former, and Rava ultimately concurs. However, R. Nahman's position has tannaitic precedent, as is evidenced by the *baraita* in B. Hagigah (T. Yadayim (Zuckermandel) 2:3) validating unintentional hand-washing (B). Furthermore, this distinction appears anonymously in the parallel *sugya* in the Yerushalmi. Y. Hagigah 78b reports R. Simeon b. Laqish's ruling that one who becomes impure by consuming impure food or liquid may purify himself without intention—though the Yerushalmi's redactors interpret this to mean without *proper* intention. Since most of the Yerushalmi *sugya* is presented anonymously, it likely belongs to a later redactional stratum that can be dated to after R. Nahman,[24] making it possible that the Yerushalmi's redactors espouse R. Nahman's opinion.[25]

---

22   Halivni also notes inconsistencies within the B. Hagigah *sugya*. Halivni, *Meqorot U-Mesorot: Erubin and Pesahim*, 598–99.
23   Alternatively, it could be argued that B. Hagigah represents the authentic context, since the more frequent connotation of *hullin* categorizes objects and not actions. R. Nahman's use of *hullin* in reference to food and tithes, as found in B. Hagigah, therefore represents the more typical usage of this term. According to this rendering, Rava and R. Nahman's back-and-forth is seemingly a redactional invention. (My thanks to Yonatan Feintuch who suggested this to me.) Nevertheless, *hullin* may refer to the more general category of profane. (B. Pesahim 69a cites Rava using *hullin* in this more general manner.) *Hullin* is also used in the context of *sihat hullin*, referring to non-Torah language: B. Yoma 19b, also in the name of Rava; B. Sukkah 28a, in the names of Yose b. R. Yehuda and R. Yohanan b. Zakkai; B. Avoda Zara 19b in the name of Rav (the last three predate R. Nahman). Furthermore, although *hullin* refers to marital relations in B. Hullin, it is contrasted with tithes and *terumah*, both following its more common usage.
24   There are several opinions as to when the Yerushalmi reached its final form, ranging from the mid-fourth to early fifth centuries (See Introduction, n. 29); in either event, the redaction post-dates R. Nahman, who is cited a number of times.
25   Alternatively, Friedman notes the phenomenon that both Talmuds attribute to named sages what in the other Talmud appears as a redactorial explanation of an amoraic statement; see Friedman, *Tosefta Atikta*, 434–35, n. 52; Friedman, "Al Titma," 128. In the case

2.3 Rava's View

R. Nahman's student, Rava, departs far more significantly and explicitly from the Mishnah's view by dispensing with the requirement of intention in the case of *shofar*.

שלחו ליה לאבוה דשמואל כפאו ואכל מצה יצא ...
אמר רבא זאת אומרת התוקע לשיר[26] יצא ...
אלמא קסבר רבא מצות אין צריכות כוונה

> They sent [the following ruling] to the Father of Samuel: if one is compelled to eat *matzah* [on Passover], he thereby performs his religious duty ...
>
> Rava[27] said: this would imply that one who blew [the *shofar* on Rosh Hashana] to make music has fulfilled his religious duty ...
>
> Consequently, Rava[28] maintained that positive commandments (ritual obligations) do not require intention.[29]

Rava bases his ruling on one received by the Father of Samuel, maintaining that one forced to eat *matzah* on Passover fulfills his obligation. It is possible that this decision refers only to the obligation of consuming *matzah* on Passover night, as articulated in a *baraita* cited in Y. Pesahim 37d (discussed below) which states "one discharges [the obligation of eating] unleavened bread, whether he intends to or does not intend to." Nevertheless, Rava extends this to another obligation and infers that one who blows a *shofar* on Rosh Hashana in order to make music fulfills his obligation. Two innovations arise from Rava's ruling: in contrast to the mishnah's ruling, one need not intend to hear the *shofar* to fulfill the *mitzvah,* and one may even listen for another purpose and still discharge his obligation.[30] Based on this ruling, the Bavli's redactors formulate

---

of the Bavli, Friedman explains this as aiming to formulate the statement in clearer, as opposed to authentic, language.

26   לשד] MSS Oxford Opp. Add. Fol. 23 (366), Munich 95. This is likewise cited by Rashi. לשיד] MS British Library Harl. 5508 (400).

27   Rav(a)[ah] Munich 140. However, all other MSS and printed ed. contain Rava. Furthermore, in the remainder of the passage of Munich 140, Rava is cited. As this ruling accords with other rulings which can reliably be attributed to Rava, it seems that Rava is the correct attribution here as well.

28   Rav(a)[a] Munich 140.

29   B. Rosh Hashana 28a-b.

30   Conceivably, Rava dispenses with intention in cases when one performs an action himself, but requires it when listening to another, following M. Rosh Hashana 3:7. The Bavli, however, does not suggest this.

a general principle regarding all ritual *mitzvot* which they see as underlying Rava's decision: *mitzvot ein tzerikhot kavvanah*, "(the performance of) positive commandments does not require intention."[31] This is consistent with the redactors' tendency to generate abstract concepts based on overt or implicit amoraic principles — often based on the teachings of Rava.[32]

Thus formulated, the redactors are forced to reconcile the principle they attribute to Rava with the aforementioned mishnayot that appear to stand in direct contradiction, by limiting their application to specific and remote cases. The overall trajectory of the *sugya* thus suggests that it is structured in support of Rava's/the redactors' approach.[33]

The first and final challenges are attributed to Abaye, while the two middle ones are raised anonymously. A response attributed to Rava appears at the end. The *sugya* thus continues:[34]

(A) איתיביה אביי היה קורא בתורה והגיע זמן המקרא אם כוון לבו יצא ואם לאו לא יצא מאי לאו כוון לבו לצאת לא לקרות לקרות הא קא קרי בקורא להגיה ...

---

31   Friedman, *Tosefta Atikta*, 434–35, n. 52. On the meaning of *mitzvot* as indicating 'ritual', see Novick, "Blessings over Miṣvot," 76.

32   Moscovitz, *Talmudic Reasoning*, 349–50.

33   The end of the *sugya*, reporting R. Zeira's directive to his attendant to have intention when blowing the *shofar*, might suggest otherwise: "We see [R. Zeira] maintained: The blower requires intention. They challenged this: (M. Rosh Hashana 3:7) 'If he was passing behind a synagogue ...'—Here we are dealing with a community reader whose mind is on everyone ... [Rather, R. Zeira's ruling] is a tannaitic dispute."

This passage is unclear, given the preceding section's efforts to defend Rava's position. If it represents a dissenting view (*Hiddushei HaRashba ad loc.* s.v. *amar*), R. Zeira's statement should be included among those rulings that contradict Rava. It is striking that, after broadly applying Rava's ruling, the redactors limit R. Zeira's directive to the *shofar* blower alone. Moreover, they limit the intention required; he need only have in mind for whom he is blowing. This differs from 'intention' discussed at the beginning of the *sugya*, to fulfill one's obligation. For these reasons, it seems that the redactors either limited R. Zeira's dissenting statement or were faced with an earlier tradition that did not cohere with the rest of the *sugya* and thus placed it at the end. Notably, in B. Rosh Hashana 33b the redactors try both to support Rava and reject R. Zeira from M. Rosh Hashana 4:8. These attempts fail, but it underscores the preference for Rava. Although R. Zeira's ruling conceivably represents the redactors' ambivalence, the overwhelming thrust of the *sugya* is that intention is unnecessary.

34   While this back-and-forth appears as a debate between Rava and Abaye, it could be redactional; its parallel appears anonymously in B. Berakhot 13a. Richard Kalmin limits the cases in which Abaye demonstrates awareness of Rava's rulings (Kalmin, *Sages, Stories*, 291–92, app. 4. Halivni accepts the attribution of Rava (Halivni, *Meqorot U-Mesorot: Erubin and Pesahim*, 404.)

(B) תא שמע היה עובר אחורי בית הכנסת או שהיה ביתו סמוך לבית הכנסת ושמע קול שופר או קול מגילה אם כוון לבו יצא ואם לאו לא יצא. מאי לאו אם כוון לבו לצאת לא לשמע לשמוע והא שמע סבור חמור בעלמא הוא

(C) איתיביה נתכוון שומע ולא נתכוון משמיע ולא נתכוון שומע לא יצא עד שיתכוון שומע ומשמיע. בשלמא נתכוון משמיע ולא נתכוון שומע כסבור חמור בעלמא הוא. אלא נתכוון שומע ולא נתכוון משמיע היכי משכחת לה לאו בתוקע לשיר[35] דלמא דקא מנבח נבוחי

(D) אמר ליה אביי אלא מעתה הישן בשמיני בסוכה ילקה[36]

(E) אמר לו שאני אומר מצות אינו עובר עליהן אלא בזמנן ...

(F) רבא אמר לצאת לא בעי כוונה לעבור בעי כוונה והא מתן דמים לרבי יהושע דלעבור ולא בעי כוונה

(G) אלא אמר רבא לצאת לא בעי כוונה לעבור[37] בזמנו לא בעי כוונה שלא בזמנו בעי כוונה

(A) Abaye[38] asked: (M. Berakhot 2:1) '[Where] one was reading the [portion of] Torah [containing *Shema*], and the time of [its] reading arrives: if he directed his heart, he has fulfilled [his obligation]; if not, he has not fulfilled [it].' Is this not 'directed his heart' to fulfill [the *mitzvah*]? No, [it means] to read. To read? But he *is* reading! It is where he is reading to proofread.

(B) Come and hear: (M. Rosh Hashana 3:7) 'One who was passing behind a synagogue, or his house was near a synagogue, and heard the sound of the *shofar* [on Rosh Hashanah] or the sound of [reading] the scroll [of Esther on Purim], if he directed his heart, he has fulfilled [his obligation]; if not, he has not fulfilled[it].' — is this not 'if he directed his heart' to fulfill [the *mitzvah*]? No, it is to hear. To hear? But he heard! He [initially] thought it was merely a donkey [braying].

(C) He raised the following [*baraita* in] objection: 'If the one who listens intends, but the one who sounds [the *shofar*] does not intend, [or] the one who sounds [intends,] and the one who listens does not intend, he does not fulfill [the *mitzvah*] unless both the one who listens and the one who sounds intend'. It makes sense that the one sounding intended and the one listening did not; he thought it was merely a donkey. Rather, how do you find [a case where] the one who listens intends and the one who sounds does not intend—is it

---

35 לשד] MSS Oxford Opp. Add. Fol. 23 (366). לשיד] MS British Library Harl. 5508 (400).
36 MS British Library Harl. 5508 (400) contains a fuller explanation: תוסיף בל משום לעבור.
37 לעבור בבל תוסיף] MS British Library Harl. 5508 (400).
38 Following all MSS. In ed. Vilna the question is posed anonymously.

not where he sounds [the *shofar*] to make music? [No,] perhaps he was making barking sounds.

(D) Abaye[39] said to him: But now, one who sleeps in a *sukkah* on the eighth day should receive lashes [for adding a *mitzvah*]?

(E) [Rava] said to him: [No,] for I maintain that obligations can only be transgressed [for adding to them] in their [proper] times …

(F) Rava said: Intention is not required to fulfill [*mitzvot*, but] intention is required to transgress [by adding]. But what of the sprinkling of blood, which, according to R. Joshua, [causes one] to transgress [the prohibition of adding commandments] and it does not require intention?

(G) Rather Rava said: To fulfill [*mitzvot*], does not require intention, [but] to transgress; [when it occurs] in its proper time, does not require intention, and [when it occurs] not during its proper time, does require intention.

In order to reconcile M. Berakhot 2:1's directive to "direct his heart" when reciting *Shema* with Rava's putative principle, intention is understood to refer to intent to perform an act of reading the Torah, as opposed to instances where one only has intention to proofread the text (A).[40] Similarly, both the mishnah requiring one to "direct his heart" to fulfill the obligation of hearing the *shofar* and a *baraita* explicitly requiring that both one sounding the *shofar* and one hearing it must intend to fulfill the *mitzvah* must be reinterpreted, as they directly contradict Rava's ruling that one who sounds the *shofar* to make music discharges his obligation (B, C). Again, the idea of intent is interpreted, as directing one's attention to the fact that the sound one is hearing is that of a *shofar* as opposed to an initial impression that it is the sound of an animal (B); intent to sound the *shofar* is correspondingly understood as merely the intent to perform the basic activity of sounding the ram's horn musically, rather than producing a barking sound (C).

One final challenge attributed to Abaye is raised against Rava, based on the injunction against adding on to a *mitzvah*, such as residing in a *sukkah* after

---

39   This attribution is uncertain. (B) is introduced with *ta shema* (come and hear), suggesting a redactional comment, while (C), beginning with *eytveyh* (he raised a challenge), is unclear. MS Munich 140 has *eytveyh Abaye*, making it possible that the redactors constructed the *sugya* so that there would be a pattern of three tannaitic rulings to question Rava. See Friedman, "Some Structural Patterns of Talmudic Sugyot," 389–402.

40   In the parallel, B. Berakhot 13a, intention may refer to concentrating on the words. Predictably, this text reports Rava as espousing the lenient tannaitic position that requires intention for only the first verse of the *Shema*.

the holiday is over and the obligation no longer applies (D). If one may fulfill a *mitzvah* without intention, then anytime a person performs an act that may be considered a *mitzvah,* he transgresses the biblical violation not to add to biblical precepts. The *sugya* offers three variations of Rava's response: first, one can only violate the prohibition of adding to precepts when doing so at the time that the act must be performed (E); second, one may fulfill an obligation without intention, but one cannot be liable for transgressions without intention (F); third, whether intention is required in order to impose liability depends on when the violation occurs (G).

Although all three statements are attributed to Rava, the general consensus is that where alternate statements by a given sage are offered, only one is authentic and the other versions are the product of redactional reworking.[41] While distinguishing which is Rava's original statement remains indeterminate,[42] what it does indicate is that Rava's ruling is not limited to the specific case of *shofar,* but applies to other areas as well. This may be inferred from the fact that Rava derives his decision regarding *shofar* via analogy from another amoraic ruling concerning Passover along with the challenges raised against Rava's putative view (in the name of Abaye and anonymously) based on rulings regarding *Shema, Sukkot,* as well as *shofar.* These suggest that it could have broader applications. Indeed, Rava dispenses with the need for intention in ritual immersion as noted above,[43] along with sacrificial offerings, by formulating the idea that a sacrifice brought without qualification discharges the owner's obligation because, "an unqualified sacrifice stands at the ready for its purpose" (*zebahim be-stam leshman omdin*).[44] Rava's ruling regarding *shofar* is thus understood to embody a broader principle that extends to all *mitzvot,* which is then used to establish a framework employed by the redactors in other *sugyot* to explain seemingly unrelated tannaitic debates.[45]

---

41   Aaron Amit and Moshe Benovitz discuss similar cases and conclude that it is more likely that the multiple versions of Rava's statements are the product of redactional reworking. Amit, *Pesahim IV,* 175, n. 79; Benovitz, *Berakhot VI,* 131, n. 44. Halivni views such exchanges between Rava and Abaye as authentic reports and hence the revised answers as recording Rava's actual statement, Halivni, *Meqorot U-Mesorot: Erubin and Pesahim,* 426. However, as noted above, Kalmin demonstrates that actual contact between Rava and Abaye was rare. *Supra* Chapter 3, n 4.
42   The fact that the answer offered in (F) parallels an explanation offered in the redactional stratum in B. Erubin 95b-96a, (discussed below) might suggest that it is a reworked version of Rava's original statement by the redactors. However, it is also possible that the redactors based their explanation in B. Erubin on Rava's statement in B. Rosh Hashana.
43   B. Hullin 31a-b, B. Keritut 7a.
44   B. Zebahim 2a.
45   Friedman, "Al Titma," 128.

For instance M. Pesahim 10:3, which obligates one to consume two servings of *maror* during the Passover meal (once at the beginning and again with the *matzah* and *haroset*), is understood in the Bavli to reflect the more fundamental issue of whether intention is necessary to fulfill *mitzvot* (B. Pesahim 114b):

(A) 1. אמר ר"ל זאת אומרת מצוות צריכות כוונה
2. כיון דלא בעידן חיובא דמרור הוא דאכיל ליה בבורא פ"ה הוא דאכיל ליה ודילמא לא איכוון למרו' הילכך בעי למהדר לאטבולי לשם מרור דאי סלקא דעתך מצוה לא בעיא כוונה למה לך תרי טיבולי והא טביל ליה חדא זימנא

(B) ממאי דילמא לעולם מצות אין צריכות כוונה ודקאמרת תרי טיבולי למה לי כי היכי דליהוי היכירא לתינוקות[46] ...

(C) ועוד תניא ... אכלן בלא מתכוין יצא ...

(D) תנאי היא דתני' רבי יוסי אומ' אף על פי שטיבל בחזר' מצוה להביא לפניו חזר' וחרוסת ושני תבשילין

(E) ואכתי ממאי דילמא קסבר רבי יוסי מצוות אין צריכות כוונה[47] והאי דבעינן תרי טיבולי כי היכי דתיהוי היכירא לתינוקות

(F) אם כן מאי מצוה

(A) 1. Resh Laqish said: This means that positive commandments (ritual obligations) require intention (*mitzvot tzerikhot kavvanah*).
2. Since one does not eat [the first portion of *maror*] at the time of the obligation of *maror,* he eats it with [the blessing] 'Who creates the fruit of the ground,' [as opposed to the blessing recited for performing the *mitzvah* of eating *maror*] and perhaps he did not intend [to fulfill the *mitzvah* of] *maror*; therefore, he is required to dip again for the sake of the *maror*. For if you would think that positive commandments (ritual obligations) do not require intention, why two dippings? He already dipped [lettuce] once!

(B) From where [do you say this]? Perhaps positive commandments (ritual obligations) do not require intention and [regarding] what you said 'why [do] I [need] two dippings'?, [it is] so that there will be a distinction for [attracting the attention of] the children ...

---

46 כי היכי ... תינוקות] absent from a number of MSS including JTS Rab 1623 (EMC 271), Vatican 134, Columbia X893-T141. They instead state הא קא משמע לן דבעינן תרי טיבולי, which does not answer the question as to why there are two servings.

47 ממאי...כוונה] absent from MSS JTS Rab 1623 (EMC 271), Columbia X893-T141, instead have דלמא משום דקא סבר ר' יוסי בעינן תרי טיבולי.

(C) And furthermore, it was taught: '... if he ate them [the bitter herbs] without intention [to fulfill the *mitzvah*], he has fulfilled [the *mitzvah*] ...'?

(D) It [whether ritual obligations require intention] is [disputed by] Tannaim. For it was taught, 'R. Yose said: Even though one has dipped lettuce, [it is an] obligation (*mitzvah*) to bring before him lettuce, *haroset*, and two cooked dishes'.

(E) But still, from where [do you say intention is necessary]? Perhaps R. Yose holds that positive commandments (ritual obligations) do not require intention, and he requires two dippings so that there may be a distinction for the children.

(F) If so, what is [meant by] 'obligation' (*mitzvah*)?

This *sugya* proceeds based on the initial supposition that the mishnah's requirement of two servings of lettuce is meant to ensure that the participants eat it with the proper intention of fulfilling the requirement of *maror*. Although the positive principle of *mitzvot tzerikhot kavvanah* is attributed to the second-generation Palestinian Amora Resh Laqish (A.1), undermining the notion that it was the redactors who formulated the inverse principle; scholars have noted the inaccuracy of this attribution based on the corresponding passage in the Yerushalmi:

(A1) חבריא בשם רבי יוחנן צריך לטבל בחזרת שני פעמים רבי זעורה בשם ר' יוחנן אינו צריך לטבל בחזרת שני פעמים

(B1) רבי שמעון בן לקיש אמר אם לא טבל פעם ראשונה צריך לטבל פעם שנייה

(C1) מתניתא פליגא על רבי שמעון בן לקיש שבכל הלילות אנו מטבלי' פעם אחת והלילה הזה שתי פעמים סבר רבי שמעון בן לקיש על הדא דבר קפרא{מתניתא פליגא על בר קפרא}[48]{שבכל הלילות אנו מטבילין אותו עם הפת וכאן אנו מטבילין אותו בפני עצמו

(1D) מתניתא פליגא על רבי יוחנן}[49] יוצאין במצה בין שכיוון בין שלא כיוון והכא מכיון שהיסב חזקה כיוון

---

48   According to Lieberman, this line should be deleted. See next note.
49   שבכל הלילות ... פליגא על ר' יוחנן] is found only in the margin of MS Leiden. See Ratner, Ahavat Zion Virushalayim, Pesahim, 131. Lieberman suspects that the note in MS Leiden was an attempt to emend the text which reads מתניתא פליגא על בר קפרא to what is written in the margin. However, the scribe mistakenly left in מתניתא פליגא על בר קפרא as well. Lieberman asserts that the correct text of the Yerushalmi is rather:
סבר ר' שמעון בן לקיש על הדא דבר קפרא שבכל הלילות אנו מטבילין אותו עם הפת ...
Thus Resh Laqish is in disagreement with M. Pesahim 10:4 which maintains that one of the four questions asked is "on all other nights we dip one time;" he rather maintains

(A1) The Scholars [said] in the name of R. Yohanan: [One] is required to dip with lettuce twice. R. Zeira[50] [said] in the name of R. Yohanan: One is not required to dip with lettuce twice.

(B1) R. Simeon son of Laqish said: if one does not dip the first time, then one is required to dip a second time.

(C1) The Mishnah (M. Pesahim 10:4) is at variance with R. Simeon son of Laqish [which states]: 'On all nights we dip once, and this night twice'? R. Simeon son of Laqish is of the same opinion like that of the son of Qappara[51] {'on all nights we dip [vegetables] with bread, and here we are dipping it by itself.'

(D1) The *baraita* is at variance with R. Yohanan} [which states] 'one discharges [the obligation of eating][52] unleavened bread, whether he intends to or does not intend to'? Here (i.e. when consuming unleavened bread), since he leans, there is a presumption that he intends ...[53]

Y. Pesahim 37c-d reports Resh Laqish as requiring lettuce to be dipped only one time (B1), compared to the first tradition of R. Yohanan, who requires that it be dipped twice (A1). It is the redactors who understand the latter as evincing a concern for proper intention in their citation and understanding of a *baraita* (D1), which states that one may discharge the obligation of eating unleavened bread on Passover night without intention to do so. The textual variants make it unclear why or to whom this *baraita* is cited.[54] The printed edition and the margin in MS Leiden clarify that it was raised as a question to R. Yohanan's ruling which requires two servings of lettuce. The redactors understood R. Yohanan's ruling to indicate that intention is necessary when consuming *maror*, making it at odds with the *baraita* that maintains that one does not need intention when consuming *matzah*. Unlike what is found in the Bavli, in the Yerushalmi the idea that a double serving of lettuce indicates a requirement for intentional action was an inference of the redactors alone, not found in the statements of either Resh Laqish or R. Yohanan. The question

---

that the question asked is "on all other nights we dip with bread," as is phrased in the *baraita* of the son of Qappara. Lieberman, *Yerushalmi Kipshuto: Shabat, 'Eruvin, Pesahim*, 1:519.

50 Presumably this refers to R. Zeira I, a third-generation Babylonian Amora who moved to Palestine.

51 See Y. Ma'aser Sheni 54b 3:5. Y. Orlah 62c 2:12. R. El'azar son of El'azar ha-Kappar is a fifth-generation Tanna.

52 See n. 49.

53 Y. Pesahim 37c-d.

54 *Supra* n 49.

is resolved by asserting that there is a presumption that one has intention—either during the whole night or while consuming unleavened bread—since one reclines and will presumably be reminded of his participation in a religious act.[55] The implication is that intention is required just as is inferred from R. Yohanan's ruling and as is consistent with other rulings predating R. Nahman and Rava. However, unlike what is found in the Bavli, the Yerushalmi does not issue a general principle regarding intention in the performance of religious obligations—neither in the anonymous nor amoraic strata.

Moscovitz therefore suggests that the redactors of the Bavli reformulated R. Yohanan's and Resh Laqish's rulings based on their conceptual understanding of it, though in all likelihood neither was concerned with intention.[56] Friedman likewise maintains that the Bavli attribution is not authentic and that the issue of intention was imposed onto Resh Laqish's ruling based on the *baraita* cited there (Section C), which contains no parallel and which Friedman identifies as late, which states the opposite, that one who consumes *maror* without intention fulfills the *mitzvah*.[57] Moreover, the concern with the general question of whether fulfilling *mitzvot* requires intention is characteristic of the later redactional strata.[58]

The Bavli's version of Resh Laqish's statement therefore appears to have developed in the following manner. The Yerushalmi's redactors understood R. Yohanan's obligation of two dippings of lettuce as reflecting a requirement of intention, which came to be regarded as his actual ruling.[59] The positions of R. Yohanan and Resh Laqish were reversed (a not unusual phenomenon),[60] Resh Laqish's ruling was articulated in terms of a principle already formulated by the redactors in B. Rosh Hashana 28a (A.1), and later redactors clarified his putative view (A.2).[61] Consequently, while earlier sages evidently required

---

55   A similar logic is found in Y. Rosh Hashana 59a, in its understanding of M. Rosh Hashana 3:5. *Supra* note 4.
56   Moscovitz, *Talmudic Reasoning*, 307–9.
57   Friedman, "Al Titma," 128.
58   For a thorough explanation of this passage and attempt to reconcile Resh Laqish's conflicting statements in the Bavli and Yerushalmi, see Halivni, *Meqorot U-Mesorot: Erubin and Pesahim*, 575; Friedman, "Al Titma," 128.
59   Friedman, "Al Titma," 129; Moscovitz, *Talmudic Reasoning*, 349–50.
60   This occurred in the course of oral transmission; see Frankel, *Mevo*, 42a-b. For alternate explanations for the reversal of their traditions, see Halivni, *Meqorot U-Mesorot: Erubin and Pesahim*, 574–76; Tabory, *Passover Ritual*, 255, nn. 17, 19. Moskowitz notes the significance of the Yerushalmi attributing conflicting traditions to R. Yohanan; Moscovitz, *Talmudic Reasoning*, 307, n. 63.
61   Friedman, "Al Titma," 128–29.

intention in the performance of individual religious acts, only the Bavli's redactors formulated a general principle.

Although the *sugya* presents intention as underlying the tannaitic requirements of double servings of lettuce at Passover, neither the mishnah nor the *baraita*'s statement of R. Yose (D) refer to it. The redactors even consider the possibility that the mishnah is concerned with creating a distinction in order to engage the children at the meal.[62] Alternatively, a second serving of lettuce may result from a need for *maror* to be consumed with *matzah* and the Passover offering (perhaps stemming from Exodus 12:8: "they shall eat it [the Passover offering] with unleavened bread and bitter herbs"). Nevertheless, in the final redacted version of the *sugya* the focus is *mitzvot (ein) tzerikhot kavvanah*.

The Bavli's redactors also apply the principle of *mitzvot ein tzerikhot kavvanah* to explain a tannaitic debate recorded in M. Erubin 10:1 regarding whether one may wear two pairs of phylacteries found on the Sabbath in a domain where carrying is prohibited. The first anonymous opinion allows a person to wear only one pair of phylacteries, while R. Gamliel permits wearing both. To explain this tannaitic dispute, multiple explanations are cited, which are noteworthy for the accretion of amoraic and anonymous material. Much like the previous case, this mishnah makes no reference to intention; it is only in the later anonymous strata that the idea of intention is introduced.

(A) זוג אחד אין טפי לא לימ' תנן סתמא דלא כרבי מאיר דאי כר' מאיר האמ' לובש כל מה שיכול ללבוש ועוטף כל מה שיכול לעטוף דתנן לשם מוציא כל כלי תשמישו לובש כל מה שיכול ללבוש ועוטף כל מה שיכול לעטוף ...

(B) א' רבא אפילו תימ' רבי מאיר התם דרך מלבושו בחול שויה רבנן והכא דרך מלבוש וכחול שוויה רבנן התם דבחול כמה דבעי לבוש לענין הצלה נמי שרו לי' רבנן הכא ובחול נמי זוג אחד אין טפי לא לענין הצלה נמי זוג אחד אין טפי לא

(C) רבן גמליאל אומ' שנים שנים: מאי קסבר אי קסבר שבת זמן תפילין הוא זוג אחד אין טפי לא ואי קסב' שבת לאו זמן תפילין הוא ומשום הצלה דרך מלבוש שרו ליה רבנן אפילו טפי נמי

(D) לעולם קסבר שבת לאו זמן תפילין הוא וכי שרו רבנן לעניין הצלה דרך מלבוש במקו' תפילין ...

(E) לימא בדר' שמואל בר רב יצחק קמיפלגי ...

---

62 Deuteronomy 6:20-21 indicates that the Exodus is recounted through question-and-answer. The rabbis instituted various practices to rouse children's curiosity; e.g., B. Pesahim 108b, 115b; T. Pesahim 10:9.

(F) לא דכולי עלמא אית להו הא דרב שמואל והכא בשבת זמן תפלין קמיפלגי ...

(G) ואיבע' אימ' דכולי עלמא שבת זמן תפלין הוא והכא במצות צריכות כונה קא מיפלגי מר[63] סבר לצאת בעי כוונה ומר סבר לא בעי כוונה

(H) ואיבעי' אימ' דכולי עלמ' לצאת לא בעי כוונה והכא בלעבור משום בל תוסיף קא מיפלגי מר סבר לעבור משום בל תוסף בעי כוונה ומר[64] סבר לא בעי כונה

(I) ואיבעי' אימ' דכולי עלמא שבת לאו זמן תפלין ולא לעבור בעי כוונה ולא לצאת בעי כוונה והכא בלעבור שלא בזמנן קא מיפלגי מר סבר בעי כוונה ומר[65] סבר לא בעי כוונה

(A) One pair, yes (one may wear), [but] no more. Let us say that the anonymous [opinion of the] mishnah is not in accordance with R. Meir? For if it was like R. Meir, he said: '[In the case of a fire on the Sabbath,] one may wear all the clothes that he can wear (put on), and wrap himself with anything that he can wrap [himself with]' (M. Shabbat 16:3) ...

(B) Rava said: You may even say [that M. Erubin 10:1 reflects the position of] R. Meir; there (M. Shabbat 16:3) the Rabbis have treated it similar to one's habit of dressing on a weekday and here the Rabbis have treated it similar to one's habit of dressing on a weekday. There, where on a weekday a man can wear as many clothes as he

---

63 MS Munich 95 makes the source of their dispute explicit: תנא קמ' סבר לצאת לא בעי כוונה ור"ג סבר לצאת בעי כוונה

Ed. Vilna likewise clarifies the positions: תנא קמא סבר לצאת בעי כוונה ורבן גמליאל סבר לא בעי כוונה

Rashi, who has the formulation of ed. Vilna, tries to make sense of their dispute. However, he ultimately concludes that the correct version should attribute the view which maintains that *mitzvot* do not require intention to the first position of the mishnah while the view which requires intention should be attributed to R. Gamliel, as is presented in MS Munich 95. Rashi *ad loc.* s.v. *ve-Rabban Gamliel*. The Ritva (*ad loc.* s.v. *ve-i*) likewise attributes the position which requires intention to R. Gamliel as appears in MS Munich 95.

64 MS Munich and ed. Vilna contain an elucidated version of the dispute:
[דתנא קמא סבר בל תוסיף לא בעי כוונה ור"ג סבר בלעבור בל תוסיף בעי כוונה] MS Munich
דתנא קמא סבר לעבור משום בל תסיף לא בעי כוונה רבן גמליאל סבר לעבור משום בל תסיף בעי כוונה] ed. Vilna.

65 MS Munich and ed. Vilna clarify:
[תנא קמא סבר בלעבור משום שלא בזמנו לא בעי כוונה ור"ג סבר לעבור שלא בזמנו בעו] MS Munich 95.
[תנא קמא סבר לא בעי כוונה, רבן גמליאל סבר לעבור שלא בזמנו בעי כוונה] ed. Vilna.

desires, the Rabbis have permitted him to do so also for the purpose of saving; here, where also on a weekday [a man may wear] one pair only [of phylacteries] but no more, for the purpose of saving also; one pair only, but no more.

(C) R. Gamliel says: 'two by two'. What is his reasoning? If he holds that the Sabbath is a time for phylacteries, one pair should be [permitted] but no more! And if he holds that the Sabbath is not a time for phylacteries, and for the purpose of saving them the Rabbis have permitted him to wear them in the manner of [weekly] attire, then even more should also [be permitted]?

(D) Really [R. Gamliel] holds that the Sabbath is not a time for phylacteries, and when the Rabbis permitted saving [them] in the manner of [weekday] attire, it [was only] in the place [on the body] of phylacteries ...[66]

(E) Shall we say that they argue with regard to R. Samuel b. R. Isaac [who holds: there is room on the head for placing two phylacteries]? ...

(F) No, everyone accepts [the ruling] of R. Samuel b. R. Isaac, but here they argue [over whether] the Sabbath is a time for phylacteries ...

(G) And if you want, I might say that everyone [agrees] the Sabbath is a time for phylacteries, but here they argue whether positive commandments (ritual obligations) require intention (*be-mitzvot tzerikhot kavvanah*). One master holds to fulfill [ritual obligations] requires intention, while one master holds it does not require intention.

(H) And if you want, I might say that everyone [agrees that] fulfilling [a *mitzvah*] does not require intention, but here they argue whether transgressing 'you shall not add' (Deuteronomy 4:2) requires intention. One master holds transgressing 'you shall not add' requires intention, while one master holds it does not require intention.

(I) And if you want, I might say: everyone [agrees] that the Sabbath is not the time for phylacteries and intention is not required to transgress, nor is intention required to fulfill [a *mitzvah*]. Rather, they argue about transgressing when it is not the proper time. One master holds it requires intention, while one master holds it does not require intention.[67]

---

66 The *sugya* continues with a short digression concerning the opinion of R. Samuel b. R. Isaac, in terms of how many pairs of phylacteries are worn and where they are placed.
67 B. Erubin 95b-96a.

Initially, the focus of the conflicting tannaitic rulings is on specific laws of Sabbath and phylacteries. Rava (B) limits the first opinion of the mishnah, which permits wearing only one set of phylacteries, to the laws of the Sabbath. In (C) the redactors continue along Rava's line of reasoning in explaining R. Gamliel's opposing view, still understanding the debate in the context of the Sabbath. In (D) and (E) the redactors delve further into the *mitzvah* of phylacteries, suggesting that the tannaitic dispute centered on whether to follow the position of the third-generation Babylonian Amora, R. Samuel b. R. Isaac, who maintains that there are two possible spots on the head on which phylacteries may be worn. In (F), the opposing positions are explained in terms of whether the Sabbath is an appropriate time to wear phylacteries.

It is notable that in the later strata the possibility that the rulings in the mishnah reflect a concern for intention is for the first time introduced in reference to a case where intention had not already been mentioned in a related tannaitic ruling.[68] Section (G) suggests that all agree that the *mitzvah* of phylacteries applies on the Sabbath; the dispute between the anonymous opinion of the mishnah and R. Gamliel turns on whether intention is required in the performance of *mitzvot*: the former maintains that the performance of rituals does not require intention. Consequently, when one wears one set of phylacteries in order to save them, he fulfills his obligation and donning a second set violates the prohibition of adding on to biblical requirements. R. Gamliel holds intention is necessary and so long as one does not intend to perform the obligation, the two pairs of phylacteries are viewed as mere ornamental attire permitted to be worn on the Sabbath.[69]

Two more possibilities are offered as to the source of this dispute. In (H) neither R. Gamliel nor the anonymous Sages requires intention when performing *mitzvot*; their argument is understood as whether intention is necessary to be guilty of adding to commandments, recalling Rava's reported distinction in B. Rosh Hashana 28b. The anonymous opinion maintains that one is guilty even without intention, so wearing an additional set is prohibited. R. Gamliel rules that one does not incur liability without intention, thus one may wear two sets, so long as the intent is only to save the lost phylacteries, not to perform the *mitzvah* of wearing the second set. In (I) the opinions agree that if one adds a second set of phylacteries at the set time of the *mitzvah*, one violates the prohibition of adding to the *mitzvot*; the disagreement centers on whether this is also true if one adds a second set at some other time. Both (H) and (I) affirm

---

68 Friedman therefore does not address this passage in *Talmudic Studies*.
69 See MS Munich 95, *supra* n. 63.

that intention is not required in the performance of *mitzvot*; in these strata it is no longer considered a matter of dispute but an accepted principle.

Although it is characteristic of the anonymous strata to present multiple interpretive possibilities without this necessarily being indicative of different redactional layers,[70] this *sugya* does appear to consist of multiple layers of material from different periods.[71] The earliest layer (A, B) is based on existing tannaitic and amoraic statements which understand the opposing positions in the mishnah to reflect concerns specific to the laws of Sabbath and phylacteries—interpretations which conform to both the context and plain sense of the mishnah. In the subsequent layers (C-F), different elements are introduced, but they are still confined to local concerns of Sabbath and phylacteries. These layers might date either from a period before *mitzvot ein tzerikhot kavvanah* was formulated, or before it had attained its status as an independent principle that redactors could apply to cases that do not explicitly address intention. In the next stage (section G), the principle had been formulated in B. Rosh Hashana and here it is introduced into an unrelated tannaitic debate regarding phylacteries. At this stage, *mitzvot ein tzerikhot kavvanah* is considered a matter of disagreement between the conflicting rulings of the anonymous first opinion of the mishnah and R. Gamliel. The final sections (H-I) may be from a later stage when *mitzvot ein tzerikhot kavvanah* was no longer in dispute, and because the *sugya* in B. Rosh Hashana discussed above had connected it to the prohibition of adding to precepts, this mishnaic debate is likewise understood to turn on whether intention is necessary in transgressing "you shall not add."

3 Rava's Ruling in Context

3.1 *The Bavli Context: Intent in Tort Law and Religious Violations*

We have seen a clear shift from tannaitic law to the Bavli's approach to *mitzvot*. Both the Mishnah and Tosefta require intention in the performance of specific rituals, and this view persists until the third generation of Amoraim. In the fourth generation, Rava departs from the tannaitic view, dispensing with intention in the case of *shofar*, despite the mishnah's explicit injunction. The Bavli's redactors subsequently articulate a general principle regarding all

---

70 Moscovitz, *Talmudic Reasoning*, chap. nine; Rubenstein, *The Culture of the Babylonian Talmud*, 43–48.
71 For another example, see Halivni, *Meqorot U-Mesorot: Erubin and Pesahim*, 348–51.

religious obligations, attributing the principle to Rava, and thenceforth seek to reconcile it with contradictory mishnayot. Later generations of redactors apply the principle to explain seemingly unconnected tannaitic debates. In sum, Rava, followed by the redactors, depart dramatically from tannaitic law by introducing the novel idea that ritual obligations may be fulfilled without a corresponding intention to perform them.

The Bavli offers no hint as to why Rava and the anonymous redactors influenced by his approach came to regard ritual performance so differently from other aspects of law. Indeed, despite the fact that it offers a statement attributed to him that explicitly juxtaposes and contrasts fulfilling and violating *mitzvot* ("Intention is not required to fulfill, but intention is required to transgress," B. Rosh Hashana 28b) at no point is such a view questioned as being inconsistent. Yet the dictum encapsulates a divergence that at this point is well attested to. The first half restates the principle *mitzvot ein tzerikhot kavvanah*, while the latter reflects Rava's consistent view seen in the previous chapter requiring intent in order to establish liability in a range of cases: in tort law, an intent to harm; in the laws of Sabbath, intent to do a forbidden action; and in laws of idolatry and martyrdom, the intent to commit (or cause another to commit) a transgression. We thus face a puzzling divergence of views in Rava's jurisprudence (or at least as formulated by the redactors), which on the one hand places great emphasis on intention for violating the law, and on the other hand diminishes the importance of intention in performing religious obligations.

An intriguing possibility for understanding this bifurcation begins with our discussion in the previous chapter which notes that something resembling Aristotelian conceptions of justice and moral blame appear to underpin Rava's views on civil law and religious violations. In Aristotelian justice, legal liability is inexorably linked to moral blame which in turn is dependent on one's intention when acting. Rava may therefore require intention only when guilt and liability is being considered and hence the moral character of the actor is at issue. When it comes to the performance of rituals, by contrast, the character of the actor is not at stake nor are there punitive legal ramifications; it is only a question of whether he has performed the precept properly. This still leaves unanswered the question of why it is that in the performance of rituals intention need not be a factor—particularly when we are accustomed to think that the significance of a religious act depends to some extent on the motivations and intentions of the actor.

In this regard, the principle *mitzvot ein tzerikhot kavvanah* may anticipate the manner in which contemporary social theorists describe 'ritual' as a category of human activity uniquely characterized by the degree to which the meaning of actions is shaped, not by the intentions of a performer,[72] but by preexisting shared agreement within a culture as to when and how certain actions are performed.[73] Rather than necessitating a shared set of beliefs or convictions, rituals are performative entities in which the internal thought processes and intentions of the participants are inconsequential.[74] So long as it is performed correctly, a ritual is valid and carries the collectively held meanings associated with it. In other words, unlike injurious acts or violations, which are morally and religiously problematic when they reflect the inner states of the actor, the physical performance of a *mitzvah* itself carries an inherent religious meaning regardless of intent or lack thereof. Having established that for Rava intent was a legal concept around which many rulings turn, in light of this we can account for why it is that these rulings turn in opposite directions depending on whether the category is ritual obligations on the one hand, or tortious conduct and violations on the other.

In the section that follows, we will explore intention in Zoroastrian texts, against which this bifurcation of ritual from other areas of law comes into even starker relief. We will then turn to Christian monastic texts which display a similar trend toward relegating the religious significance of intention, suggesting that the influence of *mitzvot ein tzerikhot kavvanah* in the Bavli does find parallel in other religious traditions developing during roughly the same period.

3.2 Cultural Context: Zoroastrian and Monastic Texts

As noted in Chapter 1, the increasing stress on intention in ritual violations and tort law parallels trends in contemporaneous Zoroastrian law.[75] Yet where Rava's influential approach to fulfilling ritual obligations diverges, the same

---

72 In his study of ancient Indian Vedic rituals, Fritz Stall explains that ritual's significance lies in "what you do, not what you think, believe, or say" and is "pure activity without meaning or goal." Stall, "The Meaninglessness of Ritual," 4–9.

73 Bell, *Ritual Theory, Ritual Practice*, 183–87. Seligman et al., Ritual and Its Consequences, 20–26, explain that the uniform practice of ritual creates an illusion of a potential ideal of order and uniformity among its participants, making the performance of the act and the illusion it creates significant, since the ritual's actions shape reality and produce meaning.

74 Harvey Whitehouse argues that there is no place for intention in rituals and that when there is intention, the ritual loses its meaning as such, instead becoming the actor's own creation; Whitehouse, "Theorizing Religions Past," 224–25.

75 For another example, only in later Zoroastrian works could one perform a vicarious *barashnum* purification ritual for the impure soul of a deceased person, even though the latter underwent no physical purification process him/herself. Early Zoroastrian texts, conversely, require physical cleansing. de Jong, "Purification in Absentia," 313–17; see also Kiel, "Cognizance of Sin and Penalty in the Babylonian Talmud and Pahlavi Literature: A Comparative Analysis" and his bibliography in n. 4.

is not true in Zoroastrian Pahlavi texts. Shaul Shaked has collected several Zoroastrian Pahlavi sources which consistently deem ritual acts and religious behavior to be valid only when performed with proper intention; otherwise, the action is rendered meaningless.[76] One telling passage from the *Šāyest nē-Šāyest* (*ŠnŠ*)[77] supplementary texts states:

> The decision is this: whoever wittingly consecrates a *dron* [sacred bread] with an unpurified *barsom* [ritual bundle] … or whoever consecrates it negligently and without knowledge, it should be regarded as not having been recited.[78]

The latter portion of this text invalidates one's recitation of the Avesta blessing if it is done negligently or ignorantly,[79] indicating that intention is a necessary element of this ritual. A similar sentiment is expressed in *ŠnŠ* 10.6, which criticizes one who recites the Gathas *pad rah* (lit. on the way), which Shaked explains to mean without concentration.[80] Doing the act in such a manner implies that there was a degree of intention to act, but not to perform the ritual. Recall that in Rava's similar case of blowing a shofar to make music instead of performing the *mitzvah*, he considers the obligation discharged.

The *Dēnkard*[81] likewise issues several rulings requiring proper intention in the performance of religious and meritorious acts — for instance: "They held this too: One who does a good deed for the sake of these four things, it is no virtue to him: sinful fame, concupiscence, disgrace, or the fear of another person."[82] (This also recalls the reverse case discussed by Rava and Abaye of one who commits idolatry due to "love-and-fear" discussed in Chapter 3). Furthermore, *Bundahišn* 14.11 states more generally that Ohrmazd, the supreme

---

76 Shaked, "Religious Actions."
77 *Šāyest nē-Šāyest*, Proper/Improper, is a ninth- or tenth-century code, based on earlier works.
78 *ShnSh* Suppl. 14, as cited in Shaked, "Religious Actions," 412.
79 Following Shaked, who interprets this line as depicting two alternative invalid recitations.
80 Shaked, "Religious Actions," 407, n. 15. See also *Nērangestān*, vol. 2: Fragard 1 Ch. 3, which invalidates recitations of sacred texts if the reciters do not pay attention to one another.
81 *Dēnkard*, "Acts of the Religions," though redacted in an Islamic milieu, draws from and preserves Sasanian and more ancient traditions. Shaked, *The Wisdom of the Sasanian Sages: Dēnkard VI*, xvii.
82 Book 6:54. Shaked, 21. See also *Dēnkard* 6: 1,a,b (Shaked, 3.) E45 e (Shaked, 215.); E45g (Shaked, 215.) for similar sentiments expressing the importance of one's mindset and thoughts.

deity, charged the first people, (male) Mashe and (female) Mashyane, to not only act correctly but to maintain proper thoughts.[83]

Rava/the redactor's rejection of intention as a necessary component of ritual performance thus departs from both rabbinic precedent and prevailing Persian views on the nature of religious acts,[84] indicating that the bifurcation between ritual fulfillment and violations was a novel turn in religious jurisprudence.

A roughly contemporaneous analogue may be found, however, in monastic texts, which demonstrate a similar turn in thinking and hence a broader context in which to view this change.[85] Like Palestinian rabbinic texts concerning prayer, early monastic writings place great emphasis on proper intention. Among the similarities that Michal Bar-Asher Siegal discusses, both include descriptions of mental preparation for prayer and of postures that reflect submission and piety, and both ask whether it is preferable to pray quietly or audibly in order to best concentrate.[86] Similar to M. Berakhot 2:1's requirement that one "direct his heart" when reading the *Shema*, Isaac the Syrian states that reading biblical texts is inadequate; one must rather be "pure of heart."[87]

A shift occurs in the first half of the sixth century with *The Rule of Saint Benedict*, which places an emphasis on action, rather than thought. Despite drawing heavily from Cassian's *Institutes*, Benedict departs significantly.

---

[83] Though the tenth-century composition of the *Bundahišn* significantly postdates the Bavli traditions, it includes older Iranian traditions, including Old Avestan as well as Sasanian material that had been transmitted orally for centuries, and that were prevalent during the Sasanian (and Amoraic) period. See, Kiperwasser and Shapira, "Irano-Talmudica I," which describes several instances in which the Bavli includes textual formulations that are found in the *Bundahišn*.

[84] Rava is reported as combating prevalent Zoroastrian dogmas; see for example B. Berakhot 11a-b, where Rava's ruling reflects the anti-dualistic doctrine of Zoroastrian belief that appears in ŠnŠ 7:4. Rava also issues rulings throughout the Bavli that ostensibly respond to challenges posed by competing religions of his day, such as Zoroastrianism and Manichaeism. (Elman, "Hercules within the Halakhic Tradition," 14–17; Elman, "Acculturation to Elite Persian Norms in the Babylonian Jewish Community of Late Antiquity," 31–56.) *Nērangestān*, Fragard 2 Ch. 23.1 deems one who does not perform a ritual due to religious defiance a serious offender, whereas Rava maintains that one who consumes improperly slaughtered meat in order to "anger (God)" (*lehakhi's*) is a valid witness (B. Sanhedrin 27a). Nevertheless, as already noted, other rulings attributed to Rava reflect aspects of Sasanian-Zoroastrian thought; see Elman, "Toward an Intellectual History of Sasanian Law."

[85] See the Introduction for a discussion on the relevance of Christian monastic texts for the study of the Bavli.

[86] Bar-Asher Siegal, "Prayer," 69–71.

[87] Alfeyev and Diokleia, *The Spiritual World Of Isaac The Syrian*, 177.

Actions that for Cassian signal one's internal state are interpreted by Benedict as primary. While Cassian repeatedly distinguishes between technically correct behavior and true, inner piety,[88] Benedict emphasizes the former.[89] By the time of the Bavli's final stages of redactional activity, *The Rule of Saint Benedict* enjoyed wide popularity and was quite influential—in the eighth century Charlemagne ordered that all monasteries adopt it. It seems that the idea that intention was not necessary for the proper performance of ritual acts as embodied in the principle *mitzvot ein tzerikhot kavvanah*, though a departure from both rabbinic and Zoroastrian doctrine, was gaining currency in late antiquity.

4 Summary

In Rava's view, the import of an action is determined differently in different contexts. In the context of civil and criminal law, the meaning is determined by the intent of the person doing the action; in ritual, by contrast, it is determined purely by the mechanics of an action. Nonetheless, even in this area it seems that Rava never disregards intention entirely, for he appears to require that, at the very least, an actor be aware of performing a particular kind of action, even if not for the purpose of fulfilling a *mitzvah*. A person forced to eat *matzah* is still aware of doing that action, as is a person blowing the *shofar* to make music, sitting in a *sukkah*, or reading the *Shema*. Awareness that one is performing an act, coupled with the fact that it is objectively being done at an appropriate time and in a proper context, is adequate. The principle of *mitzvot ein tzerikhot kavvanah* thus redefines the Mishnah's requirement of *kivein libo* (directing one's heart) with respect to ritual fulfillment — not as intent to fulfill a precept, but as intent to perform a specific action. This definition of intention in the context of ritual actually mirrors that of Abaye's with regard to violations. So long as one is aware that one is performing an action (which happens to constitute a ritual), the meaning of the action is determined objectively by its context. *Mitzvot ein tzerikhot kavvanah* thus does not simply change the parameters of ritual fulfillment; it effectively reconceptualizes ritual such that it begins to emerge as a distinct category of activity.

---

88   Gibson, *The Conferences of John Cassian*, 7; Radding, *A World Made by Men*, 105.
89   Radding, *A World Made by Men*, 106. Radding describes the Benedictine Rule's emphasis on action in allowing boys into the monastery who had been brought by their parents, as opposed to Basil, who required that boys upon maturation take a vow of chastity before witnesses to ensure that they entered the monastery willingly.

CHAPTER 5

Views in the Bavli after Rava

1   Overview: The Late Amoraim and the Bavli's Redactors

In the previous chapter we saw how the Bavli's redactors formalized Rava's innovative ruling regarding *shofar* by articulating a general principle that they understood to be underlying it. Once formalized, the redactors then set about reconciling it with earlier conflicting opinions and applying it to other cases. This activity, characteristic of the Bavli's redactors more generally, is quite prominent in discussions that focus on intention.

Following the fourth generation's interest in the concept of intention, the final two generations of Amoraim (350–425) as well as the redactors of the anonymous strata[1] continue along similar lines with an expanded emphasis on intentionality. They also maintain many of the principles that Rava had established and apply them to other aspects of law. Like Rava, they adopt positions of Amoraim from the Land of Israel that had been rejected by earlier Babylonian Sages. The Bavli's redactors similarly continue to sustain the positions promulgated by Rava as they formulate distinct legal principles and apply them to a widening range of cases.[2] Although some of this was described in earlier chapters in the framework of the relevant *sugyot* under examination, it is worth revisiting these briefly in order to highlight the activities of later generations and locate these strata in the context of several *sugyot* not yet discussed.

2   Rava's Students

2.1   *Continuity*

Given his prominence in shaping rabbinic jurisprudence, it is no surprise that Rava's students accept and apply his views on intention in many areas. We already noted in the first chapter that in the Bavli's discussion of M. Bava Qama 3:1 (exempting one who stumbles over and breaks a jug left in a public thoroughfare), Amoraim from the fifth and sixth generations exempt the pedestrian in accordance with the plain sense of the mishnah, reinterpret earlier

---

1 See Introduction, n. 4 regarding the dating of the redactional strata.
2 This is a general trend that Moscovitz described in Moscovitz, *Talmudic Reasoning*.

positions which rule otherwise, and draw on Palestinian traditions paralleling those found in the Yerushalmi.[3] Later sages similarly follow Rava's positions in other cases involving torts as we pointed out in prior chapters.[4]

In the laws of the Sabbath, the principle, *davar she-ein mitkavvein*,[5] also gains wide acceptance among subsequent generations. R. Ashi, of the sixth generation applies *davar she-ein mitkavvein* to explain tannaitic rulings and repeatedly invokes it as the crux of a debate between the Tannaim R. Simeon and R. Judah.[6]

Turning to ritual obligations, we saw that the position of Rava and his followers which discounts the need for intention fundamentally reverses the dominant conception of ritual fulfilment—shifting the emphasis from a necessary conjunction of intention and action, to a largely performative activity. Even in the laws of sacrifices, where proper intention is an explicit factor in mishnaic and earlier Talmudic law,[7] Ravina, a sixth-generation student of Rava reports his teacher's ruling that an animal offered without the intent that it serve as a particular sacrifice still discharges its owner's obligation.[8] Relatedly, R. Ashi maintains that if a person merely contemplated doing a positive commandment but was unavoidably prevented from doing so, he is credited as if he had actually fulfilled it.[9]

2.2 Innovation: Manslaughter

Fifth- and sixth-generation sages not only consider the intention of actors in cases where Rava does, they also factor it into cases where he does not. In one example R. Ada son of Ahava,[10] another student of Rava, appears to reverse generations of Babylonian precedent by following the minority opinion regarding one who intends to kill one person but kills another instead (as described in M. Sanhedrin 9:2). The immediate context is whether the owner of an ox

---

3   B. Bava Qama 27b.
4   B. Bava Metzia 96b–97a, B. Bava Qama 62a.
5   See Chapter 3, 3.2.
6   B. Sukkah 33b; B. Keritut 20b. See Kalcheim, "Davar Sh'ain Mitkaven," 118–23.
7   The first four chapters of M. Zebahim particularly 4:6 list six thoughts the officiating priest must have when offering a sacrifice. See Rosen-Zvi, "The Mishnaic Mental Revolution," 46–51.
8   B. Zebahim 2b. This is inferred from M. Zebahim 1:1 ("all sacrifices which were offered not according to their name are valid, but do not discharge the owner's obligation.") From this Rava infers that it is disqualifying because it is brought in the name of another offering—implying that if it is brought without any qualification it discharges the owner's obligation.
9   B. Berakhot 6a.
10   In B. Bava Batra 22a. R. Ada is reported as having been a student of Abaye, left to study with Rava, and encouraged others to follow suit. For an extended discussion on R. Ada b. Ahava's hostile attitude towards Abaye, see Kalmin, *Sages, Stories*, 34.

that gores a pregnant woman is obligated to pay for the loss of the fetus. The final part of the *sugya* cites Rava and Abaye's understanding of the biblical case of two men in a fight who strike a pregnant woman, causing her to miscarry. Exodus 21:22 states: "When men fight and hurt a pregnant woman so that her offspring come out, and there is no mishap (*ason*), he shall be punished in accordance with what her husband shall impose, and it will be given over to adjudication."[11] Abaye and Rava are cited as interpreting this verse as follows:

(A) אביי ורבא דאמרי תרויהו אנשים ולא אסון באשה נענשין יש אסון לא יענשו ...

(B) מתקיף לה רב אדא בר אהבה אטו באסון תליא מ[י]לתא בכוונה תליא מ[י]לתא

(C) אלא אמ' רב אדא בר אהב' אנשים כי נתכוונו זה לזה אף על גב דיש אסון באשה יענשו נתכוונו לאשה עצמה לא יענשו ...

(D) וכן כי אתא רב חנא מדרומא אתא ואיתי מתניתא בידיה כותיה דרב אדא בר אהבה

(A) Abaye and Rava both said: [With regard to 'when] men [fight'] if there is no *ason* to the woman, they are punished [with monetary damages]. If there is *ason* [to the woman], they will not be punished (monetarily) ...

(B) R. Ada b. Ahava objected:[12] is the matter dependent on *ason*? [Rather] it is dependent on intention (*kavvanah*).

(C) Rather, R. Ada b. Ahava said: 'men' when they intend [to strike and kill] each other, even if there is *ason* to the woman, they are punished [to pay for the loss of the fetus]. If they intend [to strike and

---

11 Translation follows Sarna, *JPS: Exodus*, 125. This verse is particularly ambiguous for it does not elucidate to whom the *ason* occurs or what it entails. It has therefore been subject to various interpretations, with some assigning the mishap to the loss of the fetus at different stages in its development (Septuagint Exodus 21:22–25; Philo, *The Special Laws* III: 108–109), and others relating it to the life of the mother (Vulgate Exodus 21:22–25; Josephus, *Jewish Antiquities* 4:278–280; *Mekhilta de-Rabbi Ishmael*, *Neziqin* 8: ולא יהיה אסון באשה "And there is no mishap ..." to the woman; *Mekhilta de-Rabbi Shimon b. Yohai*, 21). The latter interpretation parallels that of Abaye and Rava. For a discussion of the history of interpreting this passage, see Kugel, *The Bible as it Was*, 395–99.

12 Halivni notes that this question was likely not raised by R. Ada b. Ahava but was constructed by the redactors in order to explain why he dissented from the position of Rava and Abaye. Halivni, *Mekorot U-Mesorot: Baba Kama*, 161–62. Indeed, many of the medieval commentators struggled with how to understand R. Ada's question and interpretation (Rashi, *ad loc.* s.v. *attu*; Ra'avad *ad loc.*, Rashba *ad loc.* s.v. *matqif*, *Shita Mequbetzet ad loc.* s.v. *ve-zeh lashon HaRa'avad*).

kill] the woman herself, they are not punished [to pay for the loss of the fetus] ...

(D) And likewise, when R. Hanna[13] came from the south, he came and brought a teaching, like that of R. Ada b. Ahava.[14]

Rava and Abaye rule in this case that compensation for the loss of the fetus is dependent upon whether the pregnant bystander is killed (A). If the injury leads to her death they are exempt from paying, for as M. Ketubot 3:2 explicates (also based on Exodus 21:22), an offense that warrants the death penalty releases one from financial penalties stemming from the same action.[15] By contrast, if she survives but suffers a miscarriage, they are required to pay compensation.[16]

R. Ada b. Ahava counters that even if the woman is killed, damages for the loss of the fetus, while dependent on whether the combatants are liable the death penalty, hinges on their intention (C). If they intended to strike one another and killed her by accident, they do not receive capital punishment, but compensation is required; if they did intend to strike the woman they will receive the death penalty but are then exempt from monetary damages.

The underlying dispute between Rava and Abaye versus R. Ada is over which ruling of M. Sanhedrin 9:2 to follow:

נתכוון להרוג את הבהמה והרג את האדם לנכרי והרג את ישראל לנפלים והרג את בן קיימה פטור ... רבי שמעון אומר אפילו נתכוון להרוג את זה והרג את זה פטור

[If one] intended to kill an animal and killed a person; [or intended to kill] a non-Jew and killed a Jew; [or intended to kill] a premature infant

---

13 חגי] printed editions, Tosafot *ad loc.* s.v. *be-kavvanah*. חגא] MSS Vatican 116, Munich 95, Florence II I 7–9, Tosafot R. Samson of Sens as cited in *Shita Mequbetzet ad loc*.. חנא] MSS Hamburg, Escorial G-1-3.

14 B. Bava Qama 42a.

15 Medieval commentators understand this as resulting from the Bavli notion *qim leih be-de-rabbah mineih*, 'establish it like that which is greater than it' (B. Ketubot 33b; B. Gittin 53a; B. Bava Qama 71a; B. Makot 16a; B. Hullin 81b). Since they are guilty of a capital offense, they are exempt from paying for the loss of the fetus. See Rashi (*ad loc.* s.v. *ella*) and *Hiddushei Ha-Rashba* (*ad loc.* s.v. *matqif*).

16 It is unclear whether the monetary compensation is for the loss of the fetus or for the injury to the woman; this Bavli passage clearly assumes the former. A tradition by Rabbi Judah the Prince reported in *Mekhilta de-Rabbi Ishmael*, *Neziqin* 8 (discussed below), maintains that the penalty is for both. Philo and Josephus list two separate payments; one makes compensation for the loss to society and the other to the family of the injured party. See Josephus, *Jewish Antiquities* 4:278–280 and Philo, *The Special Laws* III: 108–109.

[that was not viable] and killed a viable baby, he is exempt[17] ... R. Simeon says, even [if he] intended to kill this one, and he killed that one, he is exempt.

Rava and Abaye appear to follow the anonymous first opinion cited in the mishnah, which only exempts in a case where killing the intended person would not have incurred the death penalty.[18] As Rashi notes, R. Ada must follow R. Simeon who always exempts one who intends to kill one person and kills another instead.

R. Ada's position is striking not only because he disagrees with his teacher, but because it departs from what appears to be the consensus of the Bavli. In all discussions of M. Sanhedrin 9:2, the anonymous opinion is identified as the majority view and is not questioned, whereas R. Simeon's opinion is said to be in discord with M. Bava Qama 4:6 and requires justification.[19]

However, R. Ada's greater emphasis on intention finds precedent in earlier teachings from the Land of Israel; as the *sugya* itself concludes with R. Hanna citing a *baraita* which accords with his view (D). Indeed, if we look at the Yerushalmi's treatment of M. Sanhedrin 9:2 (Y. Sanhedrin 27a) we find that it emphasizes R. Simeon's opinion, which is reported to be the view adopted by both Rabbi (R. Judah the Prince) and R. Nathan.[20] This is confirmed by

---

17   In rabbinic law, none of these intended targets would result in capital punishment, though it is nonetheless forbidden (see Mekhilta de-Rabbi Ishmael Mishpatim 4:17 and Schiffman, "Legislation Concerning Relations with Non-Jews in the 'Zadokite Fragments' and in Tannaitic Literature," 381. On the lack of death penalty for the killing of a gentile, see T. Avoda Zara 8:9).

18   Nevertheless, Rava's position is somewhat unclear, since on B. Sanhedrin 79b, he highlights a tradition taught by the house of Hezeqiah, which does not distinguish between intentional and unintentional acts of manslaughter. Rava, or the redactors on his behalf, explain this tradition as exonerating one who intends to kill one person but kills another person instead from both capital and monetary punishment and as therefore in accordance with the view of R. Simeon, (see also B. Bava Qama 35a). A similar teaching in the name of Hezeqiah appears in Y. Ketubot 27c, but as opposed to the Bavli version, it only distinguishes between inadvertent and malicious killing, but not between intentional and unintentional.

19   B. Bava Qama 44b; B. Sanhedrin 79a; B. Ketubot 15a. R. Ada's interpretation also contradicts *Mekhilta de-Rabbi Shimon b. Yohai,* 21:22 which states: " 'When men fight' to treat one who does not intend [to kill] like one who does intend [to kill];" Vulgate Exodus 21:22–25; Josephus, *Jewish Antiquities* 4:278–280; and *Mekhilta de-Rabbi Ishmael, Neziqin* 8: ולא יהיה אסון, באשה, " 'And there is no mishap ...' to the woman." Moreover, it conflicts with the plain sense of the biblical verse which describes two fighting men, implying that any injury to the woman is unintended.

20   B. Sanhedrin 79b also aligns R. Simeon's ruling with another teaching of Rabbi along with the tradition by the house of Hezeqiah (*Supra* n.18).

Mekhilta de-Rabbi Ishmael, which includes an interpretation of Exodus 21:22 attributed to Rabbi that accords with R. Simeon:

וכי ינצו אנשים. למה נאמרה פרשה זו ...
רבי אומר, אם נתכוון להכות שונאו זה והכה אחר שהוא שונאו פטור
המתכוון להכות שונאו והכה אוהבו דין הוא שיהא פטור אבל בא הכתוב ללמדך
שחבל אשה לבעל ודמי וולדות לבעל וכל המתחייב מיתה פטור מן התשלומין

> 'When men fight': Why is this section set forth? ...
> Rabbi says: [Given that] one who aims to kill an enemy of his, but kills another who is likewise his enemy, is free [from capital punishment], [then in the case of] one who aims to kill his enemy (the man he is fighting) but kills his friend (the pregnant woman), perforce he should be free. Rather, Scripture comes to teach you that the compensation for injuries to a wife [is to be paid to] her husband, and [compensation for] miscarriage [is paid to] the husband; and that one who incurs the penalty of death is exempt from monetary compensation.[21]

Although Rabbi is less explicit about the role that intention plays, his opinion is consistent with R. Simeon, as the Yerushalmi claims, and it is formulated in such a way that it could well be the Palestinian tradition that R. Hanna brought in support of R. Ada. Like the latter, this tannaitic view maintains that where the quarreling men intend to strike one another but instead kill the woman, they do not receive capital punishment but pay compensation for the fetus.

As noted throughout this study, a frequent characteristic of fourth- and fifth-generation Amoraim is their return to earlier traditions from the Land of Israel, in which intention plays a larger role in determining the law, and R. Ada here is no exception.[22] Rava and Abaye maintain the Bavli view (following the first opinion of M. Sanhedrin 9:2) that so long that one intends an act of murder punishable by death, the punishment holds irrespective of whether the victim was not the intended target. R. Ada by contrast revives the older Palestinian view, which requires an absolute correspondence between the intended act and the outcome.

3   The Redactors

The redactors frequently attempt to explicate the underlying reasons behind rulings of the Amoraim, and as we have seen, this is often accomplished by

---

21   Lauterbach, *Mekilta De-Rabbi Ishmael,* 3:62–63.
22   *Supra* Chapter 3, n 97.

introducing concepts pertaining to intentionality. For example, as discussed previously, in tannaitic law the validity of a *sukkah* is based on its physical structure. Although Beit Shammai invalidates an "old *sukkah*" which is not built *le-shem hag,* "for the sake of the holiday" (M. Sukkah 1:1), in the Yerushlami it is indicated that this is due to the practical concern that it will not be constructed in accordance with the specifications required for the festival.[23] In the Bavli's discussion, by contrast, Beit Shammai's position is explained by the redactors as reflecting a requirement of intention when constructing the *sukkah*.[24]

We have also noted previously that the redactors frequently follow Rava's positions with regard to intention and apply them to explain other, seemingly unrelated, earlier rulings. This was exemplified in the discussion of *mitzvot ein tzerikhot kavvanah,* where the redactors formulate this principle based on Rava's ruling and apply it to their elucidations of other areas of tannaitic law. In the remainder of this chapter we will examine some additional examples that display similar trends in redactional activity regarding other concepts pertaining to intention. In all these instances, the redactors continue to favor Rava's rulings (as opposed to Abaye's), transform them into distinct legal principles, and apply them in a range of cases.

3.1 *Intent to Derive Benefit/Pleasure:* Davar She-ein Mitkavvein *and* Hana'at Atzmo

Although Rava initially formulates the principle of *davar she-ein mitkavvein* with respect to the violation of the Sabbath, the redactors apply it to cases throughout the Bavli even in areas unrelated to the laws of the Sabbath and as a means of narrowing cases to more specific circumstances in order to resolve both tannaitic and amoraic disputes.[25] As discussed above, Abaye exempts one who receives forbidden pleasure against his will, while Rava deems him guilty. Although, as discussed in Chapter 3, their original debate likely centered on one who willingly enters a state, the redactors offer two possibilities as to the source of their disagreement, both of which reflect the principle of *davar she-ein mitkavvein* and whether the offender could have avoided benefiting from a prohibited source (such as incense offered to an idol):[26]

---

23 Y. Sukkah 4b, 1:2.
24 B. Sukkah 9a. *Supra* Chapter 2, n. 74.
25 See Kalcheim, "Davar Sh'ain Mitkaven," chap. Four. Kalcheim describes how the redactors applied *davar she-ein mitkavvein* in a variety of ways in order to explain unrelated tannaitic and amoraic disputes. For example, B. Beitzah 23a; B. Bekhorot 24b, 25a; B. Zebahim 91b, 99a; B. Shabbat 50a-b, 81b, B. Nazir 42a; B. Yebamot 4b.
26 B. Pesahim 25b-26b. We discussed this case in Chapter 3 section 6.2.

איתמר הנאה הבאה לו לאדם בעל כרחו אביי אמר מותרת ורבא אמר אסורה אפשר וקא מיכוין, לא אפשר וקמיכוין כולי עלמא לא פליגי דאסיר. לא אפשר ולא מיכוין כולי עלמא לא פליגי דשרי. כי פליגי דאפשר ולא מיכוין. ואליבא דרבי יהודה דאמר דבר שאין מתכוין אסור כולי עלמא לא פליגי דאסור.
כי פליגי אליבא דרבי שמעון דאמר דבר שאין מתכוין מותר
אביי כרבי שמעון
ורבא אמר עד כאן לא קא אמר רבי שמעון אלא היכא דלא אפשר אבל היכא דאפשר לא

It was said: [As to forbidden] benefit that comes to a person against his will:

Abaye said: it is permitted; Rava said: it is forbidden.

Where it is possible [to avoid it] and he intends [to benefit, or] if it is impossible [to avoid it] yet he intends [to benefit], none dispute that it is forbidden. If it is impossible [to avoid] and he does not intend [to benefit], none dispute that it is permitted. They differ where it is possible [to avoid it] and he does not intend [to benefit]; on the view of R. Judah, who ruled, *davar she-ein mitkavvein*, (an unintended act) is forbidden, none dispute that it is forbidden.

They differ on the view of R. Simeon, who maintained *davar she-ein mitkavvein* is permitted:

Abaye [rules] as R. Simeon (it is permitted).

But Rava says: R. Simeon rules thus only where it is impossible [to avoid], but where it is possible, no (it is not permitted).

Both Rava and Abaye ascribed to R. Simeon the position that in a case which is classified as *davar she-ein mitkavvein* one is not liable for having violated the Sabbath. Their point of disagreement is what constitutes a case of *davar she-ein mitkavvein*. Where one intentionally enjoys that which is prohibited, both Rava and Abaye were presumed to agree that R. Simeon maintained that one is liable, whether or not he could have avoided the forbidden activity. Since he willingly enjoys that which is prohibited, his action does not fall under the category of *davar she-ein mitkavvein*. Conversely, where there is no possibility of avoiding the prohibited pleasure and one does not intend to partake of it, one is exempt from violating the prohibition. They are also reputed to agree that R. Judah, whom they view to impose guilt even where one lacks intention, would have also deemed one liable where he is able to remove himself from the prohibited pleasure even if he does not intend to derive benefit from it. Their dispute was thus explained to be regarding a case in which one could have avoided the prohibited pleasure yet did not intend to enjoy it. For Rava, since the prohibited pleasure could have been avoided, his act does not qualify for R. Simeon's absolution of *davar she-ein mitkavvein*. Abaye, by contrast, maintains that since there was no intention, his act constitutes a case of *davar she-ein mitkavvein* and thus no violation has occurred.

An alternative rendering is then offered:

איכא דאמרי אפשר ולא מיכוון היינו פלוגתייהו דרבי יהודה ורבי שמעון לא
אפשר ולא קא מיכוון כולי עלמא לא פליגי דשרי
כי פליגי דלא אפשר וקא מיכוון
ואליבא דרבי שמעון דאזיל בתר כוונה כולי עלמא לא פליגי דאסור כי פליגי
אליבא דרבי יהודה דאמר לא שנא מתכוין ולא שנא שאין מתכוין אפשר אסור.
אביי כרבי יהודה
ורבא אמר לך עד כאן לא קאמר רבי יהודה שאין מתכוין כמתכוין אלא
לחומרא, אבל מתכוין כשאין מתכוין לקולא לא

> There are those who say: If it is possible [to avoid the prohibited benefit], and he does not intend [to benefit], that is [the case of] the controversy between R. Judah and R. Simeon. If it is impossible [to avoid], and he does not intend [to benefit], none dispute that it is permitted.
>
> They differ where it is impossible [to avoid] and he intends [to benefit].
>
> On the view of R. Simeon, who follows the intention, none dispute that it is forbidden. They differ on the view of R. Judah, who maintained: It makes no difference whether he intends or does not intend, if it is possible [to avoid] it is forbidden.
>
> Abaye rules as R. Judah (as long as he cannot avoid it, it is permitted).
>
> Rava would say: R. Judah rules that the unintentional is the same as the intentional only [in the direction] of stringency, but he did not rule that the intentional is the same as the unintentional [where it results in] leniency.

In this second explanation, Rava and Abaye's dispute centers on R. Judah's position. The redactors took it for granted that R. Judah disagreed with R. Simeon over the principle of *davar she-ein mitkavvein* and that he maintained that unintentional violations are treated the same as intentional ones. Rava and Abaye's dispute was understood to be regarding the reverse: Are intentional violations treated the same as unintentional ones in a case in which the prohibited pleasure cannot be avoided? The redactors conjecture that in this case both Rava and Abaye agreed that R. Simeon regarded such a person as culpable since intention is the deciding factor in determining liability. Their point of disagreement is in terms of R. Judah's position in this case and how far he applied his notion of treating unintentional acts the same as intentional ones. Abaye understood R. Judah's position to be based on whether one can avoid the prohibited pleasure, despite the presence of intention. Hence, where the prohibition cannot be avoided, the actor is exempt. Rava was understood to maintain that R. Judah only treated unintentional acts the same as intentional ones when it results in a stringent ruling. Thus, even though the prohibited pleasure is received against the will of the actor, he is liable since he willingly enjoys it. Following the two redactional interpretations of their debate, Rava and Abaye are each attributed as bringing tannaitic support for their respective rulings.[27]

As already discussed in Chapter 3, these two interpretations appear only in the redactional layer and show a great level of complexity, making it unlikely that either underlies their positions.[28] The redactors applied *davar she-ein mitkavvein* to this debate, though at its heart, the dispute is likely not concerned with the concept. What is more, this passage broadens the application of *davar she-ein mitkavvein* to idolatry.

The redactors also relate to *davar she-ein mitkavvein* in the following passage from tractate Ketubot regarding whether it is permitted to have intercourse for the first time on the Sabbath, which will likely result in rupturing the hymen. This would cause two violations of the Sabbath, drawing blood and creating an opening. The redactors pose the following questions:

(A) איבעיא להו מהו לבעול בתחלה בשבת ... ואם תימצי לומר לדם הוא צריך ופתח ממילא קאתי הלכה כר"ש דאמר דבר שאין מתכוין מותר או הלכה כרבי יהודה דאמר דבר שאין מתכוין אסור ...

(B) איכא דאמרי ואם תימצי לומר דם חבורי מיחבר לדם הוא צריך ואסור או דלמא להנאת עצמו הוא צריך ושרי ואם תימצי לומר להנאת עצמו הוא צריך ודם ממילא קאתי הלכה כרבי יהודה או הלכה כר"ש ...

> (A) They inquired, what is [the law] regarding cohabitating for the first time on the Sabbath; ... And if you will say it is the blood he is

---

27 According to Halivni, these are redactional additions. Halivni, *Meqorot U-Mesorot: Erubin and Pesahim*, 344–45.

28 Shaul Kalcheim has pointed to several indicators of the redactional origins of this passage including the variants among text witnesses and the inconsistent meaning of "it is impossible [to avoid], and he intends [to receive the forbidden pleasure]" throughout the *sugya*. He also notes that Rava's and Abaye's proof texts only discuss cases of receiving benefit and not the presence or absence of intention and that the redactional interpretations mirror other *sugyot* in the Bavli, (e.g. B. Shabbat 29b), indicating that they were likely grafted from there. Kalcheim, "Davar Sh'ain Mitkaven," 131–41.

concerned with [lit. he needs] (to prove that she is a virgin) and the opening comes of itself, is the law according to R. Simeon who says an unintended act is permitted[29] or is the law like R. Judah who says an unintended act is forbidden ...

(B) There are those who say: if you will say [that the] blood [is the result of] a wound, is it the blood he is concerned with and it is [therefore] forbidden, or perhaps is it his own pleasure he is concerned with and it is permitted? And if you are able to say that he is concerned with his own pleasure and the blood comes of itself, is the law like R. Judah or is the law like R. Simeon? ...[30]

In attempting to resolve the issue, the redactors take for granted a number of ideas that were maintained by Rava. As in the previous case, they assume (A) the principle of *davar she-ein mitkavvein* and that it applies to this case (as Rava does on B. Ketubot 6b), along with Rava and Abaye's proposal that R. Simeon and R. Judah disputed over it. In the second rendering (B), the redactors apply a phrase employed by Rava in another context "for his own pleasure," where it similarly is concerned with the purpose of a sexual act.

As discussed in Chapter 3, Rava suggests that Esther was permitted to cohabit with a non-Jew, Ahashverosh, though this was a violation that would normally mandate martyrdom, since the act of coercion was motivated by the non-Jew's intention to receive sexual pleasure rather than a desire to force her to violate Jewish law.[31] The redactors here employ the same term to suggest that one should be permitted to engage in intercourse for the first time on the Sabbath since the intention is directed at receiving pleasure and not drawing blood—a violation of the Sabbath. Rava's idea that the intention behind a sexual act (at least for a man) is pleasure might have been limited to the case of martyrdom under discussion, but the redactors clearly see it as a broader notion—one that perhaps defines the purpose of a sexual act in all cases.

A similar logic by which an act is redefined as one motivated by sexual pleasure is found in other discussions in the anonymous strata. The redactors explain on behalf of Rava that the payment of *kofer*, 'atonement', an additional fine assessed when one's animal kills a person, is dependent on the intention behind the animal's act, a condition not found in earlier rulings. This is found in B. Bava Qama 40b, in conjunction with another teaching of R. Simeon who rules that where one's forewarned animal gores and kills a person, the owner

---

29 דאמר ... מותר] absent from MSS Vatican 112, Vatican 130.
30 B. Ketubot 5b.
31 B. Sanhedrin 74a-b, see Chapter 3, 4.2.2.

is required to pay the fine of *kofer* to the heirs of the victim.³² If, however, an animal sexually penetrates a woman, the owner is exempt. The opposing views of Rava and Abaye, along with the redactional understanding of them, are recorded to explain this ruling:

(A) היכי דמי אילימא דרבעה וקטלה מה לי קטלה ברביעה מה לי קטלה בקרניה
אלא דרבעה ולא קטלה הא דלא משלם את הכופר משום דלא קטלה הוא

(B) אמ' אביי לעולם דרבעה ולא קטלה ואתיוה לבי דינא וקטלוה
1. מהו דתימא דכמאן דקטלה איהו דמי

(C) רבא אמ' לעולם דרבעה וקטלה
1. ודקשיא לך מה לי קטלה ברביעה מה לי קטלה בקרניה קרן כוונתה להזיק רביעה אין כוונתו להזיק³³

(A) How is this like (i.e. what are the circumstances of the case)? If you will say that it penetrated her sexually and killed her, what [is the difference] to me if it kills through sexual penetration or kills with its horns? Rather [it is a case] in which it penetrated her sexually and did not kill her. [But if this is so, R. Simeon's ruling is obvious; the reason] that [the owner] does not pay atonement, is because it did not kill her (why then was it necessary for R. Simeon to issue the above ruling)?³⁴

(B) Abaye said: Really, [it is a case where] it penetrated her sexually but did not kill her, and she was brought to court (on charges of bestiality) and they executed her.
1. What might you have said? It is as if [the animal] killed her.

(C) Rava said: Really, [the case is one where the animal] penetrated her sexually and killed her.
1. And as for that which was a difficulty for you, 'what [is the difference] to me if it kills through sexual penetration or kills with its horns?' [When it kills with] horns, its intent is to harm, [when it kills through] sexual penetration, its intent³⁵ is not to harm.³⁶

---

32 R. Simeon's ruling is made explicit in M. Bava Qama 4:5.
33 להנאת עצמו] MSS Vatican 116, Munich 95, Florence II I 7–9, as well as both printed editions.
34 This question reflects the approach of the redactors towards earlier rabbinic statements, which assumes that no authority issued an unnecessary or redundant statement.
35 See n. 33.
36 B. Bava Qama 40b-41a.

The anonymous stratum (A) inquires into the ruling of R. Simeon, whether he was referring to a case of bestiality, and if so, whether in the course of the act the animal kills the woman involved; neither case seems to make sense on its face because indemnity is never tied to the means of death. Rava and Abaye are cited as offering competing explanations of R. Simeon's dictum. Abaye (B) maintains that R. Simeon's ruling refers to an instance in which the woman was not killed; accordingly, there is no obligation to pay indemnity. Apparently it is the redactors (B.1) who then clarify the necessity of R. Simeon's ruling:[37] since the woman was executed for bestiality, perhaps the animal should be responsible for her subsequent death, thereby obligating its owner to pay an indemnity. R. Simeon's ruling thus makes clear that no fine is required. This is consistent with our earlier examination of Abaye's position which focuses on actions and their consequences.

Rava, by contrast, (C) explains that R. Simeon's ruling exempts the owner from indemnity even where the animal kills the woman through the act of bestiality, thus indicating that death through sexual penetration is different from death through goring.[38] Again it is apparently the redactors (C.1) who explain on his behalf: "[When it kills with] horns, its intent is to harm, [when it kills through] sexual penetration, its intent is not to harm." While I have followed MS Hamburg, the majority of MSS, as well as printed editions, make the distinction more explicit: "[when it kills with] horns, its intent is to harm, [when it kills through] sexual penetration, its intent is for its own pleasure (*de-kavvanatah le-hana'at atzmo*)," which again culls from the language of Rava's decision in the case of Esther. The variations in the MSS in which this line appears is a sign of belonging to the more fluid redactional strata. Although this explanation was likely stated by the redactors, it is clear that this was seen as a running theme in Rava's rulings.

Goring is a violent act designed to kill or maim, and therefore we can attribute a degree of violent motive to the animal's actions. Conversely, the owner is absolved from indemnity when his animal kills a person through an act that was not intended to harm. For the redactors following in the vein of Rava, intention, even in the form of an instinctual motive on the part of an animal, determined liability for the penalty of *kofer*.[39]

---

[37] That the second half of the statement is a redactorial addition is indicated by the formulaic phrase "What might you have said" which opens it.

[38] This is characteristic of the way Rava and Abaye are often cited as resolving problematic tannaitic rulings. Henshke, "Abaye and Rava," 187–90.

[39] On the biblical treatment of the goring ox, see Finkelstein, "The Goring Ox," 180–82.

Similar logic is found in the redactorial explanation of the distinctiveness of the category of 'horn', one of the primary categories of damages:[40]

מאי שנא קרן דכונתו להזיק
How is [the category of] horn different? Its intent is to damage.[41]

As in the prior case, the redactors conceptualize the category of 'horn' as describing violent acts with malicious intent. Yet, in the case of an animal penetrating a woman, it appears as an explanation of the reason behind Rava's decision in that specific scenario; in this context, it has evolved into an independent conceptual definition underpinning the category of 'horn'.[42] In the redactional layer, the intention of an actor—even of an animal—explicitly becomes the defining feature of a class of damages.

4   Summary

The later generations of Amoraim who represent the students of Rava, as well as the Bavli's redactors, adopt a number of Rava's rulings and principles regarding intention. They reject a doctrine of strict liability and determine liability based on the intention of an actor. The redactors apply Rava's logic of absolving one who commits a transgression where it is done for the purpose of receiving pleasure and not violating a prohibition. They also continue to develop and expand principles introduced by him, making intention a relevant concept throughout many discussions in the Bavli, even in instances where it previously was not. Hence *davar she-ein mitkavvein* is both taken as a given and imposed on unrelated debates. The redactors further give explicit formulation to principles only inherent in Rava's rulings. While Rava was among the first to state that one need not have intention to discharge his obligation in fulfilling specific ritual and religious obligations, the redactors articulate an explicit principle in regard to all religious obligations—though they attribute it to Rava himself. They also apply it in their understanding of seemingly unconnected tannaitic debates. This all accords with the general development of conceptualization described by Moscovitz noted above.

---

40   See p. 19.
41   B. Bava Qama 2b, 5b, 26a.
42   Alternatively, if the redactors were the first to formulate this logic in defining the category of 'horn', they might have then applied it to explain Rava's explanation in the case of bestiality.

Conclusion: Intentionality in Rabbinic Law in Historical and Cultural Perspective

1   Transitions from Subjective to Objective Standards in Legal Thought

In this study we have seen that the idea of intention as a determinant of the legal ramifications of a person's actions was gradually incorporated into the thought of the Babylonian Amoraim. The early sages of the Bavli seemed to favor an objective system of strict liability, determining responsibility primarily based on the outcome of an action rather than the intent behind it, or in accord with standards of fault and negligence. Change begins during the third generation, when subjective considerations relating to the intentions of actors along with the concept of negligence were introduced, but rulings in line with strict liability were still prevalent.

During the fourth generation there was a dramatic shift evident in rulings attributed to Rava and Abaye. Rava is a pivotal figure because he consistently ruled based on the precise intent behind an action, and in many ways appears to subscribe to an Aristotelian view of moral blame. Rava's radical departure in regard to ritual fulfillment initially appears discordant with his overall approach, but as we argued, it may reflect a revised view of the nature of ritual taking shape at the time. In subsequent generations, the students of Rava, as well as the anonymous redactors, upheld his views and formulated new principles which established intentionality as a central concept in various areas of rabbinic law.

The shift from determining liability based on objective standards to a gradual incorporation of more subjective considerations among later generations has been observed across many legal systems in different cultures, as was mentioned in Chapter 1.

In Roman tort law, for example, the *Twelve Tables* (early Roman Republic; circa 509–527 BCE)[1] states that one who is observed wrongfully handling another's property is guilty of theft and liable to pay quadruple the value of the entire object that was touched, regardless of the amount that was taken, the intention behind his action, or whether the item was removed from the owner's domain.[2] In the sixth century, the *Digest of Justinian* points out some

---

[1]   Roman history is typically divided into three periods: 1) the Monarchy (753-509 B.C.E.); 2) the Republic (509–27 B.C.E.); and, 3) the Empire (27 B.C.E. to fifth century C.E. in the Western empire, and until 1453 C.E. in the Eastern Empire).
[2]   Watson, *The Spirit of Roman Law*, 30; VerSteeg, *Law in the Ancient World*, 345.

of the injustices that ensue from such a policy,[3] and cites rulings by multiple jurists who determine liability for theft based on the intention of the accused.[4] Similarly, a slave who is appointed as his owner's heir without an explicit grant of freedom, is considered by classical jurists to be neither his inheritor nor free.[5] By Justinian's time, however, a slave could become an heir even without an explicit grant of manumission if this is deemed to have been the intent of the testator.[6]

With regard to negligence, the second-century jurist Gaius (*Institutes*, Commentary III:211) recognizes malice and negligence, in contrast to much earlier Aquilian law (third century BCE), which imposes liability only if one directly kills another's slave or animal. Moreover, whereas Aquilian law understands 'unlawfully' to mean without rightful cause, according to Gaius, "to unlawfully kill is understood to mean with malicious intent (*dolus*) or through the negligence (*culpa*) of another."[7] As we saw in Chapter 2, the evolution of the term '*peshi'ah*' in the Bavli to mean negligence followed a similar path.

Another second to third-century Roman jurist, Paulus, discusses negligence in terms of adequate precaution. *Paulus on Sabinus, Book X*, (cited in *The Digest* Book IX, 2:31) offers the following definition:

> ... it is negligence when provision was not made by taking such precautions as a diligent man would have done, or warning was only given when the danger could not have been avoided.[8]

In *On the Edict, Book XXII* (cited in *The Digest Book IX*, 30:3) Paulus considers forces of nature that may or may not be anticipated, such as a "violent gust of wind."[9] Similar reasoning appears in *baraitot* recorded in the Bavli,[10] and as we saw in Chapter 2, in rulings attributed to Rabbah.[11]

---

3   E.g. *Digest* XLVI, 2.21pr., 5, 6,8, 9, 10; 22.1, 2; .2.40; 81pr, 1, 2; *Gaius* III.196; *Institutes of Justinian* Book IV: Title 1.6.
4   See cases cited in Watson, *The Spirit of Roman Law*, 102–3.
5   Moyle, *The Institutes of Justinian*, 70 Book II: Title XIV. 1.
6   Honoré, *Ulpian*; Watson, "Slavery"; Watson, "Morality, Slavery and the Jurists in the Later Roman Republic."
7   Scott, *The Civil Law*, 1 and 2:181; Watson, *The Spirit of Roman Law*, 31. Lex Aquilia dates from circa 287 BCE. Its three sections each discuss damage to property.
8   Scott, *The Civil Law*, 1 and 2:338.
9   Ibid.
10 See B. Bava Qama 29a, 55b.
11 B. Bava Qama 27a.

Even after concepts such as intention and negligence appeared in Justinianic and juristic law, these principles were not applied systematically or consistently.[12] Jurists primarily attended to interpreting the law and deciding an appropriate action or remedy on a case-by-case basis, without developing a systematic legal doctrine.[13] The doctrine of negligence was only later applied systematically to determine liability.[14] As such, the shift from objective to subjective standards was hardly a neat linear development,[15] and echoes of strict liability remained operative even during Justinian's time.[16] Again, as we observed in the development of the Bavli, the emergence of negligence and other subjective factors did not immediately displace all earlier objective standards.

In Chapter 1 we also saw cases in which Zoroastrian law followed a similar trajectory, with early jurisconsults appearing to espouse strict liability and later ones taking intention and level of fault into account. Mariah Macuch has similarly observed that the earliest evidence of negligence in extant Sasanian legal texts can be dated to Abarg, who lived roughly half a century after Rava.[17]

2   The "Evolution" of Legal Systems

Legal and social theorists once characterized this move from objective to subject considerations as a natural evolution from 'primitive' to 'complex'. Although this kind of generalization is now rejected as a category error (there is nothing intrinsically natural about a legal system),[18] transitions from objective

---

12 This pattern typifies Roman law, which has a low level of systematization despite its high level of conceptualization. Watson, *The Spirit of Roman Law*, 117–23.
13 Many of their rulings are *ad hoc* correctives for existing rules that were no longer applicable. Watson, 110.
14 Hallebeek, "Negligence in Medieval Roman Law," 74; Watson, *The Spirit of Roman Law*, 125–26.
15 Daube, *The Deed and the Doer*, 116. Daube also notes that the boundary between 'objective' and 'subjective' considerations is often blurred.
16 VerSteeg, *Law in the Ancient World*, 348.
17 The *Frahang ī Oīm*, a later text that defines Avestan terminology, presents *bōdōzed* for "deliberate offenses" and *kādōzed* for "injury caused by negligence"—although it is unclear whether these terms are accurate reflections of Sasanian law or later retrojections, making it difficult to pinpoint when the term for negligence entered Zoroastrian law (Elman, "Toward an Intellectual History of Sasanian Law," 37.) However, *bōdōzed* likely appears in the *Hērbedestān* 2.4.1 and in the Pahlavi *Vidēvdād* in the name of Neryōsang (dates unknown, but probably lived after Abarg). Elman, 53.
18 See Riles, *Rethinking the Masters of Comparative Law*.

to more subjective legal standards appears to be something of a regularity in legal history.[19]

David Daube suggests that this can be explained by recognizing that in their early phases, legal systems are characterized by weak mechanisms and a lack of authority to investigate subjective concerns such as intention. If claimants were not guaranteed ready compensation for damages, they might elect to resolve conflicts independently (or tribally) rather than engage the courts—which would both undermine the authority of the legal regime and often involve violence. Only once a judiciary system with broad authority becomes well established and is considered reliable does it have the space to consider subjective factors in determining liability.[20] Biblical law itself reflects this tension by simultaneously condoning familial reprisals for unintentional homicide while allowing suspects to take refuge in designated cities.[21] It is precisely inside cities where established courts have authority and the unintentional act of killing can be treated more leniently.

We speculated that these factors may help to explain why the early Babylonian Amoraim may have "reverted" to a framework of strict liability when their Palestinian counterparts, following what appears to be the dominant stream of tannaitic precedent, had already adopted a more subjective approach to tort law.

3   Intention and the Self

More recently, Lawrence Rosen, who likewise rejects evolutionary explanations of legal developments, has associated the rise of intention as a determinant of liability in medieval European law with the broader emergence, post Augustine, of inwardly focused conceptions of the self, centered on the internal experience of the individual.[22] A parallel trend in recent rabbinic scholarship

---

19   This also is congruent with Yochanan Muff's findings in his philological study of volition clauses in ancient Near Eastern deeds and in a later Seleucid formulary. He states, albeit with some hesitation, that "the later the literature - be it legal, religious, or literary, the greater the stress on inner states of mind, and in legal contexts in particular, the great constitutive importance of intent and volition." Muffs, *Love and Joy*, 145.
20   Daube, *The Deed and the Doer*, 33–34.
21   Numbers 35:9–29; Deuteronomy 19:1–13.
22   Rosen, *Law as Culture*, 53–57. Rosen makes this observation in regard to medieval European law, where a break from strict liability and the recognition of intent as a factor in assessing actions occurred in the eleventh century with the "discovery of the individual" and a concept of 'self' as divinely bestowed by God.

has sought to correlate a greater emphasis on intention with various notions of the self that emerged at roughly the same time in the late Greco-Roman period.[23] Joshua Levinson associates the rise of intention in tannaitic law and narrative with the "heightened focus on self-consciousness and a new concept of self that emerges in Stoic thought of the period."[24] Mira Balberg concurs and identifies in the mishnaic laws of impurity a construction of the self, similar to one shaped by Roman Stoic accounts of self-formation, attained through constant processes of self-examination—though as opposed to the latter whose interest in the self is ethical, for the Mishnah it is shaped by religious ideals.[25]

By contrast, Ishay Rosen-Zvi argues that the various requirements of intention and awareness present in aspects of tannaitic law simply do not entail a robust self-conception and focus on interiority.[26] The mental gestures that accompany actions are activities of the mind relating to the external world, rather than inwardly-focused processes of self-reflection. In her recent book, Ayelet Hoffmann Libson suggests that while Levinson's characterization of mishnaic law fails to demonstrate a turn toward an interior self, this does occur in the Bavli.[27] Yet it is not entirely clear that what underlies such instances of subjectivity in Bavli law is an emerging conception of the interior self rather than a more general recognition of forms of knowledge (e.g. bodily sensations, aesthetic revulsion) that are inherently subjective.

4 Intention, Argumentation, and Conceptualization

Whether the emergence of a late Stoic or Augustinian conception of the self is truly evidenced in these rabbinic texts, there is an unmistakable correlation between the development of more complex and abstract modes of rabbinic legal hermeneutics from the fourth generation of Amoraim onward, coupled with a greater concern with factors such as intention. The same rabbis who incorporate intention into their rulings are those whom David Kraemer characterizes as evincing "self-awareness, attention to reasons and justification, and concern for argumentation," in ways not found in statements attributed

---

23 See Taylor, *Sources of the Self*, 111–24; Levinson, "From Narrative Practice to Cultural Poetics," 346; Rosen-Zvi, "The Mishnaic Mental Revolution," 43–44.
24 Levinson, "From Narrative Practice to Cultural Poetics," 353.
25 Balberg, *Purity, Body, and Self in Early Rabbinic Literature*, 155; Balberg, "Recomposed Corporalities."
26 Rosen-Zvi, "The Mishnaic Mental Revolution."
27 Hoffman Libson, *Law and Self-Knowledge*.

to earlier sages.[28] We should then not be surprised to find that the emergence of an amoraic discourse interested in elucidating underlying reasoning is likewise increasingly concerned with the underlying intentions of the actors who are the subject of that discourse.

28   Kraemer, *The Mind of the Talmud*, 36–37.

Bibliography

Adiel, Schremer. "Stammaitic Historiography." In *Creation and Composition*, edited by Jeffrey Rubenstein, 219–35. Tübingen: Mohr Siebeck, 2005.

Albeck, Hanoch. *Introduction To The Mishna*. Jerusalem: Bialik Institute, 1959.

Albeck, Hanoch. *The Mishna: Seder Zeraim*. Jerusalem: Bialik Institute, Dvir Publishing House, 1957.

Albeck, Shalom. "Is there a Category of Intention in Talmudic Criminal Law?" *Qovetz Haziyonot Hadatit* 5 (2002): 460–71.

Aldrete, Gregory S. *Daily Life in the Roman City: Rome, Pompeii and Ostia*. Westport, CT: Greenwood Publishing Group, 2004.

Alfeyev, Hilarion, and Bishop Kallistos Ware of Diokleia. *The Spiritual World Of Isaac The Syrian*. Kalamazoo, MI: Cistercian Publications, 2000.

Amit, Aaron. *Talmud Ha-Igud: BT Pesahim Chapter IV with Comprehensive Commentary*. Edited by Shamma Friedman. Jerusalem: The Society for the Interpretation of the Talmud, 2009.

Aquinas, Thomas, M. S Gillet, and Angelo M Pirotta. *In decem libros Ethicorum Aristotelis ad Nicomachum expositio*. Torino: Marietti, 1934.

Aristotle. *Nichomachean Ethics*. Translated by Terence Irwin. Second edition. Indianapolis: Hacket Publishing Co., 1985.

Assis, Moshe. "A Fragment of Yerushalmi Sanhedrin." *Tarbiz* 46 (1977): 29–90.

Assis, Moshe. "The Jerusalem Talmud." In *The Classic Rabbinic Literature of Eretz Israel*, edited by Menahem Izhak Kahana, Vered Noam, Menahem Kister, and David Rosenthal, 1:225–60. Jerusalem; NY: Yad Ben Zvi Press, 2018.

Bailey, H. W. *Zoroastrian Problems in the Ninth-Century Books*. Second edition. Oxford: Oxford University Press, 1971.

Balberg, Mira. *Gateway to Rabbinic literature*. Raanana: The Open University Press, 2013.

Balberg, Mira. *Purity, Body, and Self in Early Rabbinic Literature*. Berkeley; Los Angeles; London: University of California Press, 2014.

Balberg, Mira. "Recomposed Corporalities." PhD, Stanford University, 2011.

Bar-Asher Siegal, Michal. *Early Christian Monastic Literature and the Babylonian Talmud*. Cambridge; NY: Cambridge University Press, 2013.

Bar-Asher Siegal, Michal. "Prayer in Rabbinic and Monastic Literature." In *Jewish Prayer*, edited by Uri Ehrlich, 63–77. Beer Sheva: Ben Gurion University Press, 2015.

Bazak, Jacob. "The Element of Intention in the Performance of Mitsvot Compared to the Element of Intention in Current Criminal Law." In *The Jewish Law Association Studies, XIV: The Jerusalem 2002 Conference Volume*, edited by Hillel Gamoran, 9–15. Binghamton: Global Academic Publishing, 2004.

Becker, Adam H. *Fear of God and the Beginning of Wisdom: The School of Nisibis and the Development of Scholastic Culture in Late Antique Mesopotamia*. Philadelphia: University of Pennsylvania Press, 2006.

Becker, Adam H. "Positing a 'Cultural Relationship' between Plato and the Babylonian Talmud." *Jewish Quarterly Review* 101, no. 2 (2011): 255–69.

Becker, Adam H. "The Comparative Study of 'Scholasticism' in Late Antique Mesopotamia: Rabbis and East Syrians." *AJS Review* 34, no. 1 (2010): 91–113.

Beer, Moshe. *Amora'ei Bavel: Peraqim Be-Hayei Kalkalah*. Ramat Gan: Bar Ilan University Press, 1974.

Bell, Catherine. *Ritual Theory, Ritual Practice*. NY: Oxford University Press, 1992.

Benovitz, Moshe. *Talmud Ha-Igud: BT Berakhot Chapter VI with Comprehensive Commentary*. Edited by Shamma Friedman. Jerusalem: The Society for the Interpretation of the Talmud, 2015.

Bokser, Baruch M. "Jacob N. Epstein's Introduction to the Text of the Mishnah." In *The Modern Study of the Mishnah*, edited by Jacob Neusner, 13–36. Leiden: Brill, 1973.

Boyarin, Daniel. "Hellenism in Jewish Babylonia." In *The Cambridge Companion to the Talmud and Rabbinic Literature*, edited by Martin S. Jaffee and Charlotte Fonrobert, 336–63. Cambridge: Cambridge University Press, 2007.

Boyarin, Daniel. *Socrates and the Fat Rabbis*. Chicago; London: University of Chicago Press, 2009.

Brock, Sebastian P. "From Antagonism to Assimilation: Syriac Attitudes to Greek Learning." In *East of Byzantium: Syria and Armenia in the Formative Period*, edited by N. Garsoian, T. Mathews, and R. W. Thomson, 17–34. Washington DC: Dumbarton Oaks, 1982.

Brodsky, David. *A Bride Without a Blessing: A Study in the Redaction and Content of Massekhet Kallah and Its Gemara*. Tübingen: Mohr Siebeck, 2006.

Brodsky, David. "'Thought is Akin to Action': The Importance of Thought in Zoroastrianism and the Development of a Babylonian Rabbinic Motif." In *Irano-Judaica VII Studies Relating to Jewish Contacts with Persian Culture throughout the Ages*, edited by Geoffrey Herman and Julia Rubanovich, 145–96. Jerusalem: Ben Zvi Institute, 2019.

Brody, Robert. "Irano-Talmudica: The New Parallelomania?" *Jewish Quarterly Review* 106 (2016): 209–32.

Brody, Robert. "The Contribution of the Yerushalmi to the Dating of the Anonymous Material in the Bavli." In *Melekhet Mahshevet: Studies in the Redaction and Development of Talmudic Literature*, edited by Aharon Amit and Aharon Shemesh, 27–38. Ramat Gan: Bar Ilan University Press, 2011.

Brody, Robert. "The Anonymous Talmud and the Words of the Amoraim." *Iggud: Selected Essays in Jewish Studies* I (2005): 213–32.

Cantera, Alberto. *Studien Zur Pahlavi-Übersetzung Des Avesta*. Iranica, Bd. 7. Wiesbaden: Harrassowitz, 2004.

Cassuto, Umberto. *A Commentary on the Book of Exodus*. Translated by Israel Abrahams. Jerusalem: Magnes Press, 1997.

Cassuto, Umberto. *A Commentary on the Book of Genesis, Part II: From Noah to Abraham, Genesis VI 9–XI 32*]. Jerusalem: Magnes Press, 1997.

Chernick, Michael. *A Great Voice That Did Not Cease: The Growth of the Rabbinic Canon and Its Interpretation*. Cincinnati: Hebrew Union College Press, 2009.

Cohen, Barak S. *For Out of Babylonia Shall Come Torah and the Word of the Lord from Nehar Peqod: The Quest for Babylonian Tannaitic Traditions*. Leiden: Brill, 2017.

Cohen, Barak S. "In Quest of Babylonian Tannaitic Traditions: The Case of Tanna D'Bei Shmuel." *AJS Review* 33, no. 2 (November 2009): 271–303.

Cohen, Barak S. "Rav Nahman and Rav Sheshet Conflicting Methods of Exegesis of Tannaitic Sources." *Hebrew Union College Annual* 76 (2005): 11–32.

Cohen, Boaz. *Jewish and Roman Law: A Comparative Study*. Vol. 2. NY: Shulsinger Bros., Inc., 1966.

Cohen, Shaye J. D. *From the Maccabees to the Mishnah*. Louisville, KY: Westminster John Knox Press, 2006.

Cohen, Shaye J. D. "Patriarchs and Scholars." In *Proceedings of the American Academy for Jewish Research*, 48:57–85, 1981.

Cohen, Shaye J. D. *Why Aren't Jewish Women Circumcised?: Gender and Covenant in Judaism*. Berkeley; Los Angeles; London: University of California Press, 2005.

Daryaee, Touraj. *Sasanian Persia: The Rise and Fall of an Empire*. London; NY: I.B. Tauris, 2013.

Daube, David. "Negligence in the Early Talmudic Law of Contract: Talmudic Law." In *Collected Works of David Daube*, edited by Calum M. Carmichael, 1:305–32. Berkeley: University of California Press, 1992.

Daube, David. *Roman Law: Linguistic, Social and Philosophical Aspects*. Edinburgh: Edinburgh University Press, 1969.

Daube, David. *The Deed and the Doer in the Bible: David Daube's Gifford Lectures*. West Conshohocken, PA: Templeton Foundation Press, 2007.

Dor, Zvi. *The Teachings of Eretz Israel in Babylon*. Tel Aviv: Dvir Publishing House, 1971.

Eilberg-Schwartz, Howard. *The Human Will in Judaism: The Mishnah's Philosophy of Intention*. RI: Brown Judaic Studies, 1986.

Elman, Yaakov. "A Tale of Two Cities: Mahoza and Pumbedita as Representing Two Halakhic Cultures." In *Torah le-Shamma: Essays in Jewish Studies in Honor of Shamma Friedman*, edited by David Golinkin and Moshe Benovitz, 3–38. Jerusalem: Makhon Schechter, 2007.

Elman, Yaakov. "Acculturation to Elite Persian Norms in the Babylonian Jewish Community of Late Antiquity." In *Neti'ot David*, edited by David Halivni, Zvi Arie Steinfeld, and Yaakov Elman, 31–56. Jerusalem: Orhot, 2006.

Elman, Yaakov. "Hercules within the Halakhic Tradition." *Diné Israel* 25 (2008): 7–41.

Elman, Yaakov. "Middle Persian Culture and Babylonian Sages: Accommodation and Resistance in the Shaping of Rabbinic Legal Tradition." In *The Cambridge Companion to the Talmud and Rabbinic Literature*, edited by Charlotte Fonrobert and Martin Jaffee, 165–97. Cambridge: Cambridge University Press, 2007.

Elman, Yaakov. "Rava as Mara De-Atra of Mahoza." *Hakira* 11 (2011): 59–85.

Elman, Yaakov. "Rava Ve-Darkei Ha-Iyyun Ha-Eretz Yisraeliyyot Be-Midrash Ha-Halakhah." In *Merkaz U-Tefutzah: Eretz Yisrael Veha-Tefutzot Bi-Ymei Bayit Sheni, Ha-Mishnah Veha-Talmud*, edited by Isaiah Gafni, 217–42. Jerusalem: Merkaz Shazar, 2004.

Elman, Yaakov. "Scripture Versus Contemporary Needs: A Sasanian/Zoroastrian Example." *Cardozo Law Review* 28, no. 1 (2006): 153–69.

Elman, Yaakov. "The Babylonian Talmud in Its Historical Context." In *Printing the Talmud: From Bomberg to Schottenstein*, edited by Sharon Liberman Mintz and Gabriel M. Goldstein, 19–28. NY: Yeshiva University Museum, 2005.

Elman, Yaakov. "The Socioeconomics of Babylonian Heresy." *Jewish Law Association Studies* 17 (2007): 80–126.

Elman, Yaakov. "Toward an Intellectual History of Sasanian Law: An Intergenerational Dispute in 'Herbedestan' 9 and Its Rabbinic and Roman Parallels." *The Talmud in Its Iranian Context*, 2010, 21–57.

Epstein, Richard A. "A Theory of Strict Liability." *The Journal of Legal Studies* 2, no. 1 (1973): 151–204.

Epstein, Yaakov. *Introduction to Amoraitic Literature: Babylonian Talmud and Jerusalem Talmud*. Jerusalem: Magnes Press, 1962.

Epstein, Yaakov. *Introduction to Tannaitic literature*. Jerusalem: Magnes Press, 1957.

Finkelstein, Jacob J. "The Goring Ox: Some Historical Perspectives on Deodands, Forfeitures, Wrongful Death and the Western Notion of Sovereignty." *Temple Law Quarterly* 46 (1973 1972): 169–290.

Finnis, John. "Intention in Tort Law." In *Philosophical Foundations of Tort Law*, edited by David G. Owen, 229–47. Oxford: Clarendon Press, 1995.

Fonrobert, Charlotte. "Plato in Rabbi Shimon Bar Yohai's Cave (B. Shabbat 33b-34a): The Talmudic Inversion of Plato's Politics of Philosophy." *AJS Review* 31, no. 2 (2007): 277–96.

Fraade, Steven. "Rabbinic Polysemy and Pluralism Revisited: Between Praxis and Thematization." *AJS Review* 31, no. 1 (2007): 1–40.

Fraenkel, Yonah. "Aggadah in the Mishnah." In *Mehqerei Talmud: Talmudic Studies Dedicated to the Memory of Ephraim E. Urbach 3*, edited by David Rosenthal and Yaakov Sussman, 2:655–83. Jerusalem: Magnes Press, 2005.

Fraenkel, Yonah. *Darchei Ha-Aggada Veha-Midrash*. Jerusalem: Massada, 1991.

Frankel, Zecharias. *Mevo Ha-Yerushalmi*. Breslau: Shletter, 1870.

Friedell, Steven. "Nobody's Perfect: Proximate Cause in American and Jewish Law." *Hastings International and Compositional Law Review* 25 (2002): 101–31.

Friedman, Shamma. " 'Al Titma al Hosafa Shenizkar Bah Shem Amora': Shuv Lememrot Ha'Amoraim Vestam Hatalmud Besugyot HaBavli." In *Talmudic Studies: Investigating the Sugya, Variant Readings and Aggada*, 57–135. NY: Jerusalem: Jewish Theological Seminary, 2010.

Friedman, Shamma. "A Critical Study of Yevamot X with a Methodological Introduction." In *Mehqarim u-Meqorot: Texts and Studies, Analecta Judaica*, edited by H. Dimitrovski, I:275–441. NY: Jewish Theological Seminary, 1977.

Friedman, Shamma. "A Good Story Deserves Retelling – The Unfolding of the Akiva Legend." *JSIJ* 3 (2004): 55–93.

Friedman, Shamma. "Geniza Fragments and Fragmentary Talmud MSS of Bava Metzia – A Linguistic and Bibliographic Study." *Alei Sefer* 9 (1981): 5–55.

Friedman, Shamma. "Some Structural Patterns of Talmudic Sugyot." *Proceedings of the Sixth World Congress of Jewish Studies* III (1977): 384–402.

Friedman, Shamma. *Talmud Arukh: Bavli Bava Mezi'a VI: Critical Edition with Comprehensive Commentary, Text Volume and Introduction.* Vol. II. Jerusalem: Jewish Theological Seminary, 1996.

Friedman, Shamma. "Talmudic Studies, Investigating the Sugya, Variant Readings, and Aggada." In *Mehkarim u-Mekorot*, edited by Haim Zalman Dimitrovsky. NY: Jewish Theological Seminary, 1977.

Friedman, Shamma. "The Writing of the Names 'Rabbah' and 'Rava' in the Babylonian Talmud." *Sinai* 110 (1992): 140–64.

Friedman, Shamma. *Tosefta Atikta: Synoptic Parallels of Mishna and Tosefta Analyzed With Introduction.* Ramat Gan: Bar Ilan University Press, 2002.

Friedman, Shamma. " 'Wonder Not at a Gloss in which the Name of an Amora is Mentioned': The Amoraic Statements and the Anonymous Material in the Sugyot of the Bavli Revisited." In *Melekhet Mahshevet: Studies in the Redaction and Development of Talmudic Literature*, edited by Aaron Amit and Aharon Shemesh, 101–44. Ramat Gan: Bar Ilan University Press, 2011.

Frye, Richard Nelson. *The History of Ancient Iran*. München: C.H. Beck, 1984.

Furstenberg, Yair. "The Purity of Hands and Eating of Ordinary Food in Purity: A Chapter in the History of Tannaitic Halakhah." MA, Hebrew University, 2005.

Gafni, Isaiah. "Nestorian Literature as a Source for the History of the Babylonian Yeshivot." *Tarbiz* 51 (1982): 567–76.

Gafni, Isaiah. *The Jews of Babylonia in the Talmudic Era – A Social and Cultural History*. Jerusalem: The Zalman Shazar Center, 1990.

Garner, Bryan A., ed. *Black's Law Dictionary 7th Edition*. St. Paul, Minn: West Group, 1999.

Gibson, Edgar, trans. *The Conferences of John Cassian*. NY: Christian Literature Co., 1894.

Gilat, Itzhak. "Intent and Act in Tannaitic Teaching." In *Studies in the Development of Halakha*, 72–83. Ramat Gan: Bar Ilan University Press, 1992.

Ginzberg, Louis. "Mabo (Hebrew Introduction)." In *A Commentary on the Palestinian Talmud*, Vol. 1. NY: Jewish Theological Seminary, 1941.

Goldberg, Abraham. *Tosefta Bava Kamma: A Structural and Analytic Commentary*. Jerusalem: Magnes Press, 2001.

Goldenberg, Robert. "Commandment and Consciousness in Talmudic Thought." *Harvard Theological Review* 68 (1975): 261–71.

Goodblatt, David. "Towards the Rehabilitation of Talmudic History." In *History of Judaism, the next Ten Years*, edited by Baruch M. Bokser, 31–44. Chico, CA: Scholars Press, 1980.

Gordley, James. "Tort Law in the Aristotelian Tradition." In *Philosophical Foundations of Tort Law*, edited by David G. Owen, 131–58. Oxford: Clarendon Press, 1995.

Gray, Alyssa M. *A Talmud in Exile: The Influence of Yerushalmi Avodah Zarah on the Formation of Bavli Avodah Zarah*. Brown Judaic Studies; No. 342. Providence, RI: Brown University, 2005.

Green, William Scott. "What's in a Name? The Problematic of Rabbinic 'Biography.'" In *Approaches to Ancient Judaism: Theory and Practice*, edited by Jacob Neusner, Vol. 1. Missoula: Scholars Press, 1978.

Gruenwald, Ithamar. *Rituals and Ritual Theory in Ancient Israel*. Leiden: Brill, 2003.

Gutas, Dimitri. *Greek Thought, Arabic Culture: The Graeco-Arabic Translation Movement in Baghdad and Early 'Abbasaid Society*. London ; NY: Routledge, 1998.

Habba, Yaacov. "Intention as Part of the Actus Reus in Jewish Law and Israeli Law." *Mehkarei Mishpat* 20 (2003): 177–99.

Halivni, David Weiss. "Aspects of the Formation of the Talmud." In *Creation and Composition*, edited by Jeffrey Rubenstein, 339–60. Tübingen: Mohr Siebeck, 2005.

Halivni, David Weiss. "Iyunim beHitavut Hatalmud." *Sidra* 20 (2005): 117–69.

Halivni, David Weiss. *Meqorot U-Mesorot: A Source Critical Commentary on the Talmud Tractate Baba Qama*. Jerusalem: Magnes Press, 1993.

Halivni, David Weiss. *Meqorot U-Mesorot: Baba Metsia*. Jerusalem: Magnes Press, 2003.

Halivni, David Weiss. *Meqorot U-Mesorot: Bi'urim Ba-Talmud Massekhet Baba Batra*. Jerusalem: Magnes Press, 2007.

Halivni, David Weiss. *Meqorot U-Mesorot: Seder Mo'ed, Tractates Erubin and Pesahim*. Jerusalem: Jewish Theological Seminary, 1982.

Halivni, David Weiss. *Meqorot U-Mesorot: Seder Nashim*. Tel Aviv: Devir, 1969.

Halivni, David Weiss. *Meqorot U-Mesorot: Tractate Shabbath*. Jerusalem: Jewish Theological Seminary, 1982.

Halivni, David Weiss. *Meqorot U-Mesorot: Yoma to Hagigah*. Jerusalem: Jewish Theological Seminary, 1975.

Halivni, David Weiss. *Midrash, Mishnah, and Gemara: The Jewish Predilection for Justifijied Law*. Cambridge: Harvard University Press, 1986.

Halivni, David Weiss. "Sefeqei de-Gavrei." In *Proceedings of the American Academy for Jewish Research*, 46–47: 67–93, 1980.

Halivni, David Weiss. *The Formation of the Babylonian Talmud*. Translated by Jefffrey L. Rubenstein. Oxford; New York: Oxford University Press, 2013.

Hallebeek, Jan. "Negligence in Medieval Roman Law." In *Negligence: The Comparative Legal History of the Law of Torts*, edited by J. H. Schrage, 74–101. Berlin: Duncker & Humblot, 2001.

Hart, Herbert L. A. "Intention and Punishment." In *Punishment and Responsibility: Essays in the Philosophy of Law*, Second Edition, Oxford; New York: Oxford University Press, 2008.

Haut, Irwin. "Some Aspects of Absolute Liability Under Jewish Law and Particularly Under View of Maimonides." *Dinei Israel* 15 (1990 1989): 7–61.

Hayes, Christine. *What's Divine about Divine Law?: Early Perspectives*. Princeton: Princeton University Press, 2015.

Hayes, Christine Elizabeth. *Between the Babylonian and Palestinian Talmuds: Accounting for Halakhic Difference in Selected Sugyot from Tractate Avodah Zarah*. NY: Oxford University Press, 1997.

Henning, W. B. "An Astronomical Chapter of the Bundahishn." *Journal of the Royal Asiatic Society of Great Britain and Ireland*, no. 3 (1942): 229–48.

Henshke, David. "Abaye and Rava: Two Approaches to the Mishnah of the Tannaim." *Tarbiz* 49 (1980): 187–93.

Herman, Geoffrey. *A Prince without a Kingdom: The Exilarch in the Sasanian Era*. Tübingen: Mohr Siebeck, 2012.

Herman, Geoffrey. "Ahasuerus, the Former Stable-Master of Belshazzar and the Wicked Alexander of Macedon: Two Parallels between the Babylonian Talmud and Persian Sources." *AJS Review* 29, no. 2 (2005): 283–97.

Herman, Geoffrey. "Table Etiquette and Persian Culture in the Babylonian Talmud." *Zion* 77, no. 2 (2012): 149–88.

Hezser, Catherine. "Interfaces between Rabbinic Literature and Graeco-Roman Philosophy." In *The Talmud Yerushalmi and Graeco-Roman Culture*, edited by Peter Schaeffer and Catherine Hezser, II:161–87. Tübingen: Mohr Siebeck, 2000.

Hidary, Richard. *Rabbis and Classical Rhetoric: Sophistic Education and Oratory in the Talmud and Midrash*. NY: Cambridge University Press, 2017.

Higger, Michael. "Intention in Talmudic Law." PhD, Columbia University, 1927.

Hoffman Libson, Ayelet. *Law and Self-Knowledge in the Talmud*. NY: Cambridge University Press, 2018.

Holger, Zelletin. "Margin of Error." In *Heresy and Identity in Late Antiquity*, 339–63. Tübingen: Mohr Siebeck, 2007.

Honoré, Tony. *Ulpian*. NY: Oxford University Press, 2002.

Ilan, Tal. "A Menstruant 'Forced and Immersed': 'Women to Think With' about Intention in the Performance of the Commandments · BT Ḥulin 31a–b." *Nashim: A Journal of Jewish Women's Studies & Gender Issues*, no. 28 (2015): 51–60.

Jackson, Bernard S. "Eilberg-Schwartz's 'The Human Will in Judaism.'" *The Jewish Quarterly Review* 81, no. 1/2 (1990): 179–88.

Jackson, Bernard S. "Liability for Mere Intention in Early Jewish Law." *Hebrew Union College Annual* 42 (1971): 197–225.

Jaffee, Martin. "How Much 'Orality' in Oral Torah? New Perspective on the Composition and Transmission of Early Rabbinic Tradition." *Shofar* 2 (1992): 53–72.

Jaffee, Martin. "Oral Tradition in the Writings of Rabbinic Oral Torah: On Theorizing Rabbinic Orality." *Oral Tradition* 14 (1999): 3–32.

Jaffee, Martin. "Writing and Rabbinic Oral Tradition: On Mishnaic Narrative, Lists and Mnemonics." *The Journal of Jewish Thought and Philosophy* 4 (1994): 123–46.

Jaffee, Martin S. "The Oral-Cultural Context of the Talmud Yerushalmi: Greco-Roman Rhetorical Paideia, Discipleship, and the Concept of Oral Torah." In *Transmitting Jewish Traditions: Orality, Textuality, and Cultural Diffusion*, edited by Yaakov Elman and Israel Gershoni, 27–73. New Haven: Yale University Press, 2000.

Jaffee, Martin S. *Torah in the Mouth: Writing and Oral Tradition in Palestinian Judaism 200 BCE-400 CE*. NY: Oxford University Press, 2001.

Jaffee, Martin S., and Charlotte Fonrobert, eds. *The Cambridge Companion to the Talmud and Rabbinic Literature*. Cambridge: Cambridge University Press, 2007.

Jong, Albert de. "Purification in Absentia." In *Transformations of the Inner Self in Ancient Religions*, edited by Jan Assmann and Guy Stroumsa, 301–33. Leiden; Boston: Brill, 1999.

Kahana, Menahem Izhak. "Gilui Da'at ve-'Ones be-Gittin: le-Heker Heshtalshelut he-Mesorot he-Muhlaphot be-'Arikhatan ha-Magmatit shel Sugyot Me'uharot." *Tarbiz* 62 (1993): 225–63.

Kahana, Menahem Izhak. "The Halakhic Midrashim." In *The Literature of the Sages, Midrash, and Targum; Liturgy, Poetry, Mysticism; Contracts, Inscriptions, Ancient Science and the Languages of Rabbinic Literature*, edited by Shmuel Safrai, Peter J. Tomson, Zeev Safrai, and Joshua Schwartz, 3–105. Assen, Netherlands: Philadelphia: Royal Van Gorcum Fortress Press, 2006.

Kalcheim, Shaul. " 'Davar Sh'ain Mitkaven' (A Forbidden Act Which Was Produced Without Intent) in Tannaitic and Talmudic Literature." Bar Ilan University, 2001.

Kalmin, Richard. *Jewish Babylonia between Persia and Roman Palestine*. Oxford: Oxford University Press, 2006.

Kalmin, Richard. *Migrating Tales: The Talmud's Narratives and Their Historical Context*. Oakland, CA: University of California Press, 2014.

Kalmin, Richard. "Rabbinic Literature of Late Antiquity as a Source for Historical Study." In *Judaism in Late Antiquity*, edited by Jacob Neusner and Alan J. Avery-Peck, 187–99. Leiden: Brill, 1999.

Kalmin, Richard. "The Formation and Character of the Babylonian Talmud." In *Cambridge History of Judaism: The Late Roman-Rabbinic Period*, edited by Steven T. Katz, 4:840–76. NY: Cambridge University Press, 2006.

Kalmin, Richard Lee. *Sages, Stories, Authors, and Editors in Rabbinic Babylonia*. Atlanta: Scholars Press, 1994.

Kanarfogel, Ephraim. "Study of the Order of Qodashim and the Academic Aims and Self-Image of Rabbinic Scholars in Medieval Europe." In *Asufah le-Yosef: Studies in Jewish History Presented to Joseph Hacker*, edited by Yaron Ben-Naeh, 68–91. Jerusalem: Shazar, 2014.

Katz, Meir, and Eliyahu Stern. "Hithayvut Muhletet: Toldot Adam Ha'mazik." *Beit Yizhak* 31 (2000): 260–72.

Kelley, Patrick. "Restating Duty, Breach, and Proximate Cause in Negligence Law: Descriptive Theory and the Rule of Law." *Vanderbilt Law Review* 53, no. 3 (2001): 1040–69.

Kiel, Yishai. "Cognizance of Sin and Penalty in the Babylonian Talmud and Pahlavi Literature: A Comparative Analysis." *Oqimta* 1 (2013): 1–49.

Kiel, Yishai. "Creation by Emission: Reconstructing Adam and Eve in the Babylonian Talmud in Light of Zoroastrian and Manichaean Literature." *JJS* 66 (2015): 295–316.

Kiel, Yishai. "Reimagining Enoch in Sasanian Babylonia in Light of Zoroastrian and Manichaean Traditions." *AJS Review* 39, no. 02 (2015): 407–32.

Kiperwasser, Reuven. "'Three Partners in a Person' The Genesis and Development of Embryological Theory in Biblical and Rabbinic Judaism." *Lectio Difficilior* 10 (2009).

Kiperwasser, Reuven, and Dan Shapira. "Irano-Talmudica I: The Three-Legged Ass and Ridya in B. Taanith—Some Observations about Mythic Hydrology in the Babylonian Talmud and in Ancient Iran." *AJS Review* 32 (2008): 101–16.

Kraemer, David. "On the Reliability of Attributions in the Babylonian Talmud." *Hebrew Union College Annual* 60 (1989): 175–90.

Kraemer, David. *Responses to Suffering in Classical Rabbinic Literature*. Oxford: Oxford University Press, 1994.

Kraemer, David. *The Mind of the Talmud: An Intellectual History of the Bavli*. NY: Oxford University Press, 1990.

Kraemer, David. "The Mishnah." In *The Cambridge History of Judaism*, edited by William Horbury and John Sturdy, IV:299–315. Cambridge; NY: Cambridge University Press, 2006.

Kretzmer-Raziel, Yoel. "The Impact of Purity Laws on Amoraic Laws Concerning Handling on the Sabbath." *Hebrew Union College Annual* 87 (2017): 179–202.

Krupp, Michael. "Manuscripts of the Babylonian Talmud." In *The Literature of the Sages, Part One: Oral Torah, Halakha, Mishna, Tosefta, Talmud, External Tractates*, edited by Shmuel Safrai, 346–66. Assen, Netherlands; edited by Shmuel Safrai, 252–59. Assen, Netherlands; Philadelphia: Fortress Press, 1987.

Krupp, Michael. "Manuscripts of the Mishnah." In *The Literature of the Sages, Part One: Oral Torah, Halakha, Mishna, Tosefta, Talmud, External Tractates*, edited by Shmuel Safrai, 252–59. Assen, Netherlands: Philadelphia: Fortress Press, 1987.

Kugel, James. *The Bible As It Was*. Cambridge, MA: Belknap Press, 1997.

Lauterbach, Jacob Zallel, ed. *Mekilta De-Rabbi Ishmael: A Critical Edition on the Basis of the Manuscripts and Early Editions*. Vol. 3. Philadelphia: Jewish Publication Society of America, 1976.

Levine, Lee I. *The Rabbinic Class of Roman Palestine in Late Antiquity*. Jerusalem and NY: Yad Ben Zvi Press and Jewish Theological Seminary, 1989.

Levinson, Joshua. "From Narrative Practice to Cultural Poetics." In *Homer and the Bible in the Eyes of Ancient Interpreters*, edited by Maren Niehoff; 345–67. Leiden: Brill, 2012.

Levy, Jacob. *Wörterbuch Über Die Talmudim Und Midraschim*. Edited by Lazarus Goldschmidt. Second. 4 vols. Berlin: Harz, 1924.

Lieberman, Saul. *Greek and Hellenism in Jewish Palestine*. New York: Jewish Theological Seminary, 2012.

Lieberman, Saul. *On the Yerushalmi*. Jerusalem: Darom, 1929.

Lieberman, Saul. *Talmuda Shel Kesarin*. Jerusalem: Azriel, 1931.

Lieberman, Saul. *Sifrei Zuta B: Talmuda Shel Kesarin*. NY: Jewish Theological Seminary, 1968.

Lieberman, Saul. *Tosefta Kefshuta: Seder Mo'ed*. Vol. 3. Jerusalem: Jewish Theological Seminary, 1992.

Lieberman, Saul. *Yerushalmi Kipshuto: Shabat, 'Eruvin, Pesahim*. Vol. 1. Jerusalem: Jewish Theological Seminary, 1995.

Lord, Albert B. *The Singer of Tales*. Edited by Stephen Mitchell and Gregory Nagy. 2nd edition. Cambridge, Mass: Harvard University Press, 2000.

Mackenzie, D. N. *A Concise Pahlavi Dictionary*. London: Oxford University Press, 1986.

Malter, Henry. *The Treatise Ta'anit of the Babylonian Talmud*. Philadelphia: Jewish Publication Society of America, 1967.

Marx, Tzvi C. *Disability in Jewish Law*. London ; NY: Routledge, 2003.

Masek, Lawrence. "Intentions, Motives and the Doctrine of Double Effect." *The Philosophical Quarterly* 60, no. 240 (2010): 567–85.

Milgrom, Jacob. *The JPS Torah Commentary: Numbers*. Philadelphia: Jewish Publication Society, 2003.

Moazami, Mahnaz. *Wrestling With the Demons of the Pahlavi Widewdad: Transcription, Translation, and Commentary*. Leiden ; Boston: Brill, 2014.

Mokhtarian, Jason Sion. *Rabbis, Sorcerers, Kings, and Priests: The Culture of the Talmud in Ancient Iran*. Oakland, CA: University of California Press, 2015.

Monnickendam, Yifat. *Jewish Law and Early Christian Identity: Betrothal, Marriage, and Infidelity in the Writings of Ephrem the Syrian*. NY; Cambridge: Cambridge University Press, 2020.

Montefiore, C. G., and H. M. J. Loewe, eds. *A Rabbinic Anthology*. Cambridge: Cambridge University Press, 2012.

Moscovitz, Leib. *Talmudic Reasoning: From Casuistics to Conceptualization*. Tubingen: Mohr Siebeck, 2002.

Moscovitz, Leib. "The Formation and Character of the Jerusalem Talmud." In *The Cambridge History of Judaism*, edited by Steven T. Katz, 663–77. NY: Cambridge University Press, 2006.

Moscovitz, Leib. "The Formation and Character of the Palestinian Talmud." In *The Cambridge History of Judaism: The Late Roman-Rabbinic Period*, edited by Steven T. Katz, 663–77. NY: Cambridge University Press, 2006.

Moyle, John Baron, ed. *The Institutes of Justinian*. Fifth edition. Clark, NJ: The Lawbook Exchange, Ltd., 2002.

Muffs, Yochanan. *Love and Joy: Law, Language, and Religion in Ancient Israel*. NY: Harvard University Press, 1995.

Muffs, Yochanan. *Studies in the Aramaic Legal Papyri from Elephantine*. Leiden: Brill, 2003.

Naffine, Ngaire, Rosemary Owens, and John Williams, eds. *Intention in Law and Philosophy*. S.l.: Routledge, 2019.

Naomi, Koltun-Fromm. "A Jewish-Christian Conversation in Fourth-Century Persian Mesopotamia." *Journal of Jewish Studies* 47 (1996): 45–63.

Naveh, J., and Shaul Shaked, eds. *Amulets and Magic Bowls. Aramaic Incantations of Late Antiquity*. Jerusalem-Leiden: Magnes Press, Brill, 1985.

Neusner, Jacob. *A History of the Mishnaic Law of Damages, Part 1: Baba Qamma*. Eugene, Oregon: Wipf and Stock Publishers, 2007.

Neusner, Jacob. *In Search of Talmudic Biography: The Problem of the Attributed Saying*. Chico, CA: Scholars Press, 1968.

Neusner, Jacob. *Judaism and Zoroastrianism at the Dusk of Late Antiquity: How Two Ancient Faiths Wrote Down Their Great Traditions*. Atlanta, GA: University of South Florida, 1993.

Neusner, Jacob. *Reading and Believing: Ancient Judaism and Contemporary Gullibility*. Atlanta: Scholars Press, 1986.

Neusner, Jacob. "Talmudic History: Retrospect and Prospect." In *History of the Jews in Babylonia*, Vol. 1, The Parthian Period. Chico, CA: Scholars Press, 1984.

Neusner, Jacob. *The Theology of the Oral Torah: Revealing the Justice of God*. Montreal; Kingston: McGill-Queen's Press, 1999.

Noam, Vered. "Ritual Impurity in Tannaitic Literature: Two Opposing Perspectives." *Journal of Ancient Judaism* 1, no. 1 (2010): 65–103.

Norman, Cohen. "Structural Analysis of a Talmudic Story: Joseph Who Honors the Sabbath." *Jewish Quarterly Review* 72 (1982): 161–77.

Novick, Tzvi. "Blessings over Miṣvot: The Origins of a Category." *Hebrew Union College Annual* 79 (2008): 69–86.

Owen, David G. "Philosophical Foundations of Fault in Tort Law." In *Philosophical Foundations of Tort Law*, edited by David G. Owen, 201–28. Oxford: Clarendon Press, 1995.

Porton, Gary G. *The Traditions of Rabbi Ishmael*. Vol. 4. Leiden; Boston: Brill, 1979.

Quinn, Warren S. "Intentions, and Consequences: The Doctrine of Doing and Allowing." *The Philosophical Review* 98, no. 3 (1989): 287–312.

Radding, Charles M. *A World Made by Men: Cognition and Society, 400–1200*. Chapel Hill: University of North Carolina Press, 1986.

Rappel, Dov. "Greek Wisdom-Rhetoric." *Jerusalem Studies Jewish Thought* 2, (1983) 317–22.

Ratner, Dov Ber. *Ahavat Zion Virushalayim, Pesahim*. Vilna, 1909.

Rezania, Kianoosh. "The Dēnkard Against Its Islamic Discourse." *Der Islam* 94, no. 2 (2017): 336–62.

Riad, Eva. *Studies in the Syriac Preface*. Uppsala: Stockholm, Sweden: Almqvist & Wiksell International, 1988.

Riles, Annelise. *Rethinking the Masters of Comparative Law*. Oregon: Hart Publishing, 2001.

Rokeah, David. *Jews, Pagans and Christians in Conflict*. Jerusalem-Leiden: Magnes Press, Brill, 1982.

Ronis, Sara. "A Seven-Headed Demon in the House of Study: Understanding a Rabbinic Demon in Light of Zoroastrian, Christian, and Babylonian Textual Traditions." *AJS Review*, (2019), 125–42.

Rosen, Lawrence. *Law as Culture: An Invitation*. Princeton; Oxford: Princeton University Press, 2017.

Rosenberg, Michael. "Penetrating Words: A Babylonian Rabbinic Response to Syriac Mariology." *Journal of Jewish Studies* 67 (2016): 121–34.

Rosenberg, Michael. "Sexual Serpents and Perpetual Virginity: Marian Rejectionism in the Babylonian Talmud." *Jewish Quarterly Review* 106 (2016): 465–93.

Rosenthal, E. S. "*La-Milon Ha-Talmudi: Talmudica Iranica*." In *Irano-Judaica*, edited by Shaul Shaked and Amnon Netzer, 38–131. Jerusalem: Makhon Ben-Zvi, 1982.

Rosenthal, E. S., and Saul Lieberman. *Yerushalmi Neziqin*. Jerusalem: Israel Academy of Sciences and Humanities, 1983.

Rosen-Zvi, Ishay. *Demonic Desires: Yetzer Hara and the Problem of Evil in Late Antiquity*. Philadelphia: University of Pennsylvania Press, 2011.

Rosen-Zvi, Ishay. "The Mishnaic Mental Revolution: A Reassessment." *Journal of Jewish Studies* 66 (2015): 36–58.

Rubenstein, Jeffrey. "Introduction." In *David Weiss Halivni, The Formation of the Babylonian Talmud*, translated by Jeffrey Rubenstein, xvii–xxxv. NY: Oxford University Press, 2013.

Rubenstein, Jeffrey. "Talmudic Astrology: Bavli Šabbat 156a-b." *Hebrew Union College Annual* 78 (2007): 109–48.

Rubenstein, Jeffrey. *The Culture of the Babylonian Talmud*. Baltimore: JHU Press, 2003.

Rubenstein, Jeffrey L. "On Some Abstract Concepts in Rabbinic Literature." *Jewish Studies Quarterly* 4, no. 1 (1997): 33–73.

Rubin, Nissan. *The Beginning of Life: Rites of Birth, Circumcision and Redemption of the First-born in the Talmud and Midrash*. Israel: Hakkibutz Hameuchad, 1995.

Sarna, Nahum M. *The JPS Torah Commentary: Exodus*. Philadelphia: Jewish Publication Society, 1991.

Satlow, Michael. "'Try to Be a Man': The Rabbinic Construction of Masculinity." *The Harvard Theological Review* 89 (1996): 19–40.

Schäfer, Peter. *Jesus in the Talmud*. Princeton: Princeton University Press, 2009.

Schäfer, Peter. *The Jewish Jesus: How Judaism and Christianity Shaped Each Other*. Princeton: Princeton University Press, 2014.

Schiffman, Lawrence H. "Legislation Concerning Relations with Non-Jews in the 'Zadokite Fragments' and in Tannaitic Literature." *Revue de Qumrân* 11, no. 3 (43) (1983): 379–89.

Scott, Samuel Parsons. *The Civil Law: Including the Twelve Tables, the Institutes of Gaius, the Rules of Ulpian, the Opinions of Paulus, the Enactments of Justinian, and the Constitutions of Leo*. Sixth. Vol. 1 and 2. Clark, NJ: The Lawbook Exchange, Ltd., 2006.

Secunda, Shai. *The Iranian Talmud: Reading the Bavli in Its Sasanian Context*. Philadelphia: University of Pennsylvania Press, 2013.

Seligman, Adam B., Robert P. Weller, Michael J. Puett, and Bennett Simon. *Ritual and Its Consequences: An Essay on the Limits of Sincerity*. Oxford ; New York: Oxford University Press, 2008.

Shaked, Shaul. "Ambiguous Words in Pahlavi." *Israel Oriental Studies* 4 (1974): 227–57.

Shaked, Shaul. *Dualism in Transformation. Varieties of Religion in Sasanian Iran (The Jordan Lectures in Comparative Religion),*. London: School of Oriental and African Studies, 1994.

Shaked, Shaul. "Esoteric Trends in Zoroastrianism." *Proceedings of the Israel Academy of Sciences and Humanities 3* (1969): 175–221.

Shaked, Shaul. "First Man, First King: Notes on Semitic-Iranian Syncretism and Iranian Mythological Transformations." In *From Zoroastrian Iran to Islam : Studies in Religious History and Intercultural Contacts*. Aldershot: Variorum, 1995.

Shaked, Shaul. "Iranian Influence on Judaism: First Century BCE to Second Century CE." In *Cambridge History of Judaism*, Eds. W.D. Davies and Lewis Finkelstein, 308–25. Cambridge: Cambridge University Press, 1984.

Shaked, Shaul. "Judaeo-Persian Notes." *Israel Oriental Studies* 1 (1971): 178–82.

Shaked, Shaul. "Religious Actions Evaluated by Intention." In *Shoshanat Yaakov: Ancient Jewish and Iranian Studies in Honor of Yaakov Elman*, edited by Steven Fine and Shai Secunda, 403–14. Leiden; Boston: Brill, 2011.

Shaked, Shaul. "Some Notes on Ahreman, the Evil Spirit, and His Creation." In *Studies in Mysticism and Religion Presented to G.G. Scholem*, 227–54. Jerusalem: Magnes Press, 1967.

Shaked, Shaul. *The Wisdom of the Sasanian Sages: Dēnkard VI*. Colorado: Westview Press, 1979.

Shaked, Shaul. "Zoroastrian Polemics Against Jews in the Sasanian and Early Islamic Period." In *Irano-Judaica*, edited by Amnon Netzer and Shaul Shaked, II:85–104. Jerusalem, 1990.

Shaki, Mansour. "Judicial and Legal Systems Ii. Parthian and Sasanian Judicial Systems." In *Encyclopaedia Iranica*, XV:177–80, 2012.

Shaki, Mansour. "The Dēnkard Account of the History of Zoroastrian Scriptures." *Archív Orientální* 49, no. 2 (1981).

Shanks Alexander, Elizabeth. "The Orality of Rabbinic Writing." In *The Cambridge Companion to the Talmud and Rabbinic Literature*, edited by Martin Jaffee and Charlotte Fonrobert, 38–57. Cambridge: Cambridge University Press, 2007.

Shanks Alexander, Elizabeth. *Transmitting Mishnah: The Shaping Influence of Oral Tradition*. Cambridge ; NY: Cambridge University Press, 2006.

Shemesh, Aharon. "Shogeg Karov Le-Mezid in the Amoraic Law." *Shenaton Ha-Mishpat Ha-Ivri* 20 (1997 1995): 399–428.

Skjærvø, Oktar. "Counter-Manichaean Elements in Kerdīr's Inscriptions, Irano-Manichaica II." In *Atti Del Terzo Congresso Internazionale Di Studi "Manicaeismo e Oriente Cristiano Antico": Arcavacata Di Rende-Amantea, 31 Agosto- 5 Settembre 1993*, edited by Luigi Cirillo and Alois Van Tongerloo, 313–42. Louvain and Napels: Brepols, 1997.

Sokoloff, Michael. *A Dictionary of Jewish Babylonian Aramaic of the Talmudic and Geonic Periods*. Ramat Gan: Bar Ilan University Press, 2002.

Sperber, Daniel. *The City in Roman Palestine*. NY; Oxford: Oxford University Press, 1998.

Stall, Fritz. "The Meaninglessness of Ritual." *Numen* 26 (1979): 2–22.

Stein, Dina. *Textual Mirrors: Reflexivity, Midrash, and the Rabbinic Self*. Philadelphia: University of Pennsylvania Press, 2012.

Steinmetz, Devora. *From Father to Son: Kinship, Conflict, and Continuity in Genesis*. 1st edition. Louisville, Ky: Westminster John Knox Press, 1991.

Steinmetz, Devora. "Must the Patriarch Know 'Uqtzin? The Nasi as Scholar in Babylonian Aggada." *AJS Review* 23, no. 2 (1998): 163–89.

Strack, Hermann, and Gunter Stemberger. *Introduction to the Talmud and Midrash*. Minneapolis: Fortress Press, 1992.

Strauch Schick, Shana. "A Re-examination of the Bavli's Beruriah Narratives in Light of Middle Persian Literature." *Zion* 79 (2014): 409–24.

Strauch Schick, Shana. "From Dungeon to Haven: Competing Theories of Gestation in Leviticus Rabbah and the Bavli." *AJS Review* 43, no. 1 (2019): 143–68.

Strauch Schick, Shana. "Intention in the Babylonian Talmud: An Intellectual History." Yeshiva University, 2011.

Strauch Schick, Shana. "Mitsvot Eyn Tzerikhot Kavvanah: The Radical Reconceptualization of Ritual." *Jewish Studies Quarterly* 24 (2017): 1–22.

Strauch Schick, Shana. "Negligence and Strict Liability in Babylonia and Palestine: Two Competing Systems of Tort Law in the Rulings of Early Amoraim." *Dinei Israel* 29 (2012): 139–76.

Strauch Schick, Shana. "Reading Aristotle in Mahoza?: Actions and Intentions in Rava's Jurisprudence." *Jewish Law Association Studies* 25 (2014): 262–91.

Sussman, Yaakov. "Ve-shuv Li-yerushalmi Neziqin." In *Talmudic Studies*, edited by Yaakov Sussman and David Rosenthal, 1:55–133. Jerusalem: Magnes Press, 1990.

Tabory, Joseph. *The Passover Ritual Throughout the Generations*. Tel Aviv: Hakibbutz Hameuchad, 1996.

Taylor, Charles. *Sources of the Self: The Making of the Modern Identity*. Cambridge, MA: Harvard University Press, 1992.

Urbach, Ephraim. *The Halakhah : Its Sources and Development*. Translated by Raphael Posner. Israel: Massada, Yad La-Talmud Ltd., 1986.

Urbach, Ephraim. *The Sages: Their Concepts and Beliefs*. Translated by Israel Abrahams. Cambridge, MA: Harvard University Press, 1987.

van Bladel, Kevin. *The Arabic Hermes: From Pagan Sage to Prophet of Science*. Oxford ; NY: Oxford University Press, 2009.

VerSteeg, Russ. *Law in the Ancient World*. North Carolina: Carolina Academic Press, 2002.

Vidas, Moulie. "Greek Wisdom in Babylonian." In *Envisioning Judaism: Studies in Honor of Peter Schafer on the Occasion of His Seventieth Birthday*, edited by Ra'anan S. Boustan, Klaus Herrmann, Reimund Leicht, Annette Yoshiko Reed, and Giuseppe Veltri, 287–305. Tübingen: Mohr Siebrek Ek, 2013.

Vidas, Moulie. *Tradition and the Formation of the Talmud*. Princeton: Princeton University Press, 2014.

Visotzky, Burton L. *Fathers of the World: Essay in Rabbinic and Patristic Literatures*. Tübingen: Mohr Siebeck, 1995.

Wald, Stephen G. *Shabbat, Chapter VII*. Edited by Shamma Friedman. Jerusalem: The Society for the Interpretation of the Talmud, 2007.

Walker, Joel. *The Legend of Mar Qardagh: Narrative and Christian Heroism in Late Antique Iraq*. Berkeley: University of California Press, 2006.

Walker, Joel. "The Limits of Late Antiquity: Philosophy between Rome and Iran." *The Ancient World* 33 (2002): 45–69.

Watson, Alan. "Morality, Slavery and the Jurists in the Later Roman Republic." *Tulane Law Review* 42 (1968 1967): 289–303.

Watson, Alan. "Slavery and the Development of Roman Private Law." *Bullettino Dell'Istituto Di Diritto Romano "Vittorio Scialoja,"* no. 29 (1987): 105–18.

Watson, Alan, ed. *The Digest of Justinian*. Vol. 1. Philadelphia: University of Pennsylvania Press, 1998.

Watson, Alan. *The Spirit of Roman Law*. Athens; London: University of Georgia Press, 2008.

Weinrib, Ernest J. *The Idea of Private Law*. Oxford: Oxford University Press, 2012.

Weiss, Abraham. *Diyyunim u-Verurim be-Bava Kamma*. NY: Feldheim, 1966.

Weissberg, Elyakim. "Ketiv Ha-Sheimot Rabbah ve-Rava: Shitat Rav Hai Ga'on ve-Shitot Holkot." *Mehkarim Be-Lashon* 5–6, no. Jubilee Volume for Israel Yavin (1992): 181–214.

Whitehouse, Harvey. "Theorizing Religions Past." In *Theorizing Religions Past*, edited by Harvey Whitehouse and Luther H. Martin, 215–32. Walnut Creek, CA: Altamira, 2004.

Wiesehöfer, Josef. *Ancient Persia: From 550 BC to 650 AD*. Munich: I.B. Tauris, 1996.

Wright, Richard. "Substantive Corrective Justice." In Symposium on Corrective Justice and Formalism, *Iowa Law Review*, 1992, 625–711.

Wright, Richard. "The Standard of Care in Negligence Law." In *Philosophical Foundations of Tort Law*, edited by David G. Owen, 249–76. Oxford: Clarendon Press, 1995.

Zeitlin, Solomon. "Studies in Tannaitic Jurisprudence: Intention as a Legal Principle." *Journal of Law and Philosophy* 1 (1919): 297–311.

Zellentin, Holger Michael. *Rabbinic Parodies of Jewish and Christian Literature*. Tübingen: Mohr Siebeck, 2011.

General Index

Aristotle
    actions vs. states   107, 108
    acts of passion vs. deliberation   102, 103, 104
    corrective justice   100, 103
    moral blame   101, 132, 151
    unintended harm   101, 104
    virtue   100
Attributions
    reliability of   7, 8, 9

Coercion   22, 24, 26, 45, 50, 76, 92, 108
    ending in consent   105
Custodianship   62, 77, 82, 83, 84, 85

Despair (abandonment of property)   48, 72

Exile (to city of refuge)   53, 56, 75

Hellenism
    in rabbinic works from Babylonia   13, 108
    in rabbinic works from the Land of Israel   13
    in Sasanian Persia   13
    in Syriac Christian Writings   14

Intention
    and emergence of the 'self'   154
    and moral responsibility   100, 101, 102, 103, 104, 108, 132
    building a sukkah   69
    circumcision   67
    deriving benefit/pleasure   65, 86, 143, 144, 145
    double effect   95
    forbidden labor on the Sabbath   48, 53, 57, 64, 65, 66, 77, 78, 80, 81, 87, 92, 93, 95, 97, 104, 138, 144, 146
    fulfillment of *mitzvot*   67, 110, 111, 112, 113, 118, 119, 121, 123, 124, 126, 127, 130, 131
    harm   *See* tort law, intent to harm
    homicide   48, 53, 56, 76, 138, 141, 142
    idolatry   89, 104
    in Chrisitan Monastic texts   135
    in tannaitic sources   155
    in the Mishnah   2, 18, 111, 112
    in Zoroastrian texts   44, 45, 46, 99, 134
    intent to violate a prohibition   94, 96, 97
    levirate marriage   56
    Mahozan vs. Pumbeditan approaches   49, 81, 95, 97
    martyrdom   90, 91, 92, 98
    muqtzah   77
    nullification of *hametz*   69
    ritual purity   114, 116
    sacrifices   64n48, 138

Nicomachean Ethics   *See* Aristotle

Rape   91, 105, 106, 107
Ritual Theory   132
Roman Law   42, 103n120, 151, 152, 153

Sasanian Persia   12, 14, 46, 91
Syriac Christian Writings   15

Tort Law
    accidental damages   19, 20, 21, 25, 27, 29
    Bavli vs. Yerushalmi   37, 38, 40, 41, 43, 46
    gross negligence   48, 53, 54, 56
    in tannaitic sources   18, 19, 20, 21, 22, 24, 27
    in Zoroastrian texts   43, 99
    indirect damage   77
    intent to harm   53, 55, 82, 85, 86, 149
    justified intentional damage   34, 35, 82
    negligence   19, 20, 23, 48, 54, 56, 57, 58, 62, 82, 85, 103
    strict liability   18, 20, 21, 24, 25, 26, 54
    transition away from strict liability   31, 33, 34, 62, 73, 77
    transition from objective to subjective standards   42, 47, 151, 153, 154

Ye'ush   *See* Despair

Source Index

Bible
  Genesis
    3.7   42
  Exodus
    2.6   19
    12.48   68
    12.8   127
    17.11   113
    21.12-14   57n21
    21.13   52
    21.24   21n14
    21.25   24
    21.33   74
    21.36   74
    22.8   62
    22.10   84n40
    31.1-11, 12-17   66n59
    35.33   52, 66n59
  Leviticus
    4.23   66
    23.34   69n74
  Numbers
    35.11   52, 75
    35.9-34   57n21, 154n21
  Deuteronomy
    4.2   129
    6.20-21   127n62
    19.1-13   154n21
    19.4   75
    22.8   74
    22.26   77
    25.11   53, 55, 57n21
  I Kings
    3.12   112n5
  Psalms
    64.7   112n5
  Proverbs
    16.23   112n5
Mishnah
  'Arakhim
    5.1   112n5
  Beitzah
    1.8   25n32
  Berakhot
    2.1   67n65, 111, 120, 135
    5.1   67, 112
  Bava Metzia
    2.8   84
    4.12   18n5, 18n9
  Bava Qama
    1.1   19
    1.2   23n23
    1.4   22n20
    2.4   22n20
    2.6   18, 20, 21
    3.1   18n9, 20, 27, 59
    4.5   148n32
    4.6   18n3, 141
    5.4   57n21
    5.6   74
    6.2   58
    8.1   18n9, 53, 54, 57n21
  Eduyot
    2.5   65n54
  Erubin
    4.4   18n9
    10.1   127
  Keilim
    25.9   18n4
  Keritut
    4.2   66
    4.3   65n54, 88n64
  Ketubot
    3.2   140
  Kilaim
    9.5   18n8, 80
  Makhshirim
    1.2,5   18n9
    1.6   18n4
    3.4-8   18n4
    4.1-7   18n4
    5.3-8   18n4
    5.6   18n9
    6.1-8   18n4
  Makot
    2.1   61n38
    2.1-3   57n21
  Megillah
    2.2   67n65, 112
  Menahot
    13.11   112n5

SOURCE INDEX

Nedarim
   3.2   22n19
Negaim
   7.5   18n9
Parah
   4.2   112n5
Peah
   6.11   18n9
Pesahim
   3.7   69n77
   10.3   123
   10.4   124n49
Rosh Hashana
   3.7   67n65, 112, 118n30, 120
   3.8   113
   4.8   65n54, 113n10, 119n33
Sanhedrin
   9.1   51n11
   9.2   18n3, 18n9, 57n21, 138, 140
Shabbat
   7.1   22n19
   10.4   87
   10.5   66
   12.5   112n5
   16.3   128
Shabuot
   4.10   18n9
Sheqalim
   3.3   18n9
   6.2   65n54
Sukkah
   1.1   69, 143
Temurah
   7.5   69n78
Taharot
   7.8   116n19
Yebamot
   6.1   22n18, 56, 106n138
   16.5   18n9, 112n5
Zebahim
   1.1   138n8
   2.2-5   18n7
   4.6   138n7
Tosefta
  Avoda Zara
   3.12   67n67
   3.13   68n70
   8.9   141n17

Beitzah
   2.12   79n24
Berakhot
   2.2,7   112n6
   3.18   112n6
B. Qama
   2.4   60
Makhshirim
   1.1-2   18n4
   2.15-16   18n4
Me'ilah
   2.6   65n51
Pesahim
   3.12   69n77
   10.9   127n62
Rosh Hashana
   2.6   65n54
   2.6-7   112n6
Shabbat
   9.15–16   65n54
   10.19   65n54
   15.17   90n71
Taharot
   3.1   18n4
   4.8   65n54
Terumah
   3.6   112n6
Yadayim
   2.3   112n5, 112n6, 117
Bavli
  Avoda Zara
   19b   117n23
   27a   68, 68n70
   54a   92n79
  B. Batra
   22a   138n10
   22b-23a   77
   93b-94a   25n32
   144b   36n65
  Beitzah
   6a   77n17
   13b   25n32
   23a   143n25
  Bekhorot
   24b-25a   143n25
  Berakhot
   6a   138
   11a-b   135n84

13a 119n34, 121n40
20b 70n81
56a 67n66
B. Metzia
  6a 48n1, 62
  21b 72n2
  27a 56n20
  41a 62
  83a 84
  96b 82
  96b-97a 85n51, 103n117, 138n4
  106a 62
B. Qama
  2b 150
  5a-b 56n20
  5b 150
  17b 50n10
  26a 150
  26b 24, 26, 46n93, 48n3, 76
  26b-27a 51, 94n83
  27a 74, 152n11
  27b 31, 82, 97, 98, 138n3
  28a 35
  28b 60
  28b-29a 76, 84, 108n144
  29a 60, 152n10
  29b 50
  30a 92n80
  31a 84n40
  32b 48, 56
  35a 25n29, 141n18
  40b 85n51, 86, 103n117
  40b-41a 148
  42a 139
  44b 141n19
  45b-46a 73
  54a 56n20
  55b 152n10
  56a 57
  58a 85n51, 86, 103n117
  61b 103n117
  62a 85, 138n4
  66a 49n4
  66b 72n2
  67b 49n4, 72n2
  68a 49n4
  71a 140n15
  99b 84n40
  107b 48n1, 62
  111b 49n4

Erubin
  95b-96a 122n42, 127
  96a 36n65
Gittin
  2a 48n3
  37b 72n2
  53a 140n15
  72b-73a 107n140
Hagigah
  18b-19a 114
  19b 94n89
Horiyot
  6b 22n19
Hullin
  13a 64n48
  31a-b 114, 122n43
  81b 140n15
  95b 38n68
Keritut
  7a 122n43
  11a-b 63n43
  19b 48n3, 57n22, 64, 86
  20b 138n6
Ketubot
  5b 146
  6b 87n60, 147
  15a 141n19
  33b 140n15
  51b 106
  51b 107n140
  54a 106n133
Makot
  7b 48, 56, 57n21, 75
  9a 75n9
  16a 140n15
Megillah
  12b-13a 90n70
Menahot
  42a 68n67
  42b 70
  64a 95
  110a 64n48
Moed Qatan
  28a 67n66, 99n101
Nazir
  32a 70n81
  42a 143n25
Nedarim
  25b 22n19
  27a 107n140

SOURCE INDEX

Pesahim
  6b 69n77
  7a, 8a 69n77
  25b-26a 107
  25b-26b 143, 145
  31b 69
  69a 117n23
  108b 127n62
  114b 123
  115b 127n62

Qiddushin
  52b 72n2
  70a 66n62
  81b 106n135

Rosh Hashana
  28a-b 118, 130
  28b 132
  29a 113
  33b 119n33

Sanhedrin
  15b 24n28
  27a 135n84
  61b 89, 104n127
  62b 48n3, 57n22, 87n57
  72a 22n18
  74a 98
  74a-b 90, 147
  79a 141n19
  79b 141n20

Shabbat
  24b 24n28
  29b 80n29, 146n28
  37b 38n68
  41b 87n60
  44a 77n17
  45a 77n17
  46b 77n17
  46b-47a 79, 87
  50a-b 143n25
  72b 80n30, 93
  72b-73a 54, 92, 104
  81b 87n60, 143n25
  92b 87
  102a 97n96
  103a 78, 87n60
  107b 48n3, 66
  128a 77n17
  129a 67n66
  133a 87n60
  145a 38n68

Sotah
  14b 25n32

Sukkah
  8b-9a 69
  9a 143n24
  10a 69
  28a 117n23
  33b 138n6

Taanit
  29b 63

Temurah
  4b 24n28

Yebamot
  4b 143n25
  34b 64, 67n66
  52b 77n16
  53b 106
  54a 56

Yoma
  19b 117n23
  28b-29a 49
  34b 87n60

Zebahim
  2a 122
  2b 138
  47a 64n48
  91b 143n25
  99a 143n25

Yerushalmi
  Berakhot
    10b 112n7
  B. Metzia
    8b 49n4
  B. Qama
    2b 24
    3a 22, 41
    3b 27, 98
    3c 59n28
    4c 74n6
  Gittin
    45d 49n4
  Hagigah
    78b 117
  Hallah
    58a 49n4
  Ketubot
    27c 25n29, 141n18
  Kilaim
    27b 79n24
    31a 49n4

Ma'aser Sheni
   54b   125n51
Ma'asrot
   52a   49n4
Orlah
   62c   125n51
Pesahim
   28d   69n77
   30b   69n78
   37c-d   124
   37d   118
Rosh Hashana
   59a   112n4, 126n55
Sanhedrin
   23b   49n4
   27a   141
Shabbat
   6a   79n24
   12b   88n64
   14b   96n92
Shebiit
   10a-b   98
Sukkah
   4b   143n23
Terumah
   41b   37n66
Yebamot
   9a   68n70
Midrash
   Genesis Rabbah
      19.5   41
   Mekhilta de-Rabbi Ishmael
      3.62-63   142
      Amaleq 1   113n9
      Mishpatim 4.17   141n17
      Neziqin 14   19
      Neziqin 8   57n21, 139n11, 140n16,
         141n19
      Neziqin 9   57n21
      Pesah 8   69n78
   Mekhilta de-Rabbi Shimon
     b. Yohai
      17.11   113n9
      21   139n11
      21.22   141n19
      Exodus 21.22   25n30
   Sifre
      41, 86   112n5

Sipra
   Nedava 8.9   112n5
Greco-Roman
   Digest of Justinian
      Book IX 2.31   152
      Book IX 3.2   42
      Book IX 30.3   152
      Book XLVI 2.21   152n3
      Book XLVI 2.40   152n3
   Institutes of Gaius
      Commentary III. 196   152n3
      Commentary III. 211   152
   Institutes of Justinian
      Book II.XIV.1   152n5
      Book IV.I.6   152n3
   Nicomachean Ethics
      1110a27   105n129
      1110b2   105n129
      1113b   104
      1132a   100n106
      1134a   105
      1135a   100
      1135b   101, 103, 104
      1136a   101, 102n115
      1138b   103
Zoroastrian
   Bundahišn
      14.11   135
   Dēnkard
      Book IV.19   14
      Book VI.54   134
   Hērbedestān
      9.5   43
      9.7   43
      9.8   43
   Nērangestān
      2.23.1   135n84
   Nērangestān II
      1.3   134n80
   Pahlavi Vidēvdād
      6.29   44, 45
   Šāyest nē-Šāyest
      10.6   134
   Šāyest nē-Šāyest Suppl
      14   134
   Vidēvdād
      6.28   44
      6.29   44